S0-ALL-984

Also by John Munder Ross

WHAT MEN WANT

THE MALE PARADOX

TALES OF LOVE, SEX, AND DANGER *(with Sudhir Kakar)*

THE OEDIPUS PAPERS *(editor, with George Pollack)*

NEW PERSPECTIVES ON PSYCHOANALYTIC
PSYCHOTHERAPY *(editor, with Wayne Myers)*

FATHER AND CHILD *(editor, with Stanley Cath and Alan
Gurwitt)*

THE
SADOMASOCHISM
OF EVERYDAY LIFE

Why We Hurt Ourselves —

and Others — and How to Stop

JOHN MUNDER ROSS, PH.D.

Simon & Schuster

SIMON & SCHUSTER
Rockefeller Center
1230 Avenue of the Americas
New York, NY 10020

Copyright © 1997 by John Munder Ross
All rights reserved, including the right of reproduction
in whole or in part in any form.

SIMON & SCHUSTER and colophon are registered
trademarks of Simon & Schuster Inc.

Designed by Karolina Harris
Manufactured in the United States of America

1   3   5   7   9   10   8   6   4   2

Library of Congress Cataloging-in-Publication Data
Ross, John Munder.
The sadomasochism of everyday life: why we hurt ourselves — and
others — and how to stop/John Munder Ross.
p. cm.
Includes bibliographical references and index.
1. Sadomasochism. 2. Psychological abuse. 3. Self-esteem. 4. Suffering
I Title.
HQ79.R67   1997
306.77'5 — dc21   96-50196
CIP
ISBN 0-684-81049-2

Dedicated to my patients

Acknowledgments

I would like to thank Barbara Fisher and Angela Von der Lippe for their generous reading of my manuscript and thoughtful commentary. I also owe debts of gratitude to Suzanne Gluck, my agent, and Bob Asahina, who acquired the book for Simon & Schuster. Dominick Anfuso and Sarah Pinckney, my editors there, provided warm support and careful criticism. Finally, I am grateful to my personal research and editorial assistant, Laura Frost, whose keen intellect, editorial gifts, and deep knowledge of the subject matter helped me refine the form and broaden the scope of the book.

Contents

INTRODUCTION

I AM something of a sadomasochist—like everybody else. Whether they admit it or not, almost everyone is interested in pain and suffering. Scratch the most normal surface, and you will find a little fundamental erotic sadomasochism in just about everybody. Why does traffic in the opposite lane slow down when there has been a car accident? People like to look at the squashed vehicles, to search for a bloody body or two. Relieved that they are not the ones who are strewn about the pavement, they are also fascinated by the specter of death and destruction. Doesn't it feel great, or didn't it, at least when you were a kid, to pick at a scab? The itch, the dig, the final sting, the blood? Or, if not your own scab, didn't it feel good to sling rocks at innocent little birds or squirrels?

What about all those scary games people play with each other—especially parents and children? Most fathers are not actually abusive. But they still go far enough, with their mock roars and lunges and their tickling to excess. And where parents fail to fill the bill, children have found their monsters in the movies or in fairy tales. Even before the ratings and the frank sex and violence, there have been creatures like Frankenstein's monster, the Wolf Man, Count Dracula and his love slaves—victims who became vampires in their own right. There have always been ogres and bugaboos galore to scare and excite the living daylights out of children of all ages. When these children had to wait impatiently for the next movie monsters to make their appearance, they made them up, envisioning the bogeymen in the closet or the burglars outside about to break in and. . . .

A surfeit of gore seems to fascinate viewers of all ages and predilections, identifying as they do with both the ravaged and the ravagers. Perhaps more than any other medium, current movies reveal just how infused our culture is with sadomasochism. Very little can be marketed without it in one form or another.

In other contexts as well, presentations of misery and brutality are obligatory to catch the public eye. So the tabloids and television news lay before their millions of viewers daily spectacles of murder and mayhem from real life. Consider our fascination with the Bobbits, the Menendez brothers, Tonya Harding, and O. J. Simpson. We can't get enough of this sort of thing.

Dressed up for today's movies, sadomasochistic scenarios can seem pretty "normal." Most films offer up heterosexual encounters that are more like sexy daydreams. In one such encounter, a tough but suave Sean Connery beats his adversary Pussy Galore into submission before taking her, rudely but with enough power, passion and ultimate pleasure to make it all worthwhile for both himself and his former foe. In another, Sharon Stone appeals to one of most men's most *Basic Instincts*—the inclination to surrender all to the femme fatale. In most of the action movies that are the standard fare of young filmgoers, even when the obvious sexual element is missing in PG-13-rated family entertainment, the ravishment of the flesh and the reveling in its destruction are still present. . . .

I AM a psychoanalyst. After twenty years of intensive clinical practice, I continue to be surprised and frequently saddened by the extent to which people make themselves suffer. My patients' lives and those of my colleagues and students often seem so much more unhappy than they need to be.

In many different ways, they torture themselves. The people I try to help, people like you or me, either overreact to minor setbacks and worries or ignore them, making things worse for themselves. Again and again, they find themselves locked into wretched relationships or mired in terrible and unrewarding jobs. They put up with frustration and humiliation, at times even seeming to seek out disappointment and abuse. Feeling trapped by outside forces, they report their circumstances as situations that they are helpless to act upon. And they resist with all their might my efforts to get them to see themselves as actively responsible for their lives and thus capable of changing them. When they finally recognize, usually imperfectly and incompletely, that they have contributed to their suffering in some way, a way they do not understand, they seek counsel and try to change. Patients slowly realize that most pain is a gratuitous, self-inflicted form of self-punishment. Fitfully and grudgingly, they see that they are hurting themselves. But they do so only fleetingly, and they keep forgetting that they are responsible for what they do to themselves.

The world today is full of self-styled victims. Parents yield to the character assassinations and material demands of their unruly teenagers; siblings undermine themselves just so they will not make a sister or brother envious; devoted children care for the aging parent who once abused or neglected them; wage slaves remain beaten down and underpaid by imperious bosses when they could go elsewhere; employers do not fire the employees who fail to do their jobs; henpecked husbands continue to submit to the wives who, in fact, depend on them; and, perhaps most recognizable, the "women who love too much" remain devoted to the men who do not love them at all. This familiar list does not exhaust the nearly infinite variations on this central theme. People make themselves miserable in many ways, and they find almost as many ploys to convince themselves they are not the masters of their fate.

Life is hard enough without making it harder. What Sigmund Freud once called "common unhappiness"—personal losses, world calamities that afflict everyone, diseases (including biologically based depressions), and death, which finally claims all—casts its shadow on all lives no matter how well they are lived. The trouble is, many people further compound what Shakespeare called "the shocks which flesh is heir to" with what Freud referred to as "neurotic suffering."

On the surface, this suffering usually does not make sense. It often seems to come from nowhere, though it comes from within. Its logic is hidden: the logic of psychology, "psycho-logic." Let me elaborate.

Growing up is challenging and often painful. Since, as the Rolling Stones put it, "You can't always get what you want," emotional conflicts are inevitable. Every child tries to find ways to resolve these difficulties. Most of these solutions are imperfect. They may work for a while, but not throughout life. Like the medications physicians prescribe to cure people's ills, these solutions often have unwanted side effects.

Everybody tends to cling unconsciously to images of childhood and the people in it. They continue to resort to the outmoded and counterproductive strategies they developed to deal with their parents' foibles, long after these strategies have stopped working.

Children are taught and adults are required to control themselves. Self-restraint protects both individuals and those around them from their less civilized impulses. As individuals learn to anticipate and rein in these impulses, they come to judge, criticize and, at times, punish themselves for actions and, further, intentions that seem harmful and dangerous. Along with a certain degree of self-restraint and self-criticism, a tendency toward self-punishment is a necessary byproduct of becoming a socialized adult.

However, this inclination to punish oneself can outlive its usefulness and get out of hand. For some, self-restraint, self-control, self-criticism and self-punishment in the face of wishes to harm or exploit others can transform into an inclination to hurt or sacrifice oneself. Self-injury then becomes the central motif in a lifelong pattern of what is realistically unnecessary suffering.

Individuals afflicted in this way, the victims of everyday life, feel powerless to know themselves. Either people deny the unfolding self-destructive dramas in which they have cast themselves or, if they are aware of present dangers and potential disasters, they feign an impotence to avert them. Even when they have recognized their own agency in their unhappiness, they may then regard their own psyches as alien bodies and powerful enemies. They claim that they simply cannot control or help themselves. They expend energy in trying to rationalize events in order to convince themselves and others that they aren't making these things happen.

Perhaps most important, they are simply unaware of alternatives. It is their lot in life to suffer, they believe. There is no way out, they say. They expect nothing better. They are, they believe, the hapless victims of misfortunes present and past, real and unreal. The childhoods they suffered and the psychological deformities created by those childhoods are their unalterable fate. They are born to lose, they complain, to be abused and to get hurt again and again.

Such self-styled losers have an uncanny ability to find tormentors in their relationships with others. Effortlessly, even fortuitously, they happen upon their victimizers: individuals ready to use, abuse, degrade and dominate them. Having found such partners, they can then embark on a course of suffering they pretend never to have desired, much less demanded. Once the relationship is under way, both partners claim not to have predicted its direction.

There are, of course, people who are primed to torment others, people who feel best about themselves when they are degrading and dominating others. But even where not so inclined, the future aggressor can be "seduced"—as the psychoanalyst Rudolph Lowenstein put it. Ordinary people can be provoked into committing repeated acts of cruelty. In what another theorist, Otto Kernberg, has called the "private madness of the couple," these individuals, victim and aggressor, find the relationship bringing out their worst selves. They gradually lose the ability to see beyond the folie à deux of sorts that soon envelops their purview.

Such ties may be most evident and most difficult to escape in intimate relationships—in the dealings between spouses and within families, where love, sex, dependency and familiarity bind people to one other. They can also characterize relationships in school settings, workplaces and other arenas where advancement, money, longings for affirmation and approval as well as personal conflict shape and constrain the distribution of power in human transactions. In public, too, the need to suffer may move the sufferer and those around him to behave badly. Psychoanalysts from Freud on have remarked on the numbers of people who can be "wrecked by success" and who therefore sabotage themselves and make themselves fail. Issues of authority can then be invoked to explain away irrational acts and sentiments.

The perpetual victims' quest for misery and failure becomes an almost ritualized imperative. As if drawn through life, these people seem invigorated by the crises they unknowingly create in their lives and lost or emotionally numb without them. Happiness unnerves them. They need their terrible relationships. They are compelled to fail. The possibility of a change for the better upsets their expectations and threatens their equanimity. Pleasure and tranquillity unbalance them. When life proceeds smoothly, the good feeling this brings frightens them.

Perpetual victims resist common sense, friendly advice and professional counsel. At their most intransigent, they lash out at anybody who holds out the possibility of bettering rather than battering them. Their seeming stupidity about themselves can be frustrating, even enraging. Impervious and provocative, they may even try to turn "good guys" into "bad guys" and invite those who would help to hurt instead.

Such people have gotten caught up in what is commonly and correctly called vicious circles. These interactions, compelling and compulsive, constitute the sadomasochism of everyday life.

I AM merely a man of my times, like my readers. Like them, I am surprised by what our culture brings to our consciousness. When we think of S&M, a variety of bizarre images typically comes to mind. The magazines at the corner kiosk and the cable TV purveyors of midnight porn have left traces in most of our memories. We call these frankly perverse scenes sadomasochistic. In kinky images aimed to lure us into the world of the forbidden, leather-strapped dominatrices grind spiked heels into the faces, genitals and flabby bellies of fully grown naughty boys, panting in humiliation and excitement. Hard-bunned Nazi types threaten to drive fists and sundry objects between the buttocks of same-sex supplicants. It's like the Marquis de Sade—whom I will talk about later—updated and thoroughly commercialized.

Such perverse pictures at first seem removed from interpersonal problems, self-defeating patterns and habitual disappointments that can compromise and diminish the happiness of everyday life. Yet these extraordinary examples of bondage provide insights into the more ordinary, and indirect, ways in which people oppress each other. As I shall show later on, victims and martyrs who say they get no fully conscious pleasure from their suffering are nonetheless inadvertently enacting unconscious fantasies that have a good deal in common with the games played out in sadomasochistic perversions. Besides, every now and then, if only for a moment or so, the emotional truth—their joy in pain—will out.

The tableaux, at once violent and sensual, extol the bliss to be discovered either in surrendering to agony or in the abandon attained in freely inflicting it. Weird as they seem to those of us more used to what S&M types call "vanilla sex," these scenarios hold out the promise, tendered to both players, of scaling new heights of ecstasy in yielding to impulse. In actual sadomasochistic rituals, caution, dignity, morality and restraint are thrown to the winds—along with reality, since nobody *actually* gets hurt in the end. Both the prisoners and their keepers end up feeling liberated and their audience, in spite of itself, mesmerized.

Perhaps most chilling and intriguing is the willingness of the underling to be mortified, and the unabashed demand made that the dominator dominate, that the torturer torture. Much of the time, the victim runs the show. That the pretend penitent or slave should not only accede to punishment but further help choreograph it suggests an essential ambiguity in the casting of the roles in these scenes. At another place and at another time, perhaps even then and there, the two actors could exchange parts in their perverted play. In fact, as both clinicians and prostitutes well know, in actual S&M practice, the parts are often exchanged. The sadist will take on the role of the masochist and vice versa, each according to his fancy of the moment or at times simply for convenience's sake.

Sadomasochistic stereotypes and actual perversions are true to the spirit of the authors for whom they were named: the notorious Marquis de Sade, who offered up the nether side of nobility to the high-minded French Revolution and its subsequent Reign of Terror, and the less well-known Sacher-Masoch, whose *Venus in Furs* unveiled the secret sex life of the upstanding Victorian gentleman. Both writers tried to carry human desire beyond the bounds of moral convention and conscious comprehension. At the same time, they captivated their readers by speaking to something unknown but eerily familiar, to *Something Wild* in them all (as the Jeff Daniels character quickly discovers in Jonathan Demme's film by the same name). The enduring appeal of their work, inspiring later plays such as Peter Weiss's *Marat Sade* or Mishima's *Madame de Sade*, lies in the peculiar sense of revelry in the erotic dangers portrayed by them. Audiences of all eras find themselves taken aback yet enthralled by the willingness of the sadomasochistic protagonists to risk all, by the shocking and ironic shifting of the roles in the ritual enactments and by the crossing of so many boundaries to discover what is deep and dark and present in the hearts of most, if not all, men and women. For the purposes of this book, understanding and identifying with the adventures and exhilaration they portray will provide readers with deeper levels of insight into the hidden motives for more ordinary variants of sadomasochism.

I'M A clinical theorist, interested in universals, variations and particulars. Like all things psychological then, at least a little bit of basic sadomasochism is in all of us. As much as people seek pleasure and legitimate power, they also seek suffering. As much as they try to live, people aim to die. What Sigmund Freud and Melanie Klein dubbed the "death instinct"—a concept I will explain later in the book—vies with the life force for the heart and mind of the individual who is born to die. So sadomasochism becomes the moving force behind most forms of mental illness. By extension, this cracked crystal reveals something eternal buried in its infrastructure.

The perverse expressions of the urge to surrender to and inflict pain and suffering are merely extremes. They are, like actual incest, an overt expression of otherwise hidden and mysterious tendencies in everybody, which most socialized individuals repress in their cruder forms only to succumb to their more devious manifestations in other kinds of behavior. A person can inflict and suffer pain without resorting to whips and chains. Whether they know it or not, just about everybody wants to seize control of someone else. And almost everyone unconsciously seeks to submit and be punished and to suffer. What Sigmund Freud once called the "psychopathology of everyday life" is the "S&M of everyday life."

I have pragmatic ideals and notions about what is good or healthy. These help guide me as a clinician in my psychoanalytic tradition. They serve as imaginary yardsticks with which to measure neurotic states and as guidelines for getting better.

In many individuals whose personalities will be explored in this book, sadomasochistic wishes surreptitiously gain the upper hand. They dominate their lives while remaining hidden from consciousness. Without experiencing any perverse pleasure, these individuals remain stuck in the vicious circles and failures described at the outset. Breaking these vicious circles—understanding their sources, relieving the torture and finding alternatives—is not an easy task, but it is the main objective of the therapeutic enterprise.

Sadomasochistic relationships and behavior patterns are usually so sticky, people's needs for the suffering and humiliation so entrenched, their defenses so ingenious and persistent, their blindness to their own wishes and thus to any responsibility for their lives so abiding that most of the programmatic strategies devised by the self-help movement are doomed to fail. Even where the prescribed steps of these interactions seem to succeed temporarily, they do not last. As with other addictive or compulsive syndromes, the recidivism rate is remarkable.

Something more is required: genuine insight and the responsibility that accompanies it, to borrow from the psychohistorian and ethical philosopher Erik Erikson, who was *the* psychoanalyst of the sixties and my formative years. Only by embracing both self-awareness and self-determination can the individual act to mobilize the virtues that come with growing up, overcoming conflict and mastering the environment: hope, will, purpose, competence, fidelity and love, care, integrity and wisdom.

Wise we may be, especially when it comes to those around us. Yet when it comes to ourselves, it is very difficult to take the blinders off.

That is just what *The Sadomasochism of Everyday Life* is intended to do. Its aim is to get under its readers' skins, to help them look at what they choose not to see, and to call into question the emotional suffering that can overwhelm relationships.

The book begins with a presentation of sadomasochism in ordinary or everyday life. I will survey the ways in which bureaucracies, family relations, school rooms and friendships are permeated with sadomasochistic rituals that aim to maintain a balance between the forces of love and hate. The next chapter explores masochism in the culture: our fascination with the tough guys and femmes fatales of the grown-up movies, the gore and terror in PG-rated family fare, the tabloid portrayals of misfortune and mayhem. Less florid are familial, political and social trends that reveal not so much basic motives as deferred effects. When it comes to these images and their unmistakable thrust, we do and do not see what is laid before our eyes. We disavow the violent pleasures that have come to dominate our collective imaginations.

Having demonstrated the ubiquity of sadomasochism and its variants in more intimate human relations, I survey the more pathologic manifestations of this universal theme in what clinicians call "masochistic" or "self-defeating personality disorders" and "sadomasochistic perversions." Only then will it be possible to understand why the need to suffer exists as one of life's chief imperatives. I will examine sadomasochistic themes in sexual identity and gender relations. From theory I will turn back to practice. In conclusion, I will explain how treatment works and explore ways, at the level of conscious confrontation, to help ourselves as individual patients and as social beings trying to take some responsibility for our community.

SADOMASOCHISM IN ORDINARY LIFE:
FAMILIES, FRIENDS AND OTHER FELLOWSHIPS

A PERSONAL PREAMBLE.

I BEGIN this journey into darkness with snatches from my daily life at its most mundane.

I'm on my Tuesday work break: my two-and-a-half-hour exercise routine in a regimen I started six months before my fiftieth birthday, which, in concert with the Mevacor I take, has nearly halved my cholesterol, improved my posture and wind and made my middle-aged muscles rather buff. I used to hate lifting weights, but at this moment in time I find myself eager to pump iron under the watchful gaze of my twenty-three-year-old trainer, Melonie. First, however, I must do the "cardio" to keep me and my circulation youthful and lively and perhaps melt away some of the "love handles" around my waist that I have acquired over the years. I also need time to steam away the tightness afterward. I used to work all the time and ignore the bulk of my body. But now, at the half century mark, I've tried to be as sacrosanct with the time needed to keep it in shape as I was nearly twenty years ago as a young father carving out time for family and children.

First I have to go to the bank. As usual, the lines are very long. I wait in the business accounts line to make my deposits and do a couple of simple banking chores not dealt with by ATMs. I suppose I could just make my deposits into the express receptacle, but I tell myself that I had best take care of these in person. Herein lies my fatal mistake, for as luck would have it, the customer in line before me pulls out four bags filled with bills and change. I rush to the end of the longer "personal" line and wait. Precious moments and prospective laps around the reservoir vanish before my mind's eye as the minutes tick away. I'm there, and I can't move; I can feel the pounds tugging at me to get on with it.

Finally I approach the teller's cage, and, I think, I am free, free at last. But just as I arrive, I see the gates close before me as Jane Robinson, bank clerk, blocks my way. Next Teller, Please reads the rectangle that she has inserted between me and my simple goal. My protest is to no avail as Jane slides away, blank and casual. The palsied hand of the old lady at the remaining open position shakes as it reaches into an almost bottomless tote to extricate, one by one, bills, checks, slips and documents possibly relevant to this day's transaction. At some distance behind the bars, Jane chats and laughs with the three or four other tellers on their, and our, lunchtime break.

"Should I give up and get going?" I ask myself. If I don't get going, I won't even have time to warm up my muscles and stretch—imperatives at my creaky age. But when will I get to the bank? I wait.

I tell myself I have no choice. People like me used to get angry at the tellers and the bank. Now we've given up. We just wait.

It's not the employees' fault, I tell myself; they're overworked and underpaid. "The bank's understaffed because it's cheap," the man behind me, unbidden, blurts out. One would have to be crazy to think that Jane is doing this on purpose because she enjoys her power to say no.

What's the use of protesting beyond a certain point? Either it will antagonize the remaining teller and make her slower and even less willing to please or it will accomplish nothing.

Besides, your problems aren't Jane's. How could she know about your cholesterol, and why should she care? You're a grown-up, a well-established psychoanalyst and professor and not, therefore, given to childish egocentricities. Act your age. (Even if you don't feel it or want to look it!)

So what if Jane reminds you of being less grown-up, of the days when you were an impecunious and insignificant student making your way through countries such as Italy, Greece, Turkey or India—specifically, of the countless bureaucrats grinning as they peered over documents, leering even as they blocked your way at borders and teased you, before relenting and bringing down their final stamp of approval. Watch out, hold your breath. In the lands of oppositionalism and seeming indifference, "no problema" carries the same implications as those infamous words of a lover about to leave when he or she says, "I'll always care about you—we'll always be friends."

You're being paranoid. It doesn't work like that. Jane isn't on a power trip with you—not because you're a white and somewhat affluent-looking male. This isn't the Third World, despite the homeless beggars who try to staff the bank's ATMs by night. Besides, it's just a minor annoyance, a mere fifteen lost minutes in a day made up of 1440 of them.

Yes, I conclude, as I stick the deposit slips and receipts into my breast pocket and walk out onto the street at last. It's all true. It's only a matter of emphasis and of what I choose to see at any given moment. What difference does it make, in the long run? Yes, I could have made my drop in the express deposit. I could have gotten out more quickly. Why didn't I?

WHATEVER their impact, control battles, power plays and, when they are disavowed and rationalized, the subsequent games people play characterize much of our daily lives. We see them when tellers tarry, when traffic cops give nitpicking tickets, when garbage collectors manage to block unblockable streets, when Amtrak or Delta, the labor department, Medicare and Medicaid or the IRS won't answer their phones. We see them at home and at work as well as in the streets and public places—in a variety of contexts. Or rather we don't let ourselves see them because somehow we feel we're not supposed to.

On a day-to-day basis, we don't even consider all the class, racial and gender issues that come to bear on the exchanges that serve to keep people in their places. Beyond the generalities, we don't know about the current personal lives and pressures that weigh on the actions and reactions of the participants. Usually we can't begin to know what's happening in their minds or how they got to be that way unless we ask, as the psychoanalyst asks, and then spend a long time listening. Yet we sense something's happening, something unnecessary, inconvenient and rather mean-spirited: something left unsaid but often obvious.

Before plumbing the love relations and internal psychological dramas in which suffering and pleasure so readily become fused, and before opening our eyes and closed doors to explore people's intimate lives and the unconscious motives that drive them, I simply want to remind my readers of what they already know. I want to call our attention to all the ways in which family members, schoolmates, old friends and coworkers act to torture one another on a daily basis. Such torture, particularly and proverbially when it comes to sibling rivalry, seems to have been with us from time immemorial.

ALL IN THE FAMILY: SIBLINGS

"My sister," wrote the renowned poet Sharon Olds, "entered the room like Hitler entering Paris." In the verses that follow, she captures a near nightly ritual in which her older sibling used to crouch over and pee on the hapless future author. Hardly the images of a Keats or Yeats, these sorts of pictures are commonplace these days in a culture that not only acknowledges but further sanctions and, at times, extols ugliness and degradation.

Sharon Olds's sister's assault is an extreme version of the garden variety abuses taking place between sibs. Perhaps it's not even that extreme. A bit of apocrypha has it that when asked what the optimal spacing between pregnancies should be to avoid such hostilities, Sigmund's daughter Anna Freud—who had competed relentlessly with her sister Sophie for their father's attentions, and who studied and treated children throughout her long life—responded, "Twenty years!" Sibling rivalry, she implied, is unavoidable. Competition for mother love and for the other spoils of ordinary family life—special attention and privileges, power, control—is inevitable, no matter what a child's age and developmental capacities. Moreover, the hostilities within families not only have to do with competing for something, but they also derive from the primary need to inflict harm, to hurt and be hurt—and this is particularly true when somebody is littler than or simply different from somebody else, which, except for twins, is usually the case when it comes to brothers and sisters.

For example, I remember the two sisters, aged five and seven, who lived down the road from me and with whom I played during the weekends and summers our families spent in the country. They were pretty, gifted little girls from a decent home and were destined for good and "normal" enough adult lives of their own. We did all sorts of things together, although these sweet girls shunned the yukky balls I, as a six-year-old boy, liked to throw; the guns I liked to pretend-shoot; and the sundry squirming caterpillars, frogs, newts and more inanimate pebbles lining the pockets of my shorts. We dressed up, played house, even played doctor in good innocent fun. But there was a very special game, almost a ritual, that Amelia, the older girl, liked to play with Susie, the younger, when twilight and the arrival of the fireflies concluded the day. Coyly twisting some strands of her blond bangs, squinching up her nose and puckering her mouth, Amelia would ask: "Okay, Johnny, shall we tie Susie to the tree"—a weeping willow that would make Toad proud—"shall we tie Susie to the tree now and whip her?" Susie was so pretty and vulnerable with her button of a nose, rosebud lips, little dresses (Amelia wore pants) and pink-tinted plastic eyeglass frames that I would have demurred had she not been such a willing victim. Rather than recoil or protest, Susie, like a de Sade heroine, offered herself with sweet acceptance and an ingratiating smile to the lash.

We did indeed bind her to that imposing weeping willow in the Goodmans' backyard, first tying her to it with a rope gnawed and stained with dog saliva and then (I like to think now) gently slapping at her with one of the tree's pendulant branches. I pulled my punches, avoiding Susie's tender face, and restrained Amelia from going too far in her sororal zeal. Within minutes it was all over, with none the worse for wear, and we would trudge off to dinner at one family's house or the other's.

Should we eat at my house that evening, it would prove much the same with my two sisters. The same, that is, except that they were some years older than we were—adolescents close in age who vied for boys' as for my father's usually distracted attentions. Judie, the older of the two, who was smarter but less popular, lashed out at Ellen, the younger by three years, not with whips but with words ("dumb blond," "soy bean brain"). I, agreeable and bratty as the occasion demanded, chimed in with my rudimentary six-year-old's vocabulary ("Ugghy! Ygh!") and savoir faire (I would hide Ellen's napkin so she couldn't wipe her mouth). My mother would ask us to stop while Amelia and Susie giggled with embarrassment.

INFUSED with testosterone and made to be aggressive (themes I will deal with later when looking more systematically at gender relations and sadomasochism), boys can be even more crude than their sisters in their cruelty to each other. Take, as a further example, another day in the life of a loving family.

I never had any brothers of my own, though I did have a brother-in-law early on and then classmates and friends to fill in these gaps (relationships I'll turn to shortly). I found myself fairly amazed by the shenanigans and nonstop mayhem taking place among the three sons of a couple, friends I used to visit two to three times a year. From dawn until dusk Steve, the oldest; Ian, a year and a half his junior; and Billy, the baby by another three years, were at each other. The pummeling was orchestrated mostly according to the pecking order, which in turn was directly related to age. Every now and then the two underlings, heedless of the inevitable consequences of their revolt, would try to gang up on Steve, who ruled the roost with an unabashedly iron fist. But for the most part it was

Big Steve, often aided by Ian, who assaulted Little Billy and their cousins—shorting sheets, "pink-bellying" bellies, boxing ears, shoving faces into plates, nuggying triceps, all the while hurling any and all invectives at his disposal. On one occasion, checking up on my own child who, intrepid soul that he was, had toddled into the wolves' den, I made my way downstairs to the basement's family room. Perched on the wet bar, five-year-old Billy squealed with delight while Steve, astride Ian, pounded at his face. "More," screamed Billy, "more," but without an Oliver Twist's cowed decorum. In a second, Steve was up, backhanding Billy and sending him to the concrete floor four feet below his post. In no less time, Billy had scrambled back up to his formica mesa, jutting out his jaw and inviting yet another assault. "More!" he yelled, "more!" And so it went on and on.

I'm sure that my readers are familiar with this sort of "brotherly love"—with the violent teasing, assaults and sometimes even sexual brutality that brothers routinely inflict on and invite from one another. My patients regularly recount tales of their own abuses at their elder sibs' hands or rue their own tyranny over the little guys whom they learned to love only as adults. Sometimes seeing, rather than doing or acting, is believing—that is, viewing the pleasure these boys derive from the physical and emotional welts they raise.

THE sadomasochism between brothers and sisters is perhaps more complex and sometimes more subtle but certainly no less pernicious than that between siblings of the same sex. Indeed, the overtly erotic dimension of their violent interactions is quite inescapable. Discretion prevents me, as a more or less anonymous psychoanalyst, from recounting my ample familiarity with brother-sister S&M. But I am certain my readers can recall incidents similar to those told me by patients and friends: the kid sister tagging along only to be tricked into being left behind; being forced to hold her urine while standing spread-eagled over a bucket on a beach while her brothers and their cronies take bets about the endurance of her continence; and being dangled over the balcony fence by her merciless two older brothers. Or the kid brother being forced to hold his older sister's legs in the air for an hour or more, his little forearms acquiver with the strain; being left behind in the woods; being dressed in girls' dresses or summarily unveiled for her perusal and that of her friends; being "told on" when she in fact "did it"; and coming back for more—coming back again and again. In these and in other scenarios, a further agenda is involved—the battle of the sexes, initiated earlier in childhood and waged in adulthood—a subject I will return to later.

THE NEW OFFSPRING AND THEIR HOSTILITIES: CHILD VERSUS ADULT

The sexual and aggressive abuse of children, a topic whose variants I will examine more carefully later in this book, has been in the forefront of the media in the last decade. No doubt (and I speak as a clinical theorist who has studied filicide and related abuses at some length) this current preoccupation is well deserved. However, the fact remains that "the history of childhood," in the words of child psychohistorian Lloyd de Mause, "is a nightmare from which we have only recently recovered." Child abuse itself isn't new. What is new is our awareness of it, indeed our obsession with it. People have exploited, neglected, beaten and killed their babies through the millennia, and in this respect matters have only improved in modern times. As I shall emphasize in the ensuing chapter on the contemporary culture of sadomasochism, the collective consciousness gives familiar facts (such as the reported incidences of child abuse) their weight and their meaning.

These days, for all our attention to the parent's abuse of the child, a new and insufficiently noted phenomenon has begun to call itself to our attention. The battered child of past generations seems to have yielded his or her central place to the battered, or at least "bettered" parent, in an era in which the generational lines have become more generally blurred, and parents and children tend to treat each other as peers.

Children have begun to mount assaults on their caretakers, revealing a disrespect that would have stunned our grandparents as they repeatedly shock the parents and other adults charged with their care and education. Nor is this a simple variant on the proverbial adolescent rebellion that psychologists began writing about nearly a century ago. Much younger children have begun joining the revolt, calling into question their parents' authority, beginning with their entry into school and exacerbated by their contact with increasingly irreverent peer groups. These days both patients and friends fill my ears with the antisocial antics of not only teenagers chomping at the bit, but of imperious six-year-olds who won't take no for an answer. Deference to the prerogatives and wisdom of parenthood seems increasingly a thing of the past. Indeed, symposia and support groups have proliferated in efforts to help mothers and fathers deal with "the difficult child."

For example, one patient of mine, a dedicated and thoughtful father, tells me that his seven-year-old daughter Amy has made a habit of defying her devoted, disciplined, and generally polite parents. She won't get dressed or undressed if they ask her to do one or the other, won't eat or stop eating, won't go to the movies or stay home, etc. That is, not without a preliminary and often protracted power struggle most often culminating in a temper tantrum that ends up driving the whole family to distraction. One might be tempted to say that the unique dynamics of this particular couple are responsible for Amy's bad behavior, which has been defined by *The American Psychiatric Association's Diagnostic and Statistical Manual* as an "oppositional disorder of childhood." However, the Levines have discovered from other parents of second graders that there is an epidemic of such defiance among six- to ten-year olds. Psychoanalysts once called these boys and girls "latency age" children, emphasizing the pliability and modulation of middle childhood. But that too seems to be a thing of the past, with children responding in kind to the wealth of sexual, aggressive and indeed sadomasochistic stimuli to which they are exposed on a routine basis by the movies, music and television.

With that well-known maelstrom of adolescence, when some

form of cruel defiance becomes the norm, matters only get worse. Not only are parents accused by their highminded and self-righteous offspring, at least as they have been for the past two decades, of such simple spiritual and political transgressions as socially "selling out" to "the system," but now they are taunted with epithets that drive to the heart of their personal respectability and integrity. Thus, one divorced mother, a highly accomplished professional woman and devoted parent, returned from what amounted to her second or third date since the dissolution of her marriage two years earlier only to be greeted by her sixteen-year-old son with the same insult directed by Bill Murray at Dustin Hoffman in *Tootsie:* "You slut." She complained to her friend Abby, also divorced, about the slur, only to be told, "Oh, Rick and Trish call me that all the time! They torture me! Don't take it personally."

Our children of varying ages find themselves buttressed in their cruelty toward and reckless disregard of parents by their peer groups. The further problem—one I shall return to—is that the parents tend to regard themselves as their progeny's siblings. Bereft of role models, they (men in particular) lament, today's parents fail to fill these vacated shoes and instead submit to the sadism of the younger generation, whose socialization and moral development it should be their charge to encourage and direct. Grieving their own loss, they have become resigned and acquiescent in their abdication of their own authority. Despairing, they in turn fail to take on what were once believed to be traditional family roles. Their children's contempt mirrors their loss of conviction.

This, too, will require more careful consideration later in the book when I look at the historical reasons for the increasing prominence of sadomasochism in our contemporary consciousness. In the meantime, I would only underscore the progressive disempowerment, described by family historians such as Robert Griswold in his *Fatherhood in America,* of the American father. According to Griswold, over the two centuries since the colonial period in which a man's status as *paterfamilias* was a given, a patriarchal divestiture took place as a result of the mounting social processes that were set in motion by industrialization, immigration and the rise of social in-

terventionism. As the society came to overwhelm the individual eco-
nomically and socially, the social monolith, the state, presumed to
tell a man how to run his family life and intruded on his autonomy
when he did not conform to society's expectations. In such an atmosphere, a man's castle could become the courtroom in which he
stood trial and a potential prison in which he was constrained from
exercising his will, much less his authority. Immigrant fathers (of
whom there were, obviously, a multitude) were particularly at risk—
bereft of their traditions, downtrodden in the workplace, impover-
ished and estranged from acculturated children. In modern times,
further factors—economic exigencies, social movements such as
feminism and the cult of the psychosocial expert (like me)
equipped with his or her factitious behavioral norms—restructured
family life and undermined fathers' convictions in their wisdom
and right to access and exercise their paternity.

The results, among others, include the decline of the nuclear
family, the rise of the dysfunctional family and the proliferation of
households without helmsmen. For example, in the 1950s the average American household contained more than five members as
compared with less than two persons today. With divorce rates soar-
ing to over 50 percent and common law relationships commonplace, 25 percent of these American families are headed by single
parents, most of them working or welfare mothers. Within those
families remaining physically intact, new trends can be observed
that suggest that "family" as an idea or ideal has assumed a different
meaning and valence for its members than in generations past. Not
only brothers and sisters but now parents and children, their roles
blurred, find themselves drawn into states of struggle and instability
that can make for relentless mutual torture. Although such vicious
circles may be even more obvious in the dynamics of couples (I will
spend more time examining the perversion of romantic love), these
days they routinely cross generational lines in ways we often choose
to ignore.

SCHOOL DAYS

The average reader hardly needs any reminders about the S&M MOs of schoolchildren. Nor would mine be the first book to document the multitudinous and multifaceted ways in which students and teachers haze and humiliate each other as they negotiate the long and difficult preparation in the classroom for adult life. The sadomasochism of the schoolhouse is, in fact, another longlived tradition.

As in the family, it's the little guy who suffers most—hazed at the hands of upperclassmen, fraternity brothers, faculty martinets and merciless coaches. But the higher-ups can also be in for their share of abuse, typically perpetrated behind their backs by their pupils. We like to think that it's all in good fun, these "fast times" in those goofy "animal houses" away from home. However, on occasion and with increasing frequency, it gets out of hand: knives and guns in the corridors and courtyards of our junior highs and high schools, whose entrances are now protected by electronic security detectors; initiation rituals that culminate in the plebe's death; date rape; designer drugs that kill preppies; the crack that is the bane of inner-city teens. All these and many more examples betray the darker currents beneath that innocent good fun that has long ordered the social life of the school setting.

Once again I am getting ahead of myself. Instead of extremes, I'll begin with some more familiar anecdotes—again from my own experience.

My all boys' day school was a tamer version of the notorious British public (boarding) school whose violence left its imprint on generations of lonely boys deprived of the tendernesses and libidinal outlets stirred by motherly and any other feminine presences. In this exclusively male environment, the sheer violence of the male animal could emerge quite unfettered in the form of bloodied and broken noses, blackened eyes, and jammed thumbs. My classmates and I still bear the scars on our middle-aged bodies, peeking through the accumulated layers of fat and the gray hairs of midlife. I still feel the bump in my upper lip where it was temporarily torn away when Bob B clocked me with his signet ring. And I'm sure

Charlie L's collarbone still aches where I cracked it thirty-five years ago in a duel over Melissa's affections.

But the scars left by unprovoked emotional and verbal assaults probably continue to ache far more than all the sticks and stones that cracked our bones. Remembering our inevitable mortifications, I shudder to think about the damage that my cronies and I inflicted on those schoolmates less fortunate in their endowment than ourselves. There was "Bio," the seventh-grader so named because of his gynecomastia, the fatty tissue accruing underneath the swelling pubescent nipples that we'd seen in the locker room and which made him look to us like a hermaphrodite—a bisexual, we thought, a bi, Bio. In the same class resided "Matt the Masturbator," so designated after we espied him rubbing his crotch against the bottom of his desk during four successive study halls. "Vinny the Ninny" was the dumbest in the class; "Spaz Baby," "Mommy Tommy" and "Minnesota Humongus" rounded out the class list of stigmatized kids.

Nor were our teachers immune from our onslaught. Sixteen-year-old Bruce nicknamed Monsieur Slivowitz "Greasy Foot" after our reading of a Maupassant story. Monsieur Harold Slivowitz was almost bald but foolishly covered his forehead with the few strands of hair remaining in his possession. Though he was fat, his pants fell about his legs Charlie Chaplin-style. However, lacking that engaging Little Tramp's bowlegged gait, he waddled rather than walked down the halls. He also spoke French with a lisp. More than most of our unlucky masters, Slivowitz was especially fair game. The particular sobriquet assigned him was affixed after a fateful *explication de texte.* *"Il a les pied gras,"* he repeated to us, *"pas les pieds gros. Gras. Gras. Gwah. Gwah!"* To demonstrate he lifted his own ample foot, exposing a white calf above the thick black shoe and startling the class. *"Pas gros, mais gras,"* he repeated, *"Gwah!"* running his fingers to the hair held in place, we couldn't help noting, by a hair cream whose white ooze could be discerned glomming the mass together. Greasy indeed. Greezy. "Greasy foot," Bruce whispered, *"Ca veut dire, Slivowitz, c'est Greasy Foot."* We burst into guffaws but offered our confused master *"pas d'explication!"*

The fallen star was born. Thereafter—that is, for the two years that we were still in high school—the name stuck. Monsieur S. waddled ahead of us, oblivious to the insults hovering about his being, and Bruce followed him down the hall, trailing by a foot, singing sotto voce, "Greasy Foot, you got the cutest little greasy foot" while shaking his own ample jowels, Stokowski-style. Half a dozen of us followed while the rest of the class, awaiting this parade in the classroom, witnessed the spectacle from the front. We tried desperately to subdue the giggles so that Monsieur Greasy wouldn't discover the joke and end the fun. Of course, one day he did—poor nice man that he was.

With the thumbtacks, inverted kneehole desks and the encyclopedias poised for a fall between doortop and frame, the other sad sacks on the faculty suffered much the same fate as Monsieur Slivowitz. But the real coup would come—or so we imagined—when we hoisted our admired and redoubtable high school principal, Mr. Silk, on his polished petard.

Hugh Silk, the Oxford-bred rugby star first toughened in Africa by his missionary father, was as popular as any master could hope to be, far eclipsing the headmaster with his charisma. Tall, physically powerful, and erudite, he managed to both discipline and befriend us on the soccer field, in history class, in the office wherein he proffered all manner of advice on college applications and other existential choices and in the Cape Cod home where over summers he and his elegant wife entertained what we fancied to be the best of the boys, the class leaders, ourselves. To be sure, he could be mean in his British fashion—for example, when he rapped our pates with a bethimbled middle finger should we lower our legs during an excruciatingly long leg lift or fail to regurgitate the exact date of a specific battle. Yet we loved and trusted him, sought his counsel and accepted his admonitions.

However, Mr. Silk did have his fatal flaw—the sin of pride. His hubris resided in his command of geography: "Jography," he enunciated it in his clipped Rhodesian cadence designed to penetrate American ears. He could, he said, turn his head away and direct his pointer to a map of Europe during any era in its modern history of fluctuating borders and identify the name of the place on which his apparently unguided tip alighted. Such was the education that he'd brought to our crude and ignorant shores, to the "Colonies" (like Rhodesia still). We, too, were natives to be put in our places.

So we prepared a treat for him for parents' visiting day. With the trepidation typical of teenagers in those days, Danny, Bruce, Charlie and I purchased at the local stationery store a *Playboy* complete with centerfold—tame by today's standards—which we extricated from the proprietor's reluctant grip ("I've known you boys all ya lives," Mr. Ryan exclaimed, "what are yaz doing buying smut like this?" "Why are you selling it?" Bruce retorted, whisking the offensive rag away and running out the door). Having succeeded in the hunt, we affixed Miss November atop unstable continental Europe in 1805, pulled the pull cord and let the high-glossed flesh disappear in the scroll in front of the blackboard in preparation for Parents Day.

The event itself hardly matched the hilarity of our anticipation. After days of expectation, Mr. Silk unrolled Miss November before the bemused eyes of the few parents attending the show and pointed his pointer to her tits. Turning about again and again, he eyed Bruce and me before making a bon mot (in anticipation of a technology unknown in the 1950s) about the conversion of a "Jography" into a "Mammography" lesson and whisked away our lame little joke to expose the map behind her. His retort went over far better than our prank, leaving our parents chuckling and us chagrined. To make matters worse, after our parents had left, he added, with an uncharacteristic grin, we thought (glimpsing a hitherto unseen side of our master), that he would be glad to provide us with that sort of lesson. But he understood that, in our incalculable ignorance, we would, no doubt, require much in the way of preliminaries. British boys, he continued, usually practiced on themselves before treating even the facsimile of the fairer sex with untoward familiarity. Perhaps, since we seemed so inclined as well as *so* retarded, we would do best to heed his advice. "Right?" he queried, "Right, Mr. B., Mr. R., Mr. L., Mr. W.?" as he named the perpetrators. We never did learn how he had found us out, this Sherlock Holmes from the Bush, but we felt more exposed than the woman in the centerfold.

How innocent this preppy fun from the days of Madras jackets and penny loafers must seem to younger readers. However clever, cruel and contrite we might have felt—however mortified when, in the hands of a more savvy adult, the joke backfired and we were put roundly in our place—still our mischief pales in comparison with the likes of *Animal House, Porky's, Fast Times at Ridgemont High, Wildcats* and *Wayne's World* that are the cruder farcical heritage of today's generation. In those days, middle-class kids had to hide out to drink booze and didn't even know about, much less "do," the drugs of today. Despite our efforts and claims, we rarely "got laid." The bright night lights of the club scene might as well have been science fiction.

In those less disaffected Eisenhower and then over-zealous Kennedy eras, when not serving our own considerable ambition and anticipating tidal waves to come, we picketed Woolworth's, participated in freedom rides, licked stamps for the political candidates of our choice and debated their merits and our various political and ideological convictions furiously. In these purposeful ways, tamer but in spirit not unlike the protests of the sixties, we ran afoul of convention. That is, we summoned up our initiative against what we felt to be the forces of oppression and fought for them in wars of competing values. Even in our delight over boldfaced cruelties that we dared not explain or fully acknowledge, we came to lament the lapses because they violated what we believed. What we did that was bad we tried to push outside our basic frame of reference.

By today's standards, at our most cool, we were mere pranksters who didn't take many moral chances. We were nerds, dorks and wusses. Today's high school and elementary students exhibit what their parents (we) hid while they keep their high seriousness to themselves lest they invite the mockery of what they claim to believe. Today's children feel compelled to be (or at least appear to be) mean and stupid, to make fools out of themselves and of others and to trumpet the virtues of cynicism or absurdity. No longer are nihilism and anarchy, the theatrics of cruelty and of the absurd, reserved for spiritually privileged intellectual liberators, the hippies and yippies of yore. Almost all students feel free to dump on smug pretense and propriety. Yet, they tell me—my patients, my son, his friends—that they yearn for the fellowship of common purpose. They long at times for a certain naivete, for our innocence, for a sense of discovery and imminence, for illusions of efficacy in the larger world, for the ideals of the sixties' generation. They would like to count, as we did, on the ethics of truth and revelation. They would like to believe in the shared good. They don't want to be embarrassed by hopefulness.

It's only a matter of emphasis. The generations remain recognizable to one another, despite all the clichés to the contrary.

Once again, in stressing what changes and what remains constant through time, I am getting ahead of myself. What's important to note here is that the school experience provides a template on which future generations' friendships and work-related organizational behaviors are first given shape. The gaps between any two generations are as significant as their concordances. In the school context, as in the family home, balances must be struck between the forces of love and hate, community and self-promotion. As a result, sadomasochistic rituals between both individuals and groups secure the dynamic status quo. The observable forms of these traditions change somewhat from one generation to the next, but the basic structure endures.

THE BEST OF FRIENDS

Seeking and finding solace and enhancement in each other, helping and giving to one another, friends—first of all, friends of the same sex, especially where directly sexualized intimacies between them are absent—must constantly contend with the threats to their bond posed by desire, rivalry, envy, jealousy and competition. Displaced from even more significant others (such as parents and siblings), nurtured in rank order differences in settings such as classrooms, playing fields and dance floors, ambivalences take shape in unique and sometime evolving forms in longstanding friendships.

Where a bond greater than a superficial acquaintanceship is involved and deeper feelings have come into play, the histories of such relationships, rather like those of long marriages, are inevitably discontinuous. Such a story will include betrayals, abandonments, fallings-out and periods of alienation. Coming back together and forgiving each other for having committed sins of commission and mostly omission, friends must manage what they like to think of as petty angers and disappointments. They do this by ritualizations of reciprocal cruelty and humiliation, and domination and submission. Greeting and saying good-bye, friends are constantly one-upping and teasing each other.

Where the friendship's origins predate the deeper commitments of adult life—the sort of friendship forged in school, college or the army—the rules of the friendship game will resemble the sadomasochistic interplay of love and hate in the sibling relationships described earlier. That is, with this first essential difference: Unlike the brother or sister that is a given in one's life, the friend has been chosen. Friends are drawn together by certain passions. They have both the freedom and worldweariness of adults. When things get hot between adult siblings with their separate lives and diverging ties, they tend to disengage for quite some time. Friends try to stick it out, overcoming and integrating hostility into a loving relationship freely chosen. Friends sometimes can reveal emotions more directly to each other. Their relationships tend both to endure and to change over time more than sibling relationships, which are often static, bound up with issues pertaining to their common parents and defensively obscured. Nor are friends bound, except at work, by the sort of economic contingencies that constrain longstanding lovers and their families. Some other glue holds friends together.

Most of my readers will be familiar with these typical pairs: the fat girl and pretty girl grown older, one high-powered in her career, the other in her conquest of men, each deeply concerned with the void in the other's life and vociferous about it; the high school football stars, the quarterback and his running back, one of whom becomes a high school coach while the other moves on to head the derivatives desk at Salomon Brothers and continues to outdo his receiver in racquetball; the literally gay bachelor and the family man who is his best friend, each close to the other despite the differences in lifestyle—differences that are, however, derided or snidely caricatured elsewhere. In all these and other companionships, unstated professional and sexual rivalries flourish, either continuous with the participants' earliest power brokering or deriving from the various reversals of fortune in adulthood that reorder expected comparisons. Loving each other, old friends also resent and envy their bosom buddies for beating them on their own turf; for having what they do not; for not suffering and sacrificing as they feel they have suffered and sacrificed; or for simply having taken the other road. As a result, they end up either killing each other with kindness or, more flagrantly, putting each other down—or rather, up and down.

For example, one of my patients, Sarah, described her long friendship, faltering at last, with Elaine. They had met in graduate school twenty-two years earlier, become friends, gone their separate ways and reunited after finding each other in the same Elizabeth Bing Prepared Childbirth Class six years later. They then reared children together, exercising, eating lunch, talking about ideas, gossiping and seeing each other through two sets of trial separations and divorces. For a while they had told each other everything and had been inseparable, if not in reality then as "soulmates" (though this was a word both would have disdained to use). But now, without a clear falling out, but rather an accrual of casual misuses and insensitivities as the seeming cause of mounting disaffection, they mostly avoided, ignored, snubbed each other. Now and then they tried to reconcile, without any enunciation of the fact that they were on the outs, much less any statement of why. Sarah described their last encounter with evident relish.

"She *does* look like Ethel," Alison (Sarah's daughter) said to her mother after Elaine left the other day. Sarah went on to say that Alison had been watching *I Love Lucy* reruns recently and had decided that Elaine looked fat like Ethel and had the same broad lips and perky dyed hair. Elaine had stopped by for coffee and cookies: "She's always eating my food and never cooking for me, you know. She never feeds anybody, not even her own child!" She was on her way to Tarantella class and was wearing the whole regalia complete with tambourines, which Sarah and Elaine persuaded her to smack for them. The kerchief made her look even more like Ethel, Alison said. "An Ethel," Sarah added, agreeing with her, "who wasn't dressed to receive visitors much less walk the streets."

Sarah continued, "And the dress accentuated how straight up and down she's built, you know, how thick she is. Compared to me, ha, ha! She's always envied my big tits and tiny waist. And now I've got a great man, that Ed, even if he is broke, and she hasn't got anybody, only that big coop, that big, expensive coop."

Alison had also said that David, Elaine's ex, whom she saw at school when he came to watch Larry play ball, looked just like Alley Oop, with his jowels, gun metal shadow and Neanderthal hairline.

"No wonder she left him, but why did she marry him? Couldn't she find anything a little more palatable? You know, she is smart and literate despite her background. But she's not hot, not sexy—like, uh, me. And she'll turn on you at the drop of a hat. Like the time she read the second draft of my Brontë biography, and she said, 'Well, it's hardly *Anna Karenina*—KARRENYANA!' That's how she pronounced it."

It had all started the day Alison said to her brother Mikey and Sarah that Elaine looked like Ethel, and then it just struck Sarah that she did. And it stuck—every time Sarah saw her, she looked like Ethel. Then she told her parents, Gramma and Papa, who said, yes, Elaine looked just like Ethel, and they'd never be able to look at her again without thinking this. What's more, Ed had known her before they got together through work connections, and he said that instinctively he had steered clear of her and didn't really know her, but that she in fact did look just like Ethel.

Women friends tend to be like that at their meanest to each other. They backbite and gossip, get catty with words. This style has a long history, one that goes all the way back to the dress up and doll corners of the kindergartens in which little girls first negotiate group status and volatile memberships as they discover their own competitiveness and ambivalence and that of their peers. For a variety of reasons, which have to do with inherent and socially conditioned gender differences, whose nature I will explore later, they don't act the way boys do but rather speak their minds. And they do this more or less confrontationally. Words, smart ones and not epithets, are women's weapons for the most part, with one another as with men. Rarely do they actually "tear each others' eyes out," as they often threaten to. With friends, they can be solicitous and critical at the same time.

Boys, in contrast, and the men they become, tend to act on their aggression and to enjoy doing so for its own sake, taking a great deal of pleasure in violence and harm. There are individual differences and universal counterpoints to be considered (which will be addressed later when I turn to the stereotypical femininity of men and masculinity of women that become evident in the sadomasochistic scenarios that the sexes ritually reenact with each other). However, generally speaking for the time being, among themselves boys and then men like a good fight, albeit a silent one. Male friends like to joust or jostle with each other, to rib and roast without ever quite saying what it is about the other that gets their goat or simply provokes their power plays. Behaviorally direct and verbally indirect about their rivalries, the best of men friends are forever sticking it to their buddy.

Take as another example my patient Hank Kalinkowitz, who described his rivalry with Sanshay Singh, a classmate from M.I.T. and lifelong best friend. They'd each had good careers, Hank emphasized, though Sanshay's, spent mostly in India and think tanks across the world, had been, admittedly, exceptional. One of the problems was that he, Hank, had this divided life, between the lab and the fiddle, his youthful choice having been between their alma mater and Juilliard. Because of academic and research demands of his administrative duties as chairperson, he didn't have the hours to give to practice. His unhoned sound disquieted him, and so he mostly wrote for the violin now rather than tried to perform in public. Sanshay, on the other hand, had always been so dead ahead, so single-minded. Also the competition in India couldn't have been anywhere near as stiff or as daunting as it was at a major U.S. university. No matter how smart all those damned Asians were, Sanshay's

India was still a Third World country with a major league brain drain, and his ethnicity, furthermore, was one on which he could capitalize. The fact was that at the age of forty-seven Sanshay had already won a Nobel Prize. And Singh had also slept with many more women than Hank, who was bound and deprived by a more scrupulous morality—more Jewish, more Christian, more *Western*—than his best friend. Of course, there was the one woman, Trudy—constituting one of Hank's two lapses in his lifelong pledge of fidelity to the wife who nonetheless divorced him—who had also slept with his best friend and who told him that Sanshay could or would only come once in a night to Hank's three. It was a truth that Sanshay was forced to concede one boozy night of forgiveness and reconciliation.

Sanshay remained a better tennis player than Hank. He had the opportunity to practice during his upper-class childhood, unlike his Brooklyn-born colleague and pal. On the court, the scrawnier but athletically more accomplished friend from the East suffered with humor his more boorish colleague's ground strokes, coddling him along until the last devastating set of love games. "Love games" indeed! And so it had gone, even now, Hank continued. Actually, Sanshay didn't speak with him for a whole year after he slept with Trudy at the Berne conference. That was after Sanshay went fucking one night rather than commiserate with Hank about his terrible divorce. That was also the meeting at which Hank referred to him in his friend's introduction for the plenary presentation, which he himself had orchestrated in an act of supreme affection as "the inscrutable Oriental."

But after all this caddiness, they were back on good terms. Hank looked forward to spending his second lousy divorced summer at Sanshay's Hill Station summer cottage. Whatever bad things they might have done to each other, Hank concluded, they could "say anything to each other;" he could tell Sanshay anything. Anything without fearing his judgmentalism.

"Anything," I added, "except how much you envy and want to be him, anything except how much you end up diminishing yourself in relation to him when you pretend to be doing otherwise. Anything but how much pleasure you take in hurting him and being hurt by him!"

"And, no," I was tempted to add, "it's not just rivalry either. You love and hate the guy. You two enjoy your sadomasochistic games for their own sake and stir up otherwise unnecessary trouble (just like Sarah and Elaine) except that you act rather than talk."

There are far more subtle variations on these themes. For example, there are the kind-eyed killers to whom I alluded at the beginning of these few pages on friends. There is the girlfriend rushing to commiserate with her forlorn friend, whose husband has left her for another and, yes, younger (and sexier) woman, and sucking in every detail through the open mouth of solicitude. There is the "good ol' boy" who takes his out-of-shape friend to the free weights and mogul fields. And there are many ways in which friends submit to and dominate each other and derive satisfaction from the redundant rituals and reciprocal humiliations that punctuate their devotion and deep affection. Here as elsewhere, sadomasochism enters the scene as prime mover and executive director of the action that takes place between individuals drawn both to bond with and to oppose one another.

TOWARD THE WORLD OF WORK

Nowhere in daily life is sadomasochism more constantly in evidence than in the institutions that constitute the workplace. It is here that sadomasochism matters—in the professional and technological training facilities, the medical schools and hospitals, the stock exchanges, banks and investment houses, law and management consulting firms, publishing houses, advertising agencies, media behemoths, theatrical backstages, and myriad other settings wherein, increasingly, according to the statistics on leisure time, most us spend most of our time each day in the work world. It is here that the red threads of individual power and success are woven into the fabric of fixed and often labyrinthine bureaucracies whose function it is to ensure institutional stability, viability and, with luck, profitability for all concerned. In the workplace personal passions are politically exploited. The time spent at work on a daily basis, as well as the hours and years over time, wears on a person, exposing her or his underlying raw nerves. For these long hours and days, the forces of contemporary politics and cultural history bear down on the worker's capacity to provide for dependents outside its sphere.

In such a context, that is, one rife with angers, anxieties and thwarted yearnings, the demands of self-esteem collide with those of social adaptation in a perpetual state of conflict that has been long obscured by ideology and rhetoric. In such a universe, whose tendernesses and indulgences are in short supply and are doled out at best indirectly, a worker's potentially disruptive aggression must be mixed with his personal desire in a combination that can hold things and people together. Once more, sadomasochistic scenarios emerge that serve to keep everybody happy in his (or her) work.

I would call my readers' attention to how readily this sadomasochism of the work place has been revealed in recent years. Issues of sexual harassment have taken center stage in an effort to undo old sexist habits in a new sexual world and to make explicit the continuing ways in which sex and power get confounded and exploited. Films such as *Wall Street* or *Disclosure,* the latter trying to overturn sexual status quo expectations, portray the degree to which colleagues and coworkers enjoy "screwing" one another in one way or another and are manipulated by management into doing so.

Work is a world unto itself, albeit one that has its way of invading the personal lives of its employees. Angry at his boss, the disgruntled subordinate kicks the dog when he gets home. Frightened into submission, the lowly first year associate humiliates his or her lover—a subject I will return to shortly.

IMAGES TO COME

The matter of the media is the subject of the next chapter. I suspect my audience is just now a little bit confused by the usage of the term sadomasochism to describe what might simply be called competition, control battles or gameplaying in the sorts of ordinary relationships or everyday dealings just detailed. But my purposes should become clearer in the pages about to follow. In them, I shall describe how the S&M of everyday life—with all the perverse bloodlust this phrase implies—has been brought into the average American living room, which it now permeates. Every day the family members within it are treated to rather spectacular tableaux in which erotic pleasure is to be found in undisguised images of subjugation, humiliation and pain. It is there every day, staring us in the face, and all we have to do to see it is look.

The movie and TV screens into which we gaze hold the mirror up to nature, revealing to their viewers their own innermost wishes. To an extent, they are like projective tests, such as Rorschach's inkblots, offering up images of our unrecognized desires.

Chapter

3

SADOMASOCHISM TODAY

ORIENTING OURSELVES

WHEN a crystal breaks, its structure is revealed. Underneath the smooth surface are the hard angles and complex facets. These are always there, of course, but we cannot see them until the stresses mount, cracking the whole and opening its unseen parts up to view.

Then, too, we must have the inclination to look and the tools with which to see what has been unseen. Unlike the modern geologist armed with a technology, a scientific history, a point of view and certain expectations, a caveman presumably would have little interest in a broken rock and, even if he did, little capacity to make much sense of it. "The readiness is all," as Hamlet says, when it comes to understanding something that has always been: something like sadomasochism today.

My first task is to show or, better, to remind us of what we already know but disown. Surreptitious sadomasochism is to be found everywhere in the life of ordinary individuals and the institutions that organize their social lives. Moreover, it is often in the forefront of awareness, though, like sexuality in the Victorian era, it is quickly banished from consciousness and goes unsaid. It is unpleasant, disturbing and frightening, so we pretend that it's not there. Pushed to the periphery of awareness, it defies our search for a vocabulary to describe it. Unheeded, sadomasochism in so-called normal life can elude detection and thereby continue to do its work all the more effectively. Yet we stare it in the face all the time—much as the Victorians did the sexuality that they disavowed. Having demonstrated this, I will turn to my second task and call attention to the sadomasochistic crisis in our culture and to some striking popular images that are familiar but which we tend to set aside from real life.

MORE than naturalists, social scientists tend to take advantage of those historical moments when much goes wrong to come up with startling new insights into how things usually work. The Freudian revolution, which provides the base for many of the ideas and arguments to follow in this book, is a case in point.

Freud's Vienna, like so much of fin de siècle Europe, was distinguished by its seemingly unshakable sexual hypocrisy and a consensual denial of the eroticism that drives people's lives. While fathers (like Dora's) whored and philandered, often bringing syphilis back into their homes and gene pools, and while servants and nursemaids frolicked with one another and sometimes with their charges, the children in these households were regarded as utterly innocent and oblivious. Somehow, despite all the goings on about them and the liaisons in which they were enveloped, they were supposed to happen upon their sexuality only after they had come of age. Public opinion had it that upright adults were not supposed to take their lusts very seriously but rather keep their gazes focused on higher matters.

Forced by economic circumstances to abandon his career in basic scientific research and scrambling to earn a living as a practicing neurologist, Sigmund Freud took on as private patients the hysterical women—flighty, neurasthenic, often crippled or blinded without apparent physical cause—who had been dismissed and discounted by other more established physicians and designated as malingerers. It was not long before Freud capitalized on his referrals, which less prescient practitioners discarded as rejects, as a scientific opportunity. Learning how to psychoanalyze them, Freud illuminated the unconscious sexual and specifically incestuous conflicts that found symbolic expression in his patients' hitherto mysterious symptoms. It was not all that long before Freud and the intellectuals of his day found themselves identifying libidinal conflicts everywhere in the human condition. The individual and idiosyncratic neuroses of these "cracked souls" became but one variation on a universal theme that pointed Freud's and modern man's way toward an understanding of the ubiquitous Oedipus complex and the infantile neurosis that is generated in every child when first confronting "wishes forced on us by nature . . . and repugnant to morality."

Ironically, earlier eras and their chroniclers had countenanced human sexuality and its displays far more easily than the men and women of Freud's day. But they didn't quite know what to do with it, or they couldn't do with it what Freud and his followers did. By Freud's era, Romanticism, Darwinism, Marxism and positivism had come upon the scene, shedding new light on the truths reflected in Shakespeare's mirrorings of human nature during his frankly bawdy Elizabethan days. As a result of these and other accruing world views, a Freudian could now see behind any image in this mirror and detect therein a whole history of dynamic and dialectic conflicts, unconscious and thus hidden from view. The successive resolutions of these conflicts, and the new integrations and syntheses they gave rise to, determined the development of the individual and, by extension, the progress of the culture in which he or she existed. Freud would see sex in this framework.

Despite the resistance with which it was met, a protest whose degree betrayed the unwanted truth, the time was right for this new perspective. It was a time of sexual crisis and thus unexplained contradictions and dissonances. Those very Victorian gentlemen who ruled their society's establishment by day and purchased pornography and patronized the bordello by night might cavil at Freud's excessive concern with sex and the new psychoanalysis's extravagant philosophic claims. But even they could not mute the voices of other eminences just beginning to rise to the fore and clamoring to get on the Freudian bandwagon. A generation later, these intellectual leaders had become fully ensconced in sinecures of authority. Educators, policymakers, family court judges, magazine writers and others who heeded their ever more official declarations would accept as a matter of course the role of infantile sexuality in psychological and social life.

By the conformist 1950s and the unconventional 1960s, under analogous sorts of conditions and for similarly paradoxical reasons, social scientists, psychoanalysts and other commentators began to think about newer enigmas such as the divided self, the problem of identity, the ravages of role diffusion and the epidemic of alienation. However, that's another story, and one far too complex even to summarize here.

Instead, the story I would like to tell is the story of our own times, the story, that is, of sadomasochism in the contemporary and everyday life of the individual and that of his or her society—in all our lives. It's an eerie and often ugly tale that we like to leave untold—a force whose existence and impact we like to deny. I know I did, at least until I felt compelled to write this book about it.

REAL SHOCKERS

Other examples from real life, many of them shocking and new to us, are far more explicit than the more everyday power plays described in chapter 2. For instance, terrorism and fanaticism and the specter of gratuitous violence they present have come to American shores. We are repulsed and riveted by the World Trade Center, Waco and Oklahoma City debacles. The pictures of the maimed and dead children strewn across the front pages haunt newspaper readers' imaginations even as they try to marginalize the victims to some degree and to see their brutalizers as creatures alien to the modern American way of life and its so-called staunch family values. They cannot, of course—not with the lingering TV spectacles of Joel and Lisa Steinberg and the 2.5 million instances of child abuse reported annually or of O. J. and Nicole Simpson and the proliferation of programs designed to protect battered wives. Indeed, David Lynch's artistically distilled and offbeat portrayals of intimate aggression (to quote the sociologists) in *Blue Velvet* or *Twin Peaks* seem rather true-to-life renderings of Americana and its unspoken proclivity for community and family violence.

Still closer to home and even more disturbing, though less sensational, are the trends so many parents and other caretakers find themselves observing in children—trends whose ordinary manifestations were touched on in the previous chapter. A cover of *Newsweek,* inspired by the movie *Kids,* deplores the homicidal and suicidal potential of urban teenagers today. Parents everywhere have experienced the collapse of their authority. Not only do proverbially rebellious adolescents assault their rules, but indeed their very being. So epidemic is this rebelliousness and unmanageability that a variety of organizations have sponsored suburban talks and conferences on "the difficult child." Most of us could not imagine treating our own parents in the way that today's children feel free to challenge us.

There are reasons for the gradual entrance of disrespect and devaluation onto center stage, of wanton displays of power and of a delight in violence—sociopolitical reasons that I will return to in later chapters. These attitudes show the degree to which we see sadomasochism every day with increasing intensity and the degree to which we try not to acknowledge it as an aspect of our own lives. What I would like to hint at as I open our eyes is the surreptitious pleasure we find in assuming, more or less fleetingly, the roles of both victim and victimizer, as time-honored value systems and the defenses that they reinforce have started to give way. We're not quite ready to 'fess up' to it, but our acceptance of the pleasures to be found in inflicting or suffering pain and humiliation are fast being taken for granted.

CONTEMPORARY ICONS

Even where we try to deny its actuality, sadomasochism's presence in our icons betray its ubiquity. Oscar Levant used to quip that he "knew Doris Day in the days before she became a virgin." He'd have

to survey her mother's womb to find a time when today's counter-
part, Madonna, didn't try to claim that she had never been one.
The media, with exceptions here and there, of course, used to reinforce peoples' illusions of a deepseated decency. These days the
commercial imagination gives indecency free rein. Madonna's nipple rings—more precisely, those of her playmates in her sensational
book *Sex*—have replaced Doris Day's cherry lipstick. The bad girl
has replaced the virgin as an object of adulation. What's more, it's
not only a few weird aesthetes, the de Sade aficionados, but many,
many people who find themselves interested in the "kinky" images
Madonna presents. When they think about it and remember their
formative years in the forties, fifties and sixties, they realize that they
were not half so taken by Doris Day's neat and sunny composure as
they are by Madonna's funky and hard-edged erotic display. When,
in the privacy of their own homes, ordinary people open her silver
book or catch glimpses of her on MTV, they cannot help being
turned on by Madonna as they never were by Doris Day—or Sandra
Dee, Patti Page or even Annette Funicello, the various "vanilla
queens" of their youth. Somehow Madonna's telling them something about what they want. Somehow Madonna speaks to the desires inherent in the image and not just the image itself. Even as we
close the silver book in avowed dismay or perhaps feigned disinter-
est, we have found ourselves—both men and women—looking up
her legs as her toreador impales both her and his bull.

   The world of the media captures in more or less broad strokes
the images and wishes most on people's minds. The image makers,
in order to make money, must tap into their prospective audience's
collective imaginations, further shaping their responses in that
feedback loop that marketers count on to make a fit. If they miss the
mark, they will fail. This context, in what a psychoanalyst such as D.
W. Winnicott might call a "transitional space between fantasy and
reality," is found in the stuff of which real dreams and aspirations
are made, in a postmodern world writ large and made easy. Here
emotional truths can emerge from the haze of conflict and from
the smokescreens we create to hide them from ourselves. It is here,

in contemporary music and the movies, that sadomasochistic tableaux prevail.

It is just a matter of seeing. So let us look. Because I happen to know less about the music whose incendiary lyrics have become a source of public concern, I will turn now to the movies.

THE MOVIES

Mel Gibson's epic *Braveheart* concludes with a grizzly sequence designed to haunt its viewers' memories. In it, the actor-director-star, playing the Scottish patriotic rebel William Wallace, is hung by his English captors from the neck, stretched upon the rack and, with only his grimacing face visible to view, most probably disemboweled while a London throng looks on. The closing note tells us that after Wallace was drawn and quartered, his head was left impaled upon a London bridge while his other body parts were dispatched to the four corners of England as cautionaries to the locals about the deadly consequences of rising up against their sovereign. In fact, little is known about Wallace, and the rest of the film's plot was made up from a scattering of historical facts. Indeed, this image of the handsome and proud man at the moment of his dismemberment (and perhaps that of his young wife's having her throat slit summarily) startles us most. The rest of the movie's considerable violence is offered up rather decorously and cast within the terms of a familiar, indeed, quintessentially American cause: national and individual freedom. What the scene also tells us is that people's fascination with the gruesome and their capacity to hurt others has always been there, and at times with a vengeance far greater than today's.

As with so many other primal manifestations of man's instinctual drives—crude sexuality, aggression and amalgams thereof—the self-reflective self, the ego (I will return to this later), is constantly reinventing sadomasochism. We repeatedly claim that its appearance upon the contemporary scene is new and that we are taken aback by man's inhumanity and indecency. The Australian *Mad Max* trilogy, in which Mel Gibson first rose to fame, further captures the variations on this eternal theme. The trilogy projects perverse scenarios and punk cruelty into a postnuclear holocaust setting in which the medieval feudalism reminiscent of *Braveheart*'s prevails. Gibson's character, for all his disclaimers, is a paladin guided not by self-interest but by the chivalric code. The world has always been a hard, cruel place, and people have always had to suffer as they clawed their way through it. Moreover, people enjoy destroying others in helpless and vulnerable positions. Good will, like Gibson's, is a rare and precious thing.

Filmmakers have generally acknowledged the sadistic half of the equation, though they have attempted to distance themselves from this by projecting bad intentions away from themselves onto others. Like the old silents or DeMille epics, *Braveheart* has villains, most notably the tyrant Longshanks (Edward I)—a homophobe, to boot—to do the dirty work and revel in it while the heroic band of brothers assembled by Wallace, vengeful to be sure and therefore violent, remain mostly pure of heart. If they and he willingly die for their dear Scotland, it is an inspiring martyrdom, not masochism, that motivates the sacrifice of life and limb. This rousing high-mindedness sets the film apart from so many others nowadays in which the sadism is closer to home and the masochism more fully embraced. Tragic and frightening as it is, *Braveheart* feels like a breath of fresh air among the sundry films noirs that have dominated the screen since the early eighties. These films and their characters bring to the fore the extent of their viewers' fascination with suffering in one form or another and their identification with both victim and victimizer.

Iɴ the sadomasochistic images that follow, many problematic themes that warrant analysis emerge. Notable among these are gender paradoxes that have intrigued the intellectual community for the last two and a half decades. At the same time that they play upon what we find most immoral in men and women and seduce us from our avowed value systems, many of these scenarios further violate our expectations of the sexes and call into question gender stereotypes and the balances of power with which they are associated. They must do so safely and innocently enough, of course, because such films have to remain mindful of their market and the sexual politics that partly determine it. Shocking though they appear, they ultimately retain and further reinforce those gender stereotypes and power dynamics.

I will turn to these specific issues later in this book—to the prototypic development and manifestations of male masochism and female sadism in our supposedly postsexist marketplace and, more generally, to the synergy and entropy that guide and contain the manifestations of the unconscious in the evolution of a society and its culture. As a psychoanalyst, I want to begin by collecting, sifting and distilling certain impressions that operate like free associations, which are the data that I work with, before trying to interpret them. In broad strokes, I want us to discern certain patterns and leitmotivs. I want to stress the increasing cruelty and amorality of movie heroes during the course of the last generation and the use of sex as a weapon by the new wave of femme fatale heroines.

Mean Men

Movie heroes and such as straightforward tough guys, Burt Lancaster and Kirk Douglas at the O. K. Corral, have become, if not yet things of the past, matters of less interest. With exceptions here and there, for example, Robert Mitchum's ironic killers in otherwise high-minded films such as *The Night of the Hunter* or *Cape Fear,* the 1950s leading men (as cruel and diverse as John Wayne, John Garfield or Lee Marvin) were restrained from violence by the ethic of honor or fair play. They fought straight and for justice in relatively bloodless shoot-outs and fisticuffs. Only villains of the kind made famous by Richard Widmark or Jack Palance had license to kill and to enjoy it—although the good guys got them in the end.

By the 1960s, the rules of the game—the game of male movie violence—began to change. The year 1962 brought *Dr. No* and James Bond. Bond was loyal to Queen and country but made few pretenses to fair play, dispatching henchmen in any way he could, chuckling about their demises and memorializing their final paroxysms with a well-chosen bon mot. James Bond also made a virtue of promiscuity, "bedding birds" and dispatching them as well should they have been secretly working for the opposition. Yet there remained something restrained about the images used to represent this. The long fights were not particularly bloody or graphic. Nor was the sex explicit.

At the close of the sixties, a number of films had begun to linger on the aftershocks or aftermath of violence and sex. Most memorable in this regard was Peckinpah's *The Wild Bunch,* recently restored to its full glory (though other films such as *Bonnie and Clyde* or *Easy Rider* had shock value). The movie began with a scene of sweet Mexican muchachos burning a scorpion to death and concluded, unlike the more decorous *Butch Cassidy and the Sundance Kid,* with a series of cinematically beautiful montages in which blood and flesh spurted from the chests of the protagonists William Holden, Ernest Borgnine and Ben Johnson. The gore had begun, and from this point on movie audiences would hardly be satisfied with anything less.

Hollywood adopted the British censorship system, labeling films too tough for tender young eyes with R, X and, more recently, NC-17 ratings (the last for unabashedly lewd and punishing films such as *Bad Lieutenant* or *Natural Born Killers*). In this way, greedy fans could be treated to a variety of grisly or titillating spectacles while moviemakers could claim to be protecting public morals. Nonetheless, many of the movies' new men had become mean men: men for whom the cruel means justify the ends, which were usually lost sight of in the heat of battle. These action heroes relished the violent acts they committed, often adding insult to evident injury through shows of contempt and delight in the loser's humiliation. They were unabashed badasses, whose most sadistic moments were cherished by their fans. The contemporary stars include: Clint Eastwood of the Sergio Leone spaghetti westerns and *Dirty Harry* fame, Charles Bronson and his *Death Wish,* Sylvester Stallone of *Rocky* and *Rambo, Angel Heart*'s Mickey Rourke, Robert De Niro in a variety of incarnations, terminating angel Arnold Schwarzenegger, Bruce Willis dying hard, *GoodFellas* Joe Pesci and Ray Liotta, taut Tommy Lee Jones and martial artists such as Bruce Lee, Chuck Norris, Steven Seagal and more—many more.

Notwithstanding the conceit of the ratings, these new icons of powerful men inflicting harm mostly on other violent men, their putative adversaries, found their way quite easily through the supposedly seventeen-year-old barrier to our children. After all, who is more interested in conquest and mayhem than boys—preschoolers, nine- and ten-year-olds and adolescents on the biological verge of manhood? Children and teenagers snuck in regularly to see forbidden fare, sometimes abetted by ever more careless or intrigued parents, and got their taste for bloodlust. Besides, cartoon figures like the Road Runner, Sylvester, Tom and Jerry and others had suffered and served out horrible fates in animated images of brutality and silliness for years, well before real actors did. Even the fairy tales our children, like us, grew up on left ghoulish pictures in our mind's eye (most of the time, a fairy tale is not just a fairy tale). In time, standard PG films came to include the likes of *Gremlins*, the *Star Wars* and *Indiana Jones* series and family comedies such as *Home Alone*. In all of these, the flesh is ravaged in ways that stagger the imagination of today's parents: the men and women who couldn't sleep after reading *Babar* or seeing *Bambi* or *Snow White*.

And what about straightforward horror movies, the heirs to the Frankenstein's Monsters, Draculas, Wolf Men and Mummies of yore? What about the far more murderous, gory images from *Halloween, Friday the 13th, Poltergeist* or *Nightmare on Elm Street*, the originals and their numerous sequels? Here, too, the list continues to grow exponentially once we catch on to the quantity, intensity and repetitive regularity of movie violence.

ONE could argue that sadomasochism has to do with not only violence but also sex, and that there's not much of the latter in these "bad fella" films. Perhaps there is some in the list of horror movies, but it is separated from aggression itself. Indeed, the two are usually depicted sequentially, as if sexual transgressions were punishable by death. Love of violence is not enough to suggest that people are also sexually aroused by it. More evidence is needed to demonstrate an erotic melding of death and desire in the popular consciousness.

The New Femmes Fatales

Such a union of death and desire is not to be found in the brutal heroes of the movies today. It is not in the men who have been said to mistreat women but who, in fact, very often stop short of hurting the physically weaker sex. Rather, it is found in movie women, in the heroines, and more precisely, the new femmes fatales. They are the heiresses to the vamps of the silents, leggy and throaty Dietrich, barely talking Harlow in the heat of the Depression years, primly packaged Mary Astor and mannishly suited Barbara Stanwyck of the forties and fifties. But the breasts, buttocks and sometimes the vulvas of the new femmes fatales don't have to be inferred. These women frankly use their naked bodies and sex appeal to lure their lovers to their doom. They are sirens calling not from afar but from close at hand, their sexual allure in the forefront, their malevolence hovering in the air above lustful beds in which they drive men wild and, not infrequently, make them die for love.

The year 1962 not only brought us Bond, but also Ursula Andress—"Undress," we called her—the first of the new breed of femme fatale. Introduced to us in *Dr. No*, the first Bond film, she emerged from the Caribbean surf, dripping wet in her cream-colored bikini (tame by today's standards), having unsheathed the knife that had rested on her bare and tanned haunches.

I remember seeing the film with some teenaged friends and our fathers. My father—who was deaf and could never quite gauge the volume of his own voice—exclaimed in a booming baritone to the delight of the entire audience, "My god, what's she wearing—a jock strap?"

Later, in another film whose title and plot escape my recall, but certain of whose images stick in my mind, Andress did a striptease that ended when she fired two bullets at two of her onlookers from the points of her tasseled brassiere. The charges erupted in puffs of smoke and a bang about where the nipples should have been.

Boom! Boom! Just like that. Like Bernadette Peters in a Mel Brooks spoof, and the bad guy oglers were dead.

But she wasn't even that bad. *Dr. No*'s heroine had a sad story: She had been orphaned, her father a victim of the villain. Although she had been on her own, nonetheless she quickly became a scared little girl after all, a foil and helpmate to the far tougher Bond. She screamed silently when he killed one of No's henchman in a reedy stream. "Horrible," Andress said, sotto voce, and buried her head in James's hairy chest—as did Pussy Galore, Octopussy and a dozen of their kind in the two and a half decades to follow. Andress gave way. She herself posed no threat after all.

Today's femmes fatales take it *all* off. It has become routine to manipulate not only the protagonist's but also the audience's sexual feelings with naked women. Unlike the Astors or Stanwycks of the films noirs before them, these new women get away not only with murder, but with quite palpable sex and sensuality. One after another they occupy the screen, the killer women of the movies: Nastassia Kinski in *Cat People*, Glenn Close in *Fatal Attraction*, Theresa Russell in *Black Widow*, Rebecca De Mornay in *The Hand That Rocks the Cradle*, Kim Basinger in *Final Analysis*, Sharon Stone in *Basic Instinct*, Miranda Richardson in *The Crying Game*, Juliette Binoche in *Damage*, Jennifer Jason Leigh in *Single White Female*, Drew Barrymore in *Poison Ivy*, Madonna in *Body of Evidence*, Lena Olin in *Romeo Is Bleeding*, Linda Fiorentino in *The Last Seduction*, Nicole Kidman in *To Die For*, and many more.

There are variations on this major theme. In *Bull Durham*, for instance, Susan Sarandon uses her dominatrix's guile for Tim Robbins's own good. Some of these women get their hard knocks either before or after they pulverize their men. Others do not. With other leading ladies, the sex is not quite there, or it is not in itself violent; yet, interposed with nude scenes, the killing remains. Relatively undressed at one point or another, Jamie Lee Curtis in *Blue Steel*, Linda Hamilton in *Terminator 2*, Bridget Fonda in *Point of No Return* (Hollywood's version of *La Femme Nikita*) or Sigourney Weaver in the *Alien* series all prove to be resourceful and formidable adversaries.

And there are movies in which the sex and violence between man and woman become reciprocal—for example, in *Boxing Helena*. In this bizarre variant on the film noir, a quadruple amputee, whittled down to size—to a torso only—but sharp-tongued as ever, exclaims to her ex-lover and would-be rescuer when he happens upon her and her vindictive torturer.

"Get lost! We (she and her limb-severing lover) have a special thing here."

In their nakedness, all these women reveal that they have their own "balls" when it comes to action, and thus they threaten to take away the ones attached to the more physically powerful men whom they mesmerize and overpower. The havoc they produce is as directly primal as their bodies are inviting. They are descendants of the sovereign sirens who actually cut off men's heads, divided them from their humanity and made them traitors to all that they held dear: the mystic Delilahs, Judiths, Salomes, Circes and Cleopatras, sexually and supernaturally luring heroes to their deaths throughout history. But while these ancient sorceresses intoned incantations, today's temptresses use their bodies instead of words, and audiences do not have to imagine what their lovers suffer.

Choose one example. In Paul Schrader's 1980s version of the 1940s *Cat People*, starring Klaus Kinski's daughter Nastassia, the main female character was malevolent simply because she was a panther person. The virgin was a cat. She was a big black panther, in fact, and thus she killed for love.

The night I first saw the film a decade ago, a man in the audience screamed during the climactic scene. He stood up and screamed just like a kid at a horror movie. He howled out loud—as I felt like doing inwardly.

By this point in the movie, the audience knows that Nastassia, like her hybrid brother Malcolm McDowell, turns into a panther when she has sex with a person. They understand that she then has to kill a human to regain her own human form. They understand that she is likely to do so with the human who is closest at hand—her lover of the moment. They have seen Nastassia naked and stooped on the moonlit bayou searching for rodents, seen her delicious animal haunches and high hips, pert pigeon breasts, long sloping abdomen, a hint of bushy pubic hair, blood (not her own) smeared on her upper lip above that pouting and large-lipped mouth, her eyes aflurry with feral bloodlust one moment and civilized remorse and shame the next. They have seen her lose her virginity, taste her blood and change. She is, they now know, a cat person, all right, and thus a predator by nature.

However, she and zookeeper John Heard are in love. He knows everything, and still he wants to consummate his love for her. The zoologist makes love with this woman even though he knows she will turn into a blindly instinctual great cat, who will tear him limb from limb and dismember his body like those of her other ill-fated lovers we have seen in the film. She has already killed, she tells him, and still he wants her.

In the darkened shack on the bayou while unseen gators, cotton-mouths and other treacherous creatures slither and sidle through its murky swamp water, and hungry howls and bellows call from the reeds waving in the darkness spread out around them—in this swamp, Nastassia starts to undress for the second time. Her top falls away. Her face is framed in the pane of window. She parts her upper lips. She starts to unzip the fly of her jeans, spreading it apart, her crotch framed between window and window sill below. Slowly, she unfolds the denim to expose the curly, dark tangle of her pubic bush as, intercut and reflected, Heard's eyes, transfixed with desire, are held by hers. He can smell her.

"*Don't do it!* It's not worth it!" the man in the audience screamed.

Perhaps, in the anonymous darkness of that neighborhood Loews, he had felt that groin-to-cerebellum jolt of desire and fear that all men were meant to feel. Such a surge is nothing quite like the passions of his real life. The sensation is disembodied, arche-typal, elemental—a mixing of the terrors and desires of the child with the sensate pleasures of an adult man, more a matter of the imagination and its truths than of real life. Such cinematic mo-ments are designed to make us seek out our own "love death" in the suspension and safety of an illusion.

"Kill me," she implores. When Heard refuses, she begs, "Free me. . . . Let me be with my own kind."

Heard ties the naked Nastassia to the head and foot boards of an old iron bed, spreading her out before and under him. Willingly she offers her wrists and ankles to his bonds. We hear the snap of heavy rope as her limbs fall into place. Expectantly she awaits him, serene and desirous.

We do not quite see Heard take off his clothes in the dark, but we can feel his nudity and his vulnerability as we get under his skin. And all at once Heard is naked also, if not as exposed, and he is descending on her. We see his white rear end as, unseen, his penis penetrates her, sinking into the unseen folds of engorged flesh hidden in her fur.

The film cuts to the zoo that Heard keeps. There, at its beginning, a big, black panther, brother Malcolm's alter ego, tore off handsome Ed Begley, Jr.'s arm with one quick sweep of death. The audience remembers it now.

Heard approaches a cage. We hear *Cat People*'s New Age Cajun melody, the one earlier associated with metamorphosis and death. It is linked to mystic memories of the Kinski character's bestial ancestors, to her mother and father, to her orphaned and forlorn fate. Heard reaches between the bars, offering the tender underside of his hand, wrist and forearm to the creature within. She is revealed. Heard feeds raw meat to the cat Nastassia has become—a big, purring, yellow-eyed, furry black panther—a cat that looks just like the deadly woman. Lapping up the bloody morsels, she gazes up into Heard's face as only the pet we love can. He scratches under her chin as she purrs, rubbing against the metal cage. The vibrations reach through Heard's image into movie theaters' velour seats.

For years Hollywood actresses complained of the insipidness of the few roles available to them. With luck, they lamented, they might find themselves playing dumb blondes or dutiful wives, second fiddles to more interesting and assertive leading men. Times seem to have changed, and female actors have taken charge in their roles of wild, wild women.

Women, that is, of mostly men's imaginations. A feminist protest seems to be at work in the creation of these new archetypes, in which women find themselves granted—temporarily at least— greater control over their erstwhile oppressors. However, male sensibilities have also shaped and eroticized the newfound powers of women and orchestrated men's ambivalent reactions to them. Old gender roles cannot be completely discarded. Women's erotic desirability has always been a primary source of their power over men.

These sirens' fatal attraction depends on their heterosexual attraction, and this means that the old gender roles cannot be completely discarded. They must be beautiful. They must appeal to men's illusions of conquest, at least for a while, as trophies and testimony to their virile powers. And they must do so even while appealing to contradictory sentiments in him, and to what used to be called his Romanticism—the willingness to surrender all, to become a fool, to die for love.

In many of these cinematic scenarios of femmes fatales who deliberately seduce and destroy, the male lover, like Odysseus before him, is inexorably drawn to his doom (or near-doom). He may be indomitable, violent and resourceful in other contexts—a warrior, a tough cop, a litigator, a lion tamer taking on other male animals. But when it comes to women, the male protagonist finds himself transformed into a pussycat who is "pussywhipped." In the grip of a woman, a tough guy like Michael Douglas finds himself stripped of his clothes, his will and his common sense. He may know better, but he cannot help himself. On one level, the pleasure and passion are too sweet and compelling to relinquish despite their consequences. On another, it is not just the temptress's sexual thrall but the danger itself, the threat of death and the whole ethos of violence permeating sex, that draws the lover into the spider's web.

The reversal of roles and fortunes arouses ambivalence, however, and cannot be sustained. An enduring misogyny continues to lurk behind these scenes of the lover's awe of *"la belle dames sans merci."* Luring him toward his death, the temptress usually ends up dying herself. If not, she is imprisoned, punished or otherwise stigmatized for having temporarily overturned the sexual status quo. For the most part, a Glenn Close of *Fatal Attraction* or a Lena Olin of *Romeo*

Is Bleeding dies in the end. Yet the ambivalence persists, and Linda Fiorentino of *The Last Seduction* may imply changes to come.

The siren's magnetism and her willingness to use it to transform steadfast heroes into love slaves are old themes. Among the ancient Greeks and Romans, Aphrodite's emissaries on earth included a fair number of secular sovereigns. Queens and sorceresses such as Circe, Dido and Cleopatra mixed political ambition and sex appeal into a deadly brew. The foreign warriors who alit on their shores to exploit and conquer them ended up succumbing to their charms instead. Able to make men and whole nations die for them, these ancient demigoddesses were conversant with the sensual as well as the supernatural. They themselves were leftovers from the bygone days when matriarchies ruled Mother Earth and capacious fertility goddesses reigned in imaginary heavens. Femmes fatales thus come from the dawn of human consciousness.

The modern moguls have put a somewhat new spin on this theme by making women's erotic allure conform with sexual politics in the form of explicit female sexual power. Hollywood is merely resurrecting the distant past and its prehistory. Today's films call upon long-lived universal dreads and desires. Like the ancients, the current cinema speaks to the fear all men feel: their fear for their freedom and integrity, for their manhood and sometimes for their very lives, their dread of the desire to be drawn into the bed and web of a woman.

Basic Instinct's Sharon Stone epitomizes this fatal attraction. The specter of sex and death hovers about her person: the ice pick on the rumpled bed and the first murder victim's bloody limp penis. In the movie's most famous moment, Stone's character uncrosses her legs in what could be her most vulnerable and compromised position—in a police station where as a suspect she is being interrogated. Lit from below, the mesh of her pubic hair is fleetingly but unmistakably revealed. Unmistakably? Perhaps it is a mirage after all. And all at once, the balance of power shifts. Entranced, turned on, shocked and somehow afraid, her interrogators are undone. One of them, the sadistic cop played by Douglas, will soon become her fool for love. Stone's character is, and aims to be, devastating.

THE REAL THING

As I implied in the introduction and as I will elaborate on in a later chapter on perversion, S&M proper, if you will, is fast becoming commonplace on the contemporary scene. I have already noted its presence on Cable TV and in a book produced by one of rock's superstars. In addition, S&M sex clubs have been cover topics for magazines such as *New York* and *Esquire*. S&M suppliers ply their wares in big trade shows in major hotels, coincidentally right next to conventions of psychologists and orthopedists. Dominatrices tell their true stories not only on cable TV in the wee hours but now on daytime TV talk shows. Even our teenagers have for years pummeled us with jolts of punk, heavy metal, rap and more—the music of assault.

Beyond the popular media, S&M fascinates highbrow intellectuals, artists and academics who have joined more offbeat performance artists in paying it due heed. Thus, *The New Yorker* devoted a full-length article to unmasking, or rather interviewing, "Pauline Réage," author of *Story of O*, the book that became a cult classic and a compelling pornographic movie. Biographies of the prisoner, playwright and French cultural hero Jean Genet and the critical theorist Michel Foucault claim the front pages of the *New York Times Book Review*, stunning readers with their revelations about the hard edges of the writers' homoerotic lives. For one of two productions transported in 1995 from Sweden to the Brooklyn Academy of Music, Ingmar Bergman chose to mount Mishima's *Madame De Sade*, a paean to the glories of pain, bondage and humiliation, themes never before treated so directly by the great director. In academic circles, particularly among students of gender and its literary deconstruction, one sees a growing preoccupation with sadomasochism as a universal theme whose analysis, or deconstruction, is believed to proffer new and surprising insights into realms such as society or the imagination. In my own field, psychoanalysis, the late Robert Stoller, a brilliantly innovative sexologist whose ideas I will turn to later, clearly focused the field's scrutiny on what he called "the erotic form of hatred."

Although supposedly detached from the everyday life of ordinary people, but real and direct nonetheless, sadomasochism has made its appearance on the cultural scene and even, increasingly often, stands in the limelight.

CHAPTER 8 will explore more thoroughly the "battle of the sexes" portrayed in the media. In the meantime, in chapter 4, I return from this excursion into the theater of sadomasochism, as it were, to a reexamination of everyday life, where the pleasures are usually less obvious. As a psychoanalyst, I will reassert a truth most people know but do not like to admit or acknowledge when it comes to themselves and not just the antiheroes and heroines of the movies: People want to suffer. And because they unconsciously—routinely and repeatedly—seek out misery, there are no easy answers and no simple solutions to the vicious circles in which they so often find themselves entrenched.

Chapter

4

VICIOUS CIRCLES

In this chapter, I examine one of the most persistent and pernicious manifestations of the sadomasochism of everyday life. Almost all sexually and emotionally intimate relationships find themselves compromised to some degree by the satisfaction people find in suffering and subjugation both as sufferer and subjugator, in teasing and being teased, controlling and being controlled. However, in some of these relationships—indeed, in a great many more than we like to recognize—the forces of harm can spin out of control. When this happens, lovers become victims and tormentors entrapped in what amounts to vicious circles. I will schematize the parameters of these binds, which are familiar to many of my readers, reserving for later chapters an exploration of the personalities involved and their deeper motives. I will begin with some examples.

The Woman Who Loves Too Much
Meets the Man Who Can't Commit

First consider one of those familiar cases of a woman stuck in a relationship with a lousy man, and the friend who tries to pry her loose.

Consider Judy Gould, her boyfriend Bill Andrews and her friend Amy Jackson.

As far as Judy Gould is concerned, Billy's latest leave-taking is but another unfortunate and ugly turn of events. Perhaps it was predictable. Billy is just another one of the guys who is skittish, self-centered and mean. Judy seems simply "born to lose," and now she's losing him. Judy's life never seems to hold out any options to losing. Standing up for herself only makes matters worse, she declares. Though each cruel twisting of fate comes upon her as if for the first time, hurt and disappointment nonetheless loom as foregone conclusions. These are what she expects and what she gets.

Judy's self-contradictions are amazing to behold, Amy Jackson thinks to herself as she listens to her friend's latest lament. Summoned to yet another "emergency lunch" by Judy, Amy cannot help remarking on how short her friend's memory always seems. Amy was confused at first by Judy's latest installment. Despite the desperate phone call, when they got together Judy started out on what seemed to be a positive note. For the first time in eight and a half months with her boyfriend Billy, Judy Gould refused to accept the charges on a collect call from his *other* girlfriend—a call to Judy's apartment at 2 A.M. while she was lying in bed with him.

Hearing Judy's story of the night before, Amy would have liked to give her the thumbs up for this one. But somehow she still didn't believe it. So she sucked in her breath and waited, trying to be optimistic. Yes, Amy sensed at this moment a glimmer of hope. Maybe she had succeeded after all in getting Judy to think about her deflated picture of herself, and to call into question her haunting sense that she doesn't deserve better treatment. Maybe in helping Judy look at herself, she had gotten her to look at this latest boyfriend more clearly and to see that his wasn't the only act in town. Still, Amy couldn't quite believe it.

Amy has known Judy for ten years and has seen her through at least a dozen relationships like this one with Billy. Again and again Amy and other friends have urged Judy to see a therapist. Judy Gould has to figure out why she keeps getting hurt by men: used, taken for granted, kicked around, dumped: "You name it—the whole ninety-nine yards!"

"Why do you put up with it?" Amy has asked her friend over and over. "How does it keep happening to you? And where do you find these guys anyway?"

"I dunno," Judy answers dully and repeatedly. "I guess I'm some kind of magnet for them."

It seems that Judy is forever getting hurt by "Mr. Wrongs." Most of the time they get her into bed right away. Sometimes they're competent lovers, but usually they're not. And somehow it's these duds that Judy always ends up with—the men who "don't even know I'm there." In any case, once they've gotten what they want from her, they don't call for maybe a week. So Judy finds herself hanging out by the telephone or checking in every fifteen minutes to retrieve the messages that never come. When they show up again, it's for short bursts of time before the inevitable disappearing act. With almost every one of these men, it turns out that they're unavailable, usually because they're involved with somebody else. At least one other, and no doubt "superior," woman always takes precedence over Judy. In Billy's case, she lives in Santa Fe ("this Buffy or Muffy or whatever her name is"). Now that he's made her rival's existence known to her, Billy's made it a further condition of Judy's continuing to see him at all that she allow this other "Princess Chick" free access at all times.

"I've lost a lot of sleep over it," Judy concedes, recalling all the tossing and turning next to a guy who never stirs. "But what can I do? If I want Billy, I have to put up with it. And who knows"—in fact, she's certain of it—"if I love him hard enough, give him enough, he'll change. He'll find himself and love me one day."

"In the meantime, *it's torture*," Amy tells herself—for Judy certainly, but for her as well as she listens, lunch after lunch, to her friend's litany of woes. It is exasperating to see so many of her efforts to dislodge Judy from her suffering fall on deaf ears.

Just this one time it seemed that Amy and common sense might have won out. Just for a moment, Amy thought that she'd enabled her friend to say no—to Billy and her own worst self. After months of cajoling, at last Judy had done something, or so Amy hoped. She had inched forward and said no. No to something outrageous. Not a resounding no to be sure, just a little baby one, but a no nonetheless.

"Thank Heaven," Amy found herself exclaiming out loud, exhaling at last. "Thank Heaven for small blessings."

Realizing what she had said, Amy could've kicked herself. She shouldn't have lapsed and put Judy down—like almost everybody else in her friend's life. A friend shouldn't be mean, not ever, no matter how frustrated she feels, not even to a masochist.

Having slipped out, Amy's faux pas slipped by. Judy didn't hear her because as always she wasn't quite there. She was in the throes of some other, deeper hurt—something from inside, a memory of misery. It's the kind of memory that makes a person forgetful of the people who would help rather than harm her. It's the sort of painful memory that wraps around a person.

"A pitstop, that's me," Judy now continues, utterly oblivious, it seems, to Amy's instant of sarcasm. "A drub, a doormat!"

Again, potential triumph has evaporated into defeat.

Again, Judy's lower lip is curling as it always does while she buries her eyes in the crinkled Kleenex that cannot contain her tears (like a nine-year-old crybaby, Amy can't help thinking). Once more Judy's grief overtakes her in convulsive sobs and explosive sighs as she exclaims, "He walked out, the shit. He left, and I haven't heard from him in two days—the louse, the selfish fuck! What did I do wrong? Nothing!"

And damn it, Amy can't help noting, Judy is smiling now. She's congratulating herself on what she takes to be her insight, a truth of her own, another injustice to be added to her collection. She grins, smug, nodding her head as she confirms the fact for Amy, the fact that she, Judy, knows best after all.

"They're all like that! What I do doesn't matter."

"And what I do or say doesn't either," Amy adds to herself, silently this time.

•   •   •

"Hell," Bill Andrews hisses to himself as enters his apartment at 11:30 that night and is greeted by the blinking red eye of his answering machine. "Hell, she just won't take no for an answer."

Neither will his boss Hank Kleinschmidt, senior partner on the deal that Bill, perennial associate that he seems to be, has been working on into the wee hours all week. He just can't please the guy. He's always forgetting to dot a stupid "i" or cross an inane "t." Bill can't say no to the Nazi, but he can't seem to do anything right either. And he can't get himself to leave either—to the exasperation of friends and headhunters. He's stuck with Kleinschimdt, all right. The guy's exhausted him with his nitpicking, his career's careening into nowhere and he has to contend with Judy's sniveling on top of it all. He's tried to tell her what the terms were, but she just won't listen.

There's just something about her, Bill reflects, pulling off his coat and tie and eyeing that reproachful signal before responding to it. She's smart and good-looking, and loving to the nth degree. It's just that Judy's such a nudge.

Where does he find them, anyway?

All right, she did it. Here he'd been waiting to hear from Duffy for three days, and Judy refused the call. Okay, did she then have to tell Bill what she did? God, he was so drained that even then he didn't react. Then she upped the ante. Judy started her nudging, literally nudging him while he was sleeping, asking him whether he feels anything for her. He was so tired he couldn't even feel where his toes were, and here Judy was asking him whether he even likes her or desires her.

Why's he using her, she wonders at 4:20 A.M., serious and wide awake, when he's got to go to the printer at 7:00. Hell, this time he left just so that he could get some sleep.

As with Kleinschmidt, so with Judy, though the two are such opposites. There are times when her every word, her every flicker of an eyelash reproaches him, tells him something's wrong. Something's morally wrong with his bones, and Billy should feel guilty—very, very guilty. Why, the mere act of his breathing is an injustice to her. Yeah, she's always accusing him of being remiss—like that martinet who runs his work life and runs Bill into the ground. And God, does Bill hate feeling guilty.

Judy doesn't have power over him, the way that schmuck does. Quite to the contrary, with Judy the roles are reversed. Because she wants Bill so much, or says she does, Judy just asks for it. She also has a knack for making Bill feel bad about himself. Bad and mad. A lot of the time, the mere smell, sight and sound of her, even when she's not whining, gets him so infuriated his veins could pop.

The difference is that because his boss Kleinschmidt could fire him, Bill has to take it—but Judy not only takes what Bill dishes out but, in fact, she keeps coming back for more. Bill sees her and he sees red, like the flash on that answering machine. So maybe, truth be told, that's why he stays with Judy—for revenge, because he can take out his anger at the world on her, because he can't stand up to men, to authority figures. Maybe. Or perhaps it's just to get his rocks off. Maybe he's just a sadist!

It's not that Bill beats Judy up exactly. Nothing that obvious and crude. He's too much the gentleman for that sort of thing. He can't stand being held accountable for anything he's actually done or said wrong—something other people can see. He's a "passive aggressive male," out of the book that Judy left on his pillow the other night. It's what he doesn't do. It's that he stonewalls her, ices her out, flips her channel off. Like now, as he presses the "play" button and pours himself a glass of cabernet.

The messages, beginning at 7:30 A.M., start out calmly enough. Billy might even say they were mildly dignified were it not for their interminable length and the monotonous agenda of what Judy's day will be like without him or her pseudo-psychologizing about Bill's fears of her "intensity" and the "power" of her love. As the tape and the day roll on, and Bill fast forwards through the afternoon and early evening—careful not to miss the urgent message from his accountant about the damned audit, which he also got at work, his ears pricked for the sounds of Duffy's response to his last entreaty—Judy's words begin to desert her. Her punditlike pronouncements become punctuated by weeps and wails, which soon enough replace them altogether and which, sped up, sound worse than Donald Duck.

The tape concludes with a 10:45 P.M. message—no noises now, much less language. Just a hang-up, a click that isn't even a syllable. Bill turns off the machine. On his way home in the firm's car, he'd even thought of calling Judy—for a rapprochement, a little mutual solace, R and R. But *it's torture.* She's driving him nuts, this little masochist, and he isn't going to see her after all. He'll just let her stew until he decides he needs her again.

Turning off the phone's ringer, Bill settles into himself. . . .

THE PARAMETERS OF VICIOUS CIRCLES

When it comes to relationships like these, there is no such thing as bad luck. Nor are these binds a matter of mere habit or conditioning. Interactions such as Judy's and Bill's vicious circles are defined by the following parameters:

1. They are characterized by *fixed patterns of behavior.*
2. This destructive behavior is not so much reactive as *deliberate.* It is not a response to external events but an expression of *calculated provocations and power plays.*
3. The abuse and humiliation are not one-sided but are sustained because victim and victimizer are engaged in a *collusion.*
4. In these collusive patterns of abuse, the victim's and victimizer's roles tend to become *blurred and even interchangeable.*
5. A number of *defensive rationalizations and shared disclaimers* are employed by the participants in order to cover up the motives behind these hurtful behaviors and keep them going.
6. These behaviors are *symptoms* of unconscious conflicts.

These six major characteristics all point to the *compulsive* nature of the torture in question. This quality makes this behavior very hard to change. Let me elaborate:

Judy and Bill have fallen into fixed patterns of behavior in which they hurt each other repeatedly. With relationships such as theirs, it is not a question of one individual's being irritable, momentarily striking out in anger or generally having a short fuse. The aggression and destruction in these interactions are not explosive or sporadic, not results of some spontaneous (emotional) combustion. Quite to the contrary, the cruelty and abuse are stereotypic, predictable, repetitive and almost ritualistic. They are present as a monotonous hum of disappointment and dissatisfaction, like a ringing in the ear that won't go away.

Judy is always getting hurt, and Bill is always hurting somebody. As Amy and, to some extent, Judy herself recognize, she always finds indifferent and controlling men and stays with them even after the inevitable injuries, disappointments and humiliation. For his part, Bill repeatedly seeks out "losers" like Judy and ends up misusing them and taking them for granted. When one or the other tries to break the vicious circle—when Judy stands up for herself or Bill allows her to assert herself—either one or both players become tense and uncomfortable and act to restore the familiar pattern. Thus, Judy "nudges" Bill to the point that he must again dismiss her. Wanting a rapprochement with her, nonetheless Bill cannot stop himself from continuing to deprive Judy and devalue her.

The participants' need to reenact the drama again and again further reveals that the aggressor and victim are not reacting to haphazard, external events. Instead, the victim deliberately provokes mistreatment. The abuser responds to predictable provocations with calculated power plays of his or her own. The repetitive suffering and cruelty in these scenarios have a forced and, at times, arbitrary quality. Observers such as Amy notice these patterns even when the players try to attribute their unhappiness to misfortune or the other person's sins.

Claiming innocence, Judy accuses Bill. He alone is the guilty party. Avoiding introspection, she knows only that Bill is a "shit and a sadist." She does not let herself see that she stays with him, seeks him out while driving him away, gets his goat, invites rejection and mobilizes his worst self even when he fails to respond as she anticipates. Claiming honesty, Bill sets her up for humiliation, taunting her with the presence of another woman and demanding that she accept his unacceptable terms. There's nothing accidental about any of their double dealings with each other.

These sorts of manipulations are only possible, however, when the two participants are involved in a collusion. In other words, it takes two to tangle. In these cases, abuser and abused need and seek out each other.

Pop psychologists have described these interactions as a co-dependency in order to emphasize the complicity of the seemingly innocent victim in his or her victimization. But this view does not quite capture the drive on both sides. To emphasize only the attachment of the individual who is exploited to the person who does the exploiting obscures the fact that each is impelled to find the other in order to gratify individual needs and simultaneously to cover them up. A fit between victim and victimizer is essential.

For example, when Jack stands Betty up for the second time, she calls it quits, unlike Judy. She would never accept anything like Bill's absurd and demeaning terms. Another man, Abe, would never think of subjecting Judy to such mistreatment. Probably she would soon grow tired of him. Restless and nonplussed, Judy would look elsewhere for Mr. Wrongs or try to provoke a Mr. Right into wronging her. He might tolerate her manipulations for a while, or even succumb now and then to her provocations, finding himself seduced into inflicting harm. But when the tensions and unpleasant feelings prove too much for his conscience to bear, Abe would exit as quickly and gracefully as possible. In contrast, people like Billy and Judy have trapped themselves in interactions in which both of them feel angry and degraded—in behaviors that bring out the worst in both of them.

This brings me to what is the most surprising feature of all in such self-destructive and destructive interactions. When it comes down to it, the roles are ambiguous and often interchangeable. The victim is as much in control of the abuser's power plays as the more obvious perpetrator is. Both suffer, both are aggressors who act to make the other person feel bad and both find gratification in what they do to the other person and to themselves. (Why this should be so and how exactly it occurs—why the masochism and sadism of everyday life are always sadomasochism—will only be comprehensible once we have delved more deeply into the self-punishing personalities and the unconscious perverse motives of the partners in these destructive duets.)

It is evident how bad Judy makes Bill feel. His self-degradation is also evident in the degree to which his companion in misery, Judy, is herself in charge of his reactions and can push his buttons. Moreover, in the work setting Bill acts out a role like Judy's, playing the provocative underling to his mean and critical boss. With male authority figures, he submits to the sort of abuse that he directs at Judy. Still, the basic or external roles seem fairly well set in Judy's and Bill's interactions, with Judy generally playing the acquiescent doormat to Bill's muddy boot. Their's is not a complete relationship—for better or worse.

Over time, however, as a couple remains together and one partner identifies with the other, boundaries and roles break down in even more obvious ways. It becomes increasingly difficult to determine who's suffering the most and who's doing the lion's, or lioness's, share of the abuse. Time is another factor here. Bill and Judy have not cohabited long enough. They have not mired themselves in the sort of squabbles that beset and besmirch so many couples, bickering in which the blame for their mutual mess is very much at issue but is also very hard to assign.

Consider the example of another couple—Judy's friend Amy and her husband Ed.

"A fine one to give advice," Amy Jackson berates herself as she lifts the comforter and pivots out of bed. "Maybe Judy's got the right idea, after all. Maybe marriage *is* for the birds, and men *are* a bunch of sadists."

It's 3:30 A.M. She steals a glance in the bathroom mirror at her now haggard face, the eyes sunk deep and ringed with black like Ding-a-Ling's, that panda in the zoo (a simile she's borrowed from Judy's descriptions of her woebegone self), as if she'd been beaten up. Amy continues her trek to the living room where her husband Ed is sleeping without her. There he is, a mound of blanket and bundled-up flesh on the sofa, curled into himself as usual. Yes, *it's torture.* It was another of those nights that the Jacksons have come to count on once or twice a week when they go at it, when everything's gone wrong. This one was a real shame, though, with their daughter Sarah away on a sleepover, their anniversary at hand and a whole weekend of projected romance ahead.

Sometimes Amy thinks she should see a shrink. What gets into her when Ed gets home from his studio? Here she had waited for him for two hours after getting back from work herself, and before she knew it, "critical Amy" was on him. He should lose weight—what's he waiting for? He was so good-looking once. She got him the dandruff shampoo—why didn't he use it? No, why didn't he notice it? Men never see anything. Shouldn't he have tried to spend ten minutes with Jen before the little girl left? He's her father, after all. Other people have schedules, too. All in all, why is he so utterly caught up with himself? Can't he notice her, like now as he buries his face in the paper? Tonight of all nights, he could have remembered the rubrum lilies—did he think three roses from the Korean market was going to do it? And, yes, did she have to ask? Why didn't Ed just go ahead and make that reservation at the French restaurant? Does he even know what day it is? Who she is? Does he care?

So in the early morning after the anniversary celebration that never was, Amy stares at this blob of snoring oblivion. As she fleetingly calls up in her mind the warmth of that once sweet, hairy chest in which she used to love to snuggle, she thinks she could take that brass lamp from the end table and bludgeon him. Yes, she could kill him!

Forgetting herself, Amy pads into the kitchen. Too late. Forgetting her bare feet and the evening's crescendo four hours earlier, she is painfully reminded of both. A shooting pain, a sweet and burning slash—a shard of shattered crystal has cut into her sole, and her soul. Only then is Amy reminded of the tumbler she hurled at Ed's feet in the heat of battle and of the volcanic outburst that

drove her mate from her arms for yet another night of shared loneliness.

"Who started it all?" Amy wonders as, shivering, she tries to find
the offending sliver in the gash in her foot. Whoever starts it anyway? How did it go bad? Whose fault is it?

WHATEVER their more obvious part in these cruel dramas, active
perpetrator or passive victim, the actors cover up their roles and
their motives for entering the scene. Owning up to the uglier impulses and feared outcomes being played out would upset most
people's views of themselves and of their essential goodness. So they
protect their self-esteem, appease their consciences and permit
themselves to keep on doing what they're doing by externalizing
blame and concocting convenient rationales for staying in abusive
interactions. These individual defenses are reinforced and corrob-
orated by the other player's disavowal of what he or she is doing and
why. In their collusive relationship, both people act to create and
confirm shared disclaimers in which they pretend to have no other
choice except to remain mired in misery. Because of this defensive
complicity, the masochist can avoid the guilt that would come with
owning up to his or her own vindictive or sadistic urges. And the apparently invulnerable sadist is able to escape the injury to his self-esteem that would result from embracing his own helplessness and
humiliation at being manipulated into being bad. Blind to themselves, denying their own motivation, the collusive pair persists in
gaslighting each other and can remain impervious to an outsider's
insight and advice. Other people may see through the rationales,
the disclaimers and defenses, but the injured and offending parties
can not.

Thus, Amy's understanding of the ambiguities of the evening's
debacle comes to her only later when, in solitude, she can reflect on
herself. Hours earlier, caught up in her tantrum with Ed, who kin-
dles and rekindles her rage with his passive aggression and who continues to withdraw from her as she gets angrier, she knew only that
he is depriving, belittling and enraging her.

Similarly, when he is alone, Bill fleetingly comprehends that he is misusing Judy in order to puff himself up and to exact his revenge on the people who have pushed him around, reversing the subservient roles in which he's cast with his boss and with Duffy. Fleetingly, he can own up to his fragile and flagging self-image and to the cruel gamesmanship he employs to buttress it. However, the minute Judy makes contact with him—either in the flesh or in the whining, accusatory voice on the answering machine's tape—he becomes caught up again in her provocations, gets defensive and loses his bearings. Because of her desperate horror of loss, or so she believes, Judy just cannot be alone. So she cannot stand back in order to look at herself—not yet.

Advice, cajolery, reason and even a certain level of insight usually fall flat in these circumstances because both chronic victim and habitual oppressor are in the throes of repressed unconscious conflict. They are acting in response to emotional tensions and to inner agendas that derive from their forgotten childhood relationships. They are driven to do what they do. For each individual, the torture of everyday adult life is really a reenactment—both of actual experiences from their earliest years and of fantasies about them. Forgetting their past, they are doomed to repeat it.

In clinical terms, these reenactments are symptoms, or "compromise formations," as the psychoanalyst Charles Brenner has put it. Such psychological inventions permit the sufferer to act out forbidden wishes in a disguised form, such as masochistic compulsions, in a way that is mindful of the dictates of social propriety as well as the constraints of reality. They can do what they are doing without knowing what they want, indeed without even consciously feeling what they are truly feeling.

To some extent, closet masochists are seeking the same sort of gratification as the practicing sadomasochistic pervert (a topic I'll elaborate on in chapter 6). But they do so deviously or symbolically so they will not consciously experience the sort of pleasure that makes a person feel guilty, ashamed, foolish or plain crazy. Sometimes one of their unconscious aims is to atone for real and imaginary sins, misdeeds or sins of the heart and to punish themselves.

Unhappy souls such as these may value themselves too much to let loose their baser instincts, but not enough to protect themselves from inviting pain and humiliation in their day-to-day relationships.

Sometimes, by moving others to act badly toward them, they are trying to take the moral high ground and feel superior and power-ful. Sometimes such habitual victims strive to relieve a certain ill-de-fined tension in themselves. Or perhaps they are trying to fill an inner emptiness and feel important by creating crises in their lives. Or it may be that they simply want to feel alive in feeling hurt—you know, "Pinch me, I must be dreaming." (All are themes I will deal with at greater length in chapters 6 and 7.) Most often, all these mo-tives combine in compulsions to get hurt and to be made miserable.

But these remain compulsions, not quirks of fate. Like the sub-stance abuser addicted to self-destruction, the sufferer is addicted to suffering. And like the genuine addict, the compulsive victim is emotionally dishonest, particularly in efforts to convince others of his or her innocence. The compulsive sufferer tries to pull the wool over his or her and other people's eyes so that he or she can keep on finding his emotional fix.

At this point the depth psychologist proceeds beyond the behav-iorist or the 12-step recovery advocate who tries to understand this neurotic behavior as a function of reinforcement or habit and at-tempts to modify it through reconditioning, support or exhorta-tion. As the psychodynamic clinician sees it, the conflicts from which these manifest symptoms and consequent interactions derive are not completely revealed in the behavior itself. What people do or say is merely the tip of the iceberg. Instead, the practitioner has learned, one must listen with "the third ear" to what the individual is communicating between the lines of the conscious script, to what is unconscious. Then the extant past, the masochist's childhood, comes to life. Then we learn how much this grown-up still clings to the parents who brought him or her into the world and defined it for him or her.

A HINT AT THE FORGOTTEN TRUTHS

Attentive in this way to a person's feelings and self-deceptions, we learn, for instance, that Judy Gould's problems with men predate Billy. Indeed, her troubles can be traced back to well before the dozen or more men who seduced and abandoned her during her adult years. For Judy, life—her love life—began with Daddy. Or so she begins to learn when, some months later, with Billy gone, Judy begins to make sense of her life in her psychotherapy.

Judy's father was never home—especially as far as her mother was concerned. Mrs. Gould was forever complaining about her husband Jim's disappearances, his philandering, his drinking, his unreliability, his indifference toward her. Her daughter Judy "didn't have a lot of him exactly," but she did have "some." That is, before he died and abandoned the family altogether and forever. She didn't have enough to help her not fear losing him or anybody else later on in her life. But what she did have from her father was more than what her mother got and just enough to make her feel guilty. What Judy felt when he was around made her feel even worse—excited and happy, yes, but also terrible at the same time.

Alone at last in her bed, tossing and turning as usual, unable to sleep, confronted now with herself, Judy remembers:

It's eight in the evening, dinner's over, bedtime's approaching and little Judy Gould, aged four, is playing with her daddy. Huddled between the foot of her bed and her closet, the curly-haired little girl is aquiver with anticipation. In a sudden burst, echoing the "surprises" of the nights past when he has been home, Jim Gould, swaying slightly, an acrid odor about him, flings open the closet door. Erupting in a roar, his arms outstretched Frankenstein style, he towers over his daughter before lurching toward her. Shrieking, the child flees the "monster," scurrying out of her room and down the hall, her lips jiggling and voice shaking with each jarring footfall, until she finds another nook in the space between the living room sofa and the wall behind it. Judy chews her fingers, tense but enthralled as she listens to the thunderous and rhythmic footsteps of her dad in the corridor down which she has just fled. Jim opens the door to the living room, slowly this time so its hinges creak. But before her father can complete the process of discovering her, Judy vacates her hiding place as she routinely does. Catapulted by her delicious terror, she vaults into his arms and buries her face in his woolly smothering trunk, the legs beneath her nightgown straddling his waist as she giggles hysterically. It takes some minutes before the convulsions subside into sighs and, quieting down, Judy can be carried off to bed.

To bed, where she cannot fall asleep, where she can never sleep alone.

To an onlooker, Judy's and Jim's carryings-on look normal enough—another instance of the garden variety teasing and horseplay of a delectable daughter and her playful dad. Certainly it is not incest as we usually think of it.

It is just that this is all there is to their relationship. It is a matter of context and of meaning. Jim doesn't father Judy, he only plays with her and teases her. He is never around, except now and then and at night. He never talks with her, never takes her places, never knows what she is doing when he's not there. He is never there to husband his wife, Judy's mother—not in any way his daughter can see or want to know. It seems the only thing Jim Gould does is excite Judy, and this stimulation, which he controls, defines and delimits their relationship. Besides, in the flush of her little girl's excitement, Judy has felt what she ought not—a bittersweet tingle between her legs. Jim and little Judy stay glued together just a little too long, and long enough to communicate what they should not—the body heat they should not know together. Usually never around, now Jim lingers. It is too long, too drawn out, too known, this pleasure, and so it begins to hurt. Pleasure and pain . . . before being left alone . . . again and again.

No, this overstimulation doesn't qualify as child abuse in the strict sense. But it isn't nothing. It is something. Its thrust is to control and overwhelm, to seduce and abandon. It will establish a paradigm for this little girl's love life for years to come.

Summarizing Judy's case, her psychotherapist concludes that Judy's father overstimulated her. This made her feel excited, afraid and guilty, especially in relation to her forlorn mother. Although gratifying her, Jim Gould also deserted her and made her feel bad about herself and fearful of losing those she loves. So later in life Judy is compelled to repeat what she made of her earliest experience with the man who was her first love, her father. She has gotten hooked on men who have other women in the background, who are unpredictable and therefore exciting and who are always threatening to leave her. Judy submits to their mistreatment and, guiltily putting herself in her mother's place, acts to provoke it. Her relationships, the clinician continues, are sadomasochistic. The way to change them, he tells Judy, is to deal with them directly in psychoanalysis, and he refers her to another doctor to do this job.

JUDY fits the stereotype of a masochistic woman in the thrall of the sadistic man. But are women more masochistic than men, and are men more sadistic? Or are these simply sexist stereotypes that derive from gender politics and the typical distribution of power accorded by a male-dominated society?

I shall return to these issues of gender later. What I can say at this juncture is that, despite the prevailing ideology, most women (not all, but most) tend to be more comfortable being or feeling immediately dependent, needy, and subject to being hurt in their dealings with men. In contrast, men, with their harsh consciences, more readily sabotage themselves than find themselves sabotaged by others. In their relationships they try to hide their masochism, which they find unmanly. They try, that is, but without success.

In all events, as a relationship cements, the roles tend to fluctuate and then change. Over time, especially when they find themselves frustrated in fulfilling their own ambitions, women often lash out and belittle their men. The men may flee, into work or adulterous affairs, but they tend to surrender to the control, castigations and authoritarianism of the women who loom so large in their everyday lives.

Take Ed and Amy Jackson as an example of how the roles become blurred over time in two people. In younger days, before adult life set in, Amy had enjoyed her power "to make men die" for her. She had loved driving them wild, forcing them to force themselves on her. She had loved men in extremis. She had loved feeling liberated by yielding to their impassioned entreaties. Feminist that she was, nonetheless Amy could not help herself. She secretly loved films like *Cat People.* She loved being a sex object.

Back in Ohio, before an Eastern college education and then New York City changed her mind, her consciousness, her sensibilities and her official pronouncements, Amy had even had a stint as a high school cheerleader, and a prize-winning one to boot. She had loved wearing those breast-hugging sweaters, the short pleated skirts and the skimpy panties. She had loved twirling and bouncing and kicking so high that the boys and even the grown men in the stands—men old enough to be her father—fastened their eyes on her crotch. She had loved catching men's eyes, the way the guys caught footballs. She had loved taking these eyes off the game. She had loved doing her Gypsy Rose number that night after the guys won the championship (alas, if only it hadn't gotten out of hand and gone too far—so far that she'd nearly gotten herself gang-raped).

Amy had suppressed all this at Holyoke and then Columbia, where she transferred in search of "gender integration and parity." She didn't let her cheerleading and everything else be known when she got her first job at Harrison House. She most certainly did not by the time she had risen to the position of senior editor, one with a "special interest in women's issues and gender in general." She had stopped seducing men with her body. Instead, she tried "arresting their attention with [her] mind's wit."

As time wore on, Amy had grown to miss the old sexiness. She had come to miss Ed's attentions—Ed, the author (working with another editor) whose interest she had garnered at a book party so many years ago, it seemed, and whose heart and soul she had then won in bed. Once work and parenthood overtook them, the only way to captivate him, to drive him wild, had been with a fight, a family fight.

How does the joke go? Newlyweds have "house sex" (all over the place). A little later, this becomes "bedroom sex," confined to the bedroom. After that comes "hall sex": the husband and wife pass each other in the hallways and say "Fuck you!"

Ed had also loved *Cat People.* Stoned for his fortieth "Big Chill" birthday party, he had stood up and screamed when Nastassia started to strip. Perhaps it was Ed I heard in the row behind me that afternoon.

Ed had felt that same shot of adrenaline when Lisa seduced—before abandoning—him. As he drove her up to Vermont, the winter air streaming through the top of his aging MGA, she had lifted his hand from the gear shift and placed it inside her angora sweater, and inside her bra. There Lisa's nipple had kissed Ed's palm. Veering toward the shoulder on the empty highway, he had exclaimed, "I love you—forever." One-handed, Ed lit the Lucky dangling loosely and wetly from his lips. They sped on toward Stowe Mountain where he would, he thought, claim her as his own.

A month later, having hit on another of Harvard's literati, Lisa dropped him. Ed had simply been yet another notch in the widening belt that corseted Lisa's slim waist—"the slimmest waist in three colleges," he had told her lovingly, implying some conquests of his own. The only guy who ever dumped her was the one Lisa loved. And he, Roger, was gay or bi, AC/DC as they said disparagingly in those days.

The irony was that when they had sex, Lisa did not come. In bed, a wan diffidence settled upon her and gave the lie to her hellion's image. She felt nothing, she said, when he entered her, "nothing." It was because she was frigid, Ed comforted himself, that she had danced away from him into the arms of another man, a less manly man. Lisa tarried there as with Ed, only until her secret was known, and she left. Maybe he was to blame—though other girls' responses testified to the contrary. No, no doubt about it, Lisa, for all her blush and promise, was uptight. She was a fifties girl in the sixties. She was not a new woman, but an age-old femme fatale, Ellen Barkin-style, with seas of love in which a lover could drown.

Then Amy came along, seducing him as well, in the full bloom of her mesmerizing eroticism. Yet Ed retreated from Amy as the years passed, for reasons he could not understand. Instead of having foreplay and tenderness, they found themselves bickering. A wall came down as Ed tried but failed to let himself respond to her beauty. He resisted her thrall, turning her into the domestic enemy his mother had been to his father. Before long, they found themselves numbed, simmering with rage rather than ardor.

KNIGHT WITHOUT HONOR IN HIS OWN HOUSE

Another and more extreme example of such a reversal is a CEO who rules the boardroom by day and whose wife rules him by night. Returning home, Dick Knight becomes a different person. No longer the power broker, he releases his hold on himself with a sigh of relief only to find himself a powerless prisoner in a suburban house that has become his torture chamber. No sooner has Dick opened the front door than Ethel is on him, haranguing her husband with a catalog of all that he has failed to do, she says, or done badly in the last day and a half. Forgetting his wife's struggle with her self-doubts and inadequacies (her fearfulness, her inability to find a job, her battles to lose weight, quit smoking, give up her afternoon scotches), forgetting his successes and power on the work front, forgetting his devotion and competence as a family man— Dick Knight finds himself surrendering to his wife's authority at home. Ethel looms larger than life.

Night after night, he has had to accept his wife's rejections—her rebuffs of his halfhearted sexual advances and affectionate overtures. He has even taken to heart her criticisms of his "rough skin" and "bad kissing." Most of his time at home, Dick simply stews in sulky silence, like a needy child waiting for his mother's mood to mend.

In point of fact, Dick's mother was a good deal more indulgent than his wife. She turned to "Dicky," as she called him, as a personal confidant and a family scion for the future. In the evenings before her husband came home, dressed only in a flimsy negligee, she would invite her son to sit with her on the bed in the master bedroom, a place from which his father, who slept in the den, had long been excluded. There she would deluge her future star with her laments about her husband's crude sexual demands of her and infidelities with other women. She would fill his ears with stories about the uprightness and grand accomplishments of her own father, on whom she doted, and his family, which was much higher up the social ladder than their own. One day, she hoped, Dick would become a powerhouse like his esteemed grandfather and thus vindicate her and redeem the legacy she had abandoned in marrying down.

As a result, the boy developed a strong attachment to his mother, one with erotic overtones that he took great pains to deny. A quiet and good teenage boy, Dick found himself avoiding sex. Fighting off homosexual thoughts and anxieties, he masturbated to fantasies that involved being stripped and beaten by women of Amazonian proportions. In real life, Dick was drawn to tough, handsome, forthright women. He married one of these, losing his virginity while also claiming hers—sort of—on their honeymoon. Before he knew it, Dick, for all his work successes, found himself beaten down and henpecked by his wife in much the same way as his father had been.

Thus, Dick allowed his identification with his mythic maternal grandfather to go only so far. He punished himself for having won the heart of the unseen old man's daughter. He stayed with Ethel because she was an incarnation of his mother, an object of illicit desire. He also stayed with her because she served as an emissary of rigid "superego" (conscience). At the same time Ethel was an avenging angel angered by this unhallowed union between her and Dick. To find his way into another woman's heart would have been, he later said to his analyst, "to open Pandora's box."

This typical evening's medley of emasculation comes to a climax when instead of relenting and inviting him into her bedroom and her heart as he hopes—hopes that are almost always doomed—Ethel quite literally socks her husband in the balls. It's just a playful gesture, she claims with a chuckle, a moment of silliness punctuating her more serious onslaught of legitimate complaints and accusations, a little lightheartedness brought on by the lightheadedness of a tad too much to drink. But she does it all the same right in front of the Knights' sixteen-year-old daughter, Sue Ann. Ethel drives her left fist right into Dick's grey flannel crotch. He collapses at last into one of his "temper tantrums" as his wife calls them. Dick clobbers Ethel over the head with a cushion from the couch (a soft down one) before storming out the front door and heading for the local tavern.

The extraordinary thing is that Dick does not run off into the arms of a mistress. Fit and fifty, a catch in anybody's eyes, he has nobody else. Nor could he conceive of another woman. Ethel is the only woman in his life. When his therapist listens to and talks with him long enough, he comes to understand that there could be no other. This man needs his Ethel. But that's another story, a story to be told later in this book.

Unconscious psychodynamics help explicate bizarre but all too frequent scenarios like this one. In the meantime, however, the ironies and the blurring of roles become evident in vicious circles like this one. For example, in abusing the husband with whose power she has identified and on whom she depends, Ethel diminishes and even symbolically castrates herself. In allowing her the freedom to do so, Dick in fact encourages his wife to regress and to remain imprisoned by her own childish impulses. The masochism and sadism of everyday life, particularly when it comes to couples, are always one—always *sadomasochism*.

Chapter

5

EVERYDAY SADOMASOCHISTS: BASIC CHARACTERISTICS

IN this chapter, I will discuss the types of individuals who most easily get caught up in the vicious circles described in the previous chapter. For reasons that will be made clear in chapter 7, almost everybody has enough sadomasochistic potential to succumb to such behavior at one point or another and to one degree or another. Nonetheless, certain neurotic individuals are more vulnerable and predisposed to become mired in misery than others. These sadomasochistic or self-defeating personalities, people suffering from what psychiatrists call "masochistic character disorder," are, in fact, familiar to most people. The individuals in question are not weird, like the "perverts" described in chapter 6. They are merely miserable. We all recognize the Judy Goulds and Dick Knights of the world, people in whom we can see something of ourselves. As I have already emphasized, whether they know it or not, just about everybody, at some time or another, wants to seize control of someone else. Almost everybody unconsciously seeks to submit to punishment and pain. As I have tried to demonstrate at the outset, almost everybody finds vicarious pleasure in spectacles of suffering and destruction.

Still, not everybody makes sadomasochism into a way of life. Most people are sufficiently self-preservative to protect themselves from getting hurt repeatedly. Most people are decent enough to refrain from hurting others, even if they are so inclined. They want something more out of life. They are comfortable and satisfied with themselves and their wishes. They enjoy living up to their ideals. So they are able to succeed in the give and take of love and work, the two most important components of life, according to Sigmund Freud.

In contrast, the individuals who need to immerse themselves in suffering are distinguished by certain typical histories, conflicts and personality traits, which, in combination, tip the balance toward self-destructiveness. I have already suggested some of these features in the concluding pages of the preceding chapter. These unconscious conflicts of which such relationships are symptomatic find more direct and more sensual expression in the dangerous and endangered heroines and heroes of today's movies. I will now be more specific and explicit. People who find themselves chronically tortured in their lives or are repeatedly moved to hurt others reveal most, if not all, of the following features:

1. They have a history of what might be called *lowgrade or mild childhood abuse*—sexual, aggressive and, most important, emotional abuse that falls short of actual incest or beatings.

2. As a result of this abuse, they have created *unconscious sadomasochistic and specifically sexual fantasies,* which have much in common with actual perverse practices. Masochistic characters find surreptitious *pleasure in pain.*

3. The victims' pleasure in being hurt, their hostile feelings and impulses and their more acceptable desires simply to succeed and find happiness in life make them feel guilty. This is an *irrational guilt* that leads to discomfort with contentment, denial of their own desires and a need to be punished.

4. Behind their sleepy or abject facades, masochists simmer with *unconscious rage and the desire for revenge.* For a variety of reasons, they disown this rage and project their vindictiveness onto the sadist who abuses them and whose vindictiveness is obvious.

5. A profound fear of loss leads them to cling to the people who hurt them while also provoking these people to reject them in the end. Thus masochists *repeat and reenact the initial and feared traumas of their early life.*

6. Their *poor self-esteem* allows them to feel that they do not deserve better treatment anyway, whatever they say to the contrary.

7. Masochists have a fairly *fragile sense of identity*. This makes for *uncertain personal boundaries* and facilitates a less obvious blurring of the sadistic and masochistic roles.

8. Lacking a sense of themselves, they also *lack self-awareness*. This deficiency, along with their defenses, makes it seem that bad things keep happening to them.

A History of Abuse

Child abuse, sexual and aggressive, is very much in the public eye these days. The media have made their audience aware of the numbers of sexual violations perpetrated by parents, day care workers, teachers and priests on young and impressionable children. In the wake of the infamous Steinberg case, professionals charged with the care of the young have become more sensitive to child battering. In many states, they are mandated by law to report even the mere suspicion of its occurrence. As a result, reported instances of suspected aggressive or sexual abuse have increased to over 2.5 million cases annually. "Incest survival" has become a rather dangerous fad, with many self-declared victims impugning and sometimes suing the parents who, they assert, betrayed their innocence. (This trend, at times resembling a sort of mass hysteria, has made for serious misrepresentations of reality and legal catastrophes, as well as a more general tendency, abetted by ill-trained therapists, to externalize blame and indulge in character assassination of innocent caretakers. Although this is a very serious problem, I will not address it specifically here.)

Parents and authorities outside the home may try to cover up these betrayals of their young victims, often succeeding for many years in hiding the truth of their indiscretions. The victims tend to collude with the victimizers, forgetting for many years the fact of their betrayal. Nonetheless, when fact can be separated from fantasy, the terrible truth becomes unmistakable and undeniable. Remembering the beatings, the rapes, the unwanted manipulations of their bodies, the recovering victims can make sense of a whole life of mistrust, fear, inhibition, inexplicable guilt and demoralization. Remembering the past, they may be freer not to repeat it.

Other forms of abuse, which are harder to see, can sometimes be harder to get over. Such abuse is not manifest in acts of incest and battering. It is found in subtler physical, sensual and emotional manipulations. These manipulations, often occurring sub rosa so that the adult perpetrators can escape blame, make being hurt and feeling helpless addictive and guilt-inducing all at once. At the very least, in a process that psychoanalysts call a "hysterical identification with the aggressor or transgressor," the child assumes the guilt and responsibility for the sins of the parent. At the worst, having been subjected not to actual intercourse but to a sort of "mind fuck," he or she becomes the victim of what psychoanalyst Leonard Shengold has called "soul murder."

Judy Gould, who was described in greater detail in chapter 4, is one case in point. Her father neither beat her nor molested her. But their play was both scary and sexy, and she, if not he, lost control of her sensations and feelings. Night after night until her father died, while Mrs. Gould lay alone in her room, Jim and Judy carried on together. They did not have genital sex, but Jim excited his daughter's more childish sexual sensations and desires. Hence Judy's self-punishing addiction to nighttime dramas and scenes, triangles and doomed intimacies with unreliable men: For Judy, being in a relationship came to mean being subjected to a confusing mixture of pleasure and pain, jealousy and rejection.

Unconscious Sadomasochistic Fantasies

Children have a hard time understanding the nature of sex between their parents, and other adults—what Sigmund Freud called, rather dramatically, "the primal scene." When they overhear loud noises from the bedroom, or glimpse bodies writhing and seemingly pounding at each other, young boys and girls may infer that the two people are attacking each other. Incapable of experiencing lubrication, ejaculation, intercourse itself and other adult sexual responses and pleasures, girls and boys further try to make sense of what they see or imagine. They refer these pictures to the bodily experience that is available to them, to activities that they know firsthand. Perhaps these grown people are beating, eating or excreting on each other, they conclude, as they themselves might do, especially when they are angry. (I will elaborate on primal-scene fantasies in chapters 7 and 8.)

As far as their own sexual activity is concerned, the vast majority of boys and girls remains incapable of relieving sexual tensions in orgasms. These tensions mount. And though these tensions begin by being pleasurable, sexual frustration soon leads to painful sensations, to a loss of control, to a sense of physical and emotional helplessness and to anger and destructive wishes.

Bad parental relationships and chronic overstimulation further compound these painful consequences of physical stimulation. A child may withdraw altogether, becoming emotionally dead and anhedonic (incapable of any pleasure). Otherwise, in an effort to stay emotionally and sensually alive, he or she will draw an equation between pleasure and the hurt and pain that always seem to accompany it. What otherwise might be more incidental fancies and erotic sideshows then become the dominant feature of this child's erotic imagination. The future victim of everyday life becomes fixated on sadomasochistic sexual fantasies. In these scenarios, he or she imagines being beaten by his or her partner, violently misused, humiliated, driven to the brink of helplessness and despair while finding sexual satisfaction all the while. Pleasure is to be found in pain.

Some individuals, people lacking in moral constraint and the ideal of an erotic relationship with another whole and loved person (people whom I will describe in the next chapter), end up giving more or less free rein to such impulses to be hurt and humiliated. They become practicing "perverts," either exclusively or as a compulsory behavior that helps maintain an otherwise normal enough sex life. Others, whose consciences and sexual ideals stop them from yielding to their forbidden impulses, energetically repress their sadomasochistic fantasies. However, what is repressed has a way of returning and betraying itself in many ways. Sadomasochistic fantasies, which find full expression on the psychoanalyst's couch, may be revealed in thoughts, images and activities: in conscious but utterly private masturbation fantasies during adolescence and adulthood; in a particular pornographic preoccupation; in specific sexual aversions and inhibitions aimed at keeping unwanted desires from awareness (as in homophobia); in a fleeting but often persistent image or unwanted thought during sexual intercourse; or in circumscribed or sporadic perverse activity akin to the kinds described in the next chapter. For the most part, however, these fantasies are expressed not in specific sexual acts but in the individual's love relationships. Unlike the pervert, the sadomasochist of everyday life acts out his compelling fantasies without knowing that he or she is doing it and without much pleasure.

Rather than have a woman spank him or squeeze his testicles or dump her urine and feces on him, a man like this (for example, Dick Knight) constantly submits to the humiliation of her harsh criticisms and verbal tirades. Rather than being stripped and raped, a woman (for example, Judy Gould) repeatedly allows herself to be exploited, humiliated and abandoned. Rather than experiment with bondage, partners in a sadomasochistic couple, such as Amy and Ed, take turns provoking each other. They tie each other up in emotional knots, not leather thongs, and make their home into a degrading prison from which there is no exit.

Dick, Judy, Amy and Ed would be shocked to know their hearts, much less reveal them to others. Striving to be good men and women, they labor hard to keep from acknowledging the secret desires satisfied every day in their unhappy lives. When these truths of the heart leak out every now and then, they quickly slam the lid back on and pretend that they never thought or wanted such things. For people such as these, feelings of satisfaction in suffering, along with the nature of their wishes, are banished from consciousness. Yet their needs to master traumas through the compulsion to repeat them make for a "return of the repressed" suffered again and again in their lives.

Any attempt to expose their buried pleasures arouses terror and rage, for two opposing reasons. First, these people need to maintain their sense of themselves as "good" and thus cannot do or even want anything "bad," that is, anything that will make them feel guilty. Their abiding guilt and tenuous self-esteem make it very difficult for them to own up to wishes, much less actions, that are outside what they believe to be bounds of normalcy and decency. Besides, common sense requires that nobody else becomes aware of these dirty little secrets.

Second, not only do the dictates of morality and reality demand repression, but the "pleasure principle" (in Freud's terms) also comes into play. These closet, or neurotic, sadomasochists do not want to know what they are doing because, unconsciously at least, they want to be able to keep on doing it. They do not want to give up the hidden pleasure that they find in obvious pain and emotional agony. In fact, whereas the practicing sexual masochist can often limit his or her humiliation to an occasional or routine ritual, one that need not disrupt his or her life as a whole, the sadomasochist of everyday life has made his or her whole life into an encompassing perverse enactment.

Self-Punishment

Describing King Oedipus' tragic plight in *The Interpretation of Dreams,* Sigmund Freud referred to the sexual and aggressive impulses with which all people struggle as "wishes forced upon us by nature" yet "repugnant to morality." We are fated, he wrote, to be wracked by conflicts between our inborn instinctual drives and no less pressing categorical imperatives—the moral absolutes, the do's and don'ts that also determine how we become socialized. Guilt, he continued years later in *Civilization and Its Discontents,* is an inevitable byproduct of becoming a civilized adult. In other words, all people need their superegos, or consciences, to protect others as well as themselves from their baser instincts. Superegos help people adapt to social reality, to the fact that not only can we not always get what we want but that what we want is often bad for ourselves and for everybody else.

However, a psychological structure or function that is created to meet the demands of one environment—the world of childhood— can outlive its usefulness and become maladaptive in another—the life of the adult. Some people's consciences can get out of control and attack them for no apparent fault. These consciences can become like policemen—never around when you need them and there when you don't. Or, to use another analogy, irrationally guilty people have a psychological version of an autoimmune disease: Their virulent superegos turn against their healthy parts and attack them. In a word, morality can become malignant.

Overstimulated and underprotected by parents, many manifest sadomasochists take extreme psychological measures to protect themselves, measures that outlive their usefulness. As I have already noted, they assume the transgressing parents' guilt as if it were their own so they can continue to idealize and rely on their realistically untrustworthy caretakers. In addition, lacking role models and external restraints, they develop precocious, rigid and, indeed, sadistic superegos in order to control and direct themselves. Their superegos become all the more vigilant because of the unconscious sexual fantasies to which masochists fall prey, fantasies that the parents' actions have made dangerously real.

Mistreated, they nonetheless may have been treated better than their parents, who are also their emotional rivals. Paradoxically, in having been or felt favored and seduced, future masochists can become more and more guilty about the unwanted greatness thrust upon them—guilty about what clinicians call their apparent premature "Oedipal victories." Rather than the father or mother who should lay claim to his or her spouse, the child can become or feel like the apple of the parent's eye. There's a lot of gratification to be found in this status, to be sure, but a lot of fear at having one's desires seemingly reciprocated and beyond external control. When this happens, it is up to the child to clamp the lid on. To the extent that any alloyed happiness or pleasure becomes associated in the mind with these forbidden parricidal victories and incestuous pleasures, masochists such as these, *moral masochists* (I will define moral masochism in chapter 7), become guilty about anything good in their lives. Not only their desires but also their compunctions compel them to make themselves unhappy, to trip themselves up.

Like the sadomasochistic desires themselves, the masochists' guilt about these wishes is unconscious. To admit to the one would mean to own up to the other and take responsibility for his or her life. Instead, perpetual victims believe that fate and other people are punishing them rather than that they are punishing themselves. Because self-punishment of this kind is a double-edged sword, it expresses both the guilt over the penitents' unconscious sins of the heart and the sinful wishes themselves.

In chapter 4, I began to look at how and why a woman such as Judy Gould punishes herself by maintaining her terrible relationships. In these relationships, I implied, she unconsciously identifies with her rejected mother. In the process, Judy accomplishes two opposing objectives (this is always how the mind works—by reconciling and synthesizing opposites). On one hand, she puts herself in her mother's place, implicitly displacing her in her father's sexual affections. On the other, she denies herself the possibility of having a better life than her mother's. Unconsciously Judy continues to take a beating at her father's hands as her mother did and, in the same breath, punishes herself for the gratification she gets as a result.

Dick Knight is another case in point. He has achieved much more in his work life than did his ne'er-do-well father. But in staying with Ethel and allowing her to lambast him, he punishes himself for his success. He is, as Freud put it, "wrecked by success." What is more, Dick identifies with his father after all, a man who was constantly harangued by his wife for being such a failure at work, irresponsible provider and terrible and inadequate man. As far as his conscience is concerned, his accomplishments in the real world don't count.

The Unconscious Desire for Revenge

Almost everybody gets angry at parents who excite their desires but inevitably tease, frustrate and belittle them. Incestuous feelings are experienced as a sort of "erotic horror," in the words of psychoanalyst Ivri Kumin, and the parents who stimulate them make their children uncomfortable and vindictive. When they have failed or hurt them in other ways, seducing and abandoning their sons and daughters, these parents add fuel to the fires of their rage. This is yet another reason that sexual desires and destructive urges combine in a sadistic thirst for revenge toward those who have betrayed the child—and those who will.

Once more, the future sadomasochistic personality tries to remain unaware of vindictive impulses. For one thing, as I have noted, he or she feels guilty about all instinctual impulses, particularly those aggressive urges that might lead to the destruction of those people whom he or she needs and loves. For another, his or hers was a precarious family life growing up, one haunted by the specters of rejection and loss, and he or she is loath to drive people away by showing them how angry he or she is at them. Because the sadomasochist's self-esteem is shaky and he or she tries so hard to be good, he or she repudiates anything bad, retreating from any feeling or urge that might call into question his or her decency.

Instead of acting vindictively, sadomasochists project their hostility onto the people whom they invite to torment them. In the process, they meet the demands of the forces that required them to disown their aggression in the first place. They obey their consciences by getting themselves punished while escaping its censure by being good. Since they are so accepting of abuse, nobody need leave them—or so they sometimes think. Placing blame outside themselves, they spare themselves recognition of their own baser instincts.

To some degree, they do get their revenge. Seeing others as bad, sadomasochists make them behave badly; provoking them to do so, they debase others. To the extent that people in sadomasochists' adult lives represent their miscreant parents, their enlistment as selfish abusers effects a confrontation that was impossible in childhood. Symbolically, the victim repeatedly holds the mirror up to the nature of the other, not his own. Through tormentors, sadomasochists reveal to their parents their cruelty and their shame, showing them how much they have despised them all along.

For instance, when she examined her relationship in retrospect, Judy Gould realized she had hated Bill Andrews from their very first date—no, even before she met him, certainly before he acted like the cad he was. After all, Bill was a man, and therefore in her mind a man like her father. Even before meeting him, she had imagined his betrayal of her and felt jealous. Telling him her story, her long lament of "love's labor's lost," she set herself up for exploitation and rejections.

Similarly, once in treatment, Dick Knight began to plumb the less than altruistic feelings behind his Christlike tolerance of Ethel's assaults on his manhood and his steadfast refusal to abandon her. He came to understand that he had contempt for his wife and could expect no better from her. With this insight into his marriage, he explored more fully his hitherto unacknowledged feelings for the mother whom he had tried to rescue from his father's failures. He hated her as well. He hated their little intimacies together and his being encouraged to disparage a father he wanted to admire and emulate. He hated her constant complaints. He hated the flaunting of her body, her disavowal of this, the implicit toying with his young manhood, inhibitedness and joylessness that resulted from her seductiveness toward him. Every time Dick allowed Ethel to slug him in the balls, figuratively (and now and then literally), he was dragging her down, humiliating her. She was a slob, a disgruntled harpy, just like his mother. Women were all the same. In submitting to women, he was getting his revenge on them.

The Fear of Loss

The first and most compelling danger in a child's life, according to Freud, is the danger of losing the people on whom he or she depends for survival and comes to love in their own regard. Babies fear losing their caretakers and, as they grow into toddlerhood, cling desperately to them. At first infants lack a sense of time so each separation seems like a final leave-taking. As they gain more experience of their parents' comings and goings, they tend to master these seeming traumas by way of what is called the "repetition compulsion." In activities such as peekaboo and hide-and-seek games, they themselves make disappearances and reappearances happen repeatedly in efforts to take active control of the process.

So powerful is any child's fear of losing his parents, and subsequently their love and approval, that he will hold on to even the worst of them. In physically abusive households, for instance, rival victims will compete for the attention evinced in bruises and welts. In adulthood, by way of what is called "transference," people will hold on to these parents by finding partners who are like them or by making different sorts of people act as their parents did.

As I have already suggested, their terror of separation and need to cling to others at all costs are particularly pressing imperatives for sadomasochists. Having been subjected to their parents' inconsistencies, they hold on for dear life to the people with whom they become involved. They will put up with almost any indignity rather than lose them.

An irony here makes these self-styled losers indeed losers. Clinging to their contemporaries, they are also clinging to the past. Many sadomasochists find themselves holding on to the parents who seduced and abandoned them. Nobody is allowed to be different from these parents, the people who first deserted them. To find another kind of person—someone loving, steadfast and loyal—is to acknowledge what they either lost or, worse still, never had. Fearful as they may be of loss, ironically these individuals invite rejection and abandonment in their choices of lovers and other strangers. Or they actively provoke it by behaving in ways that drive people away.

In chapter 4, I demonstrated how Judy Gould acts to repeat the central trauma of her childhood—the loss of her father. In subtler ways, her friend Amy does something similar when she acts to bring out her husband Ed's worst self. She gets his goat, making of him not the romantic and considerate lover he once was and whom she consciously desires, but a man like her father—a withdrawn and uncaring father whose attentions she could never win. Whereas Judy's father overstimulated her, Amy's paid little heed. As a teenager, she strove desperately to get men to admire her sexy body and to "knock their socks off." Retreating from her exhibitionistic displays later on, particularly in an era that rejected the idea of woman as sex object, she came to provoke anger instead of desire and then rejection in the form of indifference. Ed's inattention, repeating her father's, became for her a paradoxical form of engagement with the father of her early years.

The fear of loss in their current life and the sense that they walk on egg shells is more conscious in the sadomasochists of everyday life than some of the other wishes and fears I have already described. What they fail to realize is their need to bring this dreaded fate upon themselves. Sadomasochists refuse to see that they are holding on to a past that, on the surface at least, they claim to have tried to escape.

Low Self-Esteem

Bound up with the problem of rejection is the sadomasochist's low self-esteem. His or her consequent need for approval leads to contradictory attitudes toward and inconsistent estimations of him or herself. He or she may feel worthless as a truly desirable person, but absolutely virtuous as a moral being.

Growing up, according to most psychologists, means becoming independent and self-sufficient. In order to become self-sufficient, the developing individual must become self-contained, must replace many of the functions first performed by parents with his or her own capacities to take care of him or herself. One aspect of this process, which clinicians call "internalization," is the replacement of a need for approval from others with an ability to approve of oneself. The mature individual is governed by what psychoanalysts call his "ego ideal," by his or her own values and not by the opinions, real or imagined, of the rest of the world. As long as he or she lives up to these personal standards and morals, he or she maintains self-esteem.

Dependent, guilty and unconsciously identifying with their failed parents, sadomasochists do not feel good about themselves and do not value themselves. Their neediness and uncertainty make it difficult for them to take a stand and to tolerate being out there on their own, alone in their conviction and devotion to principle. What is more, because they unconsciously feel unworthy they will put up with a partner's abuses. Sometimes they will invite mistreatment "just to get it over with," to get what they feel they deserve and expect in the end.

At the same time, masochists can be remarkably narcissistic in their own peculiar way. They are especially self-serving when it comes to their simplistic and self-congratulatory belief that they are good while everyone else is bad. As one such patient of mine put it, they treasure their "injustice collections in the museums of disappointments." It is a mark of honor for them to be injured and to deny any malevolent intent on their own part. They take pains (as it were) to deny any selfishness and cruelty, attributing these venal sins to those who misuse them. They are subtle misanthropists when it comes to almost everybody except themselves.

For example, Judy Gould congratulates herself for being a victim. Feeling like a "pit stop in the fast track of Bill Andrew's race against love," nonetheless her suffering at his callow and callous hands served to vindicate her. Her misery serves to prove her innocence while she proves him, like all men, guilty beyond the shadow of a self-doubt. Though she is "treated like a doormat," she remains the "better person in the end." She has always been the better person. "Always," she tells herself. Despite all the men who have ever treated her "like shit," she remains innocent.

Similarly, Dick Knight, whose gratifying worldly power deserts him at the front door to his house, nonetheless finds grace in his domestic martyrdom. With Ethel he is the son he had been to his mother. He has no needs, no flagrant desires. He is not a male animal like his father. Dick is a good Christian, for he suffers. He does not reap the instinctual rewards of his worldly success but serves mankind, or rather womankind. Every time Ethel assaults and demeans him, he feels wonderful in his forbearance and his martyrdom. Were Dick to have or even want to have an affair—with anyone, any sex—he would sink from grace. He would sink into the mire, his father's muck, whence he came.

Sadomasochists such as these lack the basic self-love with which to withstand the fact of their own repugnant but naturally ordained desires. Surreptitiously acting on these desires in the ways I have described, they often feign being pure altruists and ascetics.

Fragile Identities

As observers of infants have documented, it takes some time before babies know who is who in their world or, to put this another way, where they begin and others end. At first, the child has little or no awareness of any difference between the self and the people and objects in the environment. Helpless as the infant in fact is, he or she still feels all-powerful. For example, a pain in the gut and a cry magically make Mother appear. Mother, who is hardly a person as we adults might know her, is there simply to meet the baby's needs. What is more, the boundaries, as Freud described them, between the baby's image of his body and the people who tend to it seem vague, blurred, porous, permeable. In this state, which he called a "buzzing confusion," there is little sense of inside and outside, and no clear definition of the individual and those around him or her.

As the brain and mind mature and as the child's body becomes capable of sitting and looking, standing and then moving about in the environment, a toddler becomes better able to picture and define himself or herself as a distinct entity in a world of persons, animate objects and other things. Emotionally charged, initially nonverbal and often mysterious interpersonal exchanges, particularly in relationship to the mother, contribute to this process of "separation-individuation" in complicated ways. Initially, the child experiences their dyadic relationship as a "dual unity," in the words of infant observer Margaret Mahler. Mother and child are engaged in a (near) symbiotic relationship in which images of self and mother are but partially differentiated from each other. As the mother helps meet the child's needs and manage his or her frustrations, and as she herself begins to perceive and treat the baby as an individual, her child builds up better pictures of himself or herself and of the mother as different beings. In the baby's mind, mother and self gradually become separate and distinct beings who are nonetheless still related to each other. By the time the child has acquired the language with which to talk to the parent about what he or she feels and wants and has become emotionally able to remain apart from the mother for periods of time, the child has consolidated a rudimentary sense of self in relation to others.

This sense of self and of other continues to evolve as the individual develops. With what adolescent expert Peter Blos has called the "second individuation of adolescence," it is tested once again. Adolescents tend to regress, to go backward, to become uncertain about their independence and sexuality. In this identity crisis, often they hit what Blos's boyhood friend, psychoanalyst Erik Erikson, called a "rock bottom," becoming confused once again about the basics of who they are. With luck, teenagers come out of the crisis with a deeper and firmer sense of who they are as men and women, sons and daughters and future parents and workers with their own values, interests, wishes and abilities. Stronger in their individuality, they have forged their sense of ego identity as responsible adults.

In certain circumstances, a transient "dedifferentiation of self from other," a return to one's boundless beginnings, can be a normal and useful experience. The religious mystic, the nursing mother and the orgasmic lover all profit from losing themselves now and then in the other. However, if such regressions become permanent rather than temporary, they can interfere with what these individuals have so exquisitely achieved—transcendence and aspiration, empathy and tenderness, sexual functioning and a capacity to love another human being as a real and complete person.

As clinicians well know, the sense of identity and of self remain vulnerable in many individuals. Much can go wrong during those earliest years when the self is consolidated, leaving "basic faults," in the words of Michael Balint, that may go undetected until the individual faces later life challenges: sexual relations, love, commitment, occupational choices, marriage and parenthood. Many people who succumb to neurotic inhibitions and compulsions find it scary and at times impossible to assert their own desires and convictions. They cannot stand firm in their own identity.

At the extreme, the psychotic individual is often unable to distinguish his or her thoughts from external events and separate out what the rest of the world differentiates as reality and fantasy. Imagining castles in the sky, or a personal hell, the psychotic lives in it. Less far out is the pervert, including the practicing sadomasochist, much of whose sexual activity is aimed at drawing more sharply the boundaries that protect a beleaguered and imperiled self from damage and dissolution (a theme I will turn to in the next chapter). Even more common are the sadomasochists of everyday life, who cast others in roles that often properly belong to their internal world.

While maintaining a hold on what is real, sadomasochistic characters do so much externalizing and projecting of what they do not want to see in themselves that they attribute to others intentions and potential moral failings that are their own. Sometimes, based on experiences of pain early in their lives with frustrating or inconsistently present mothers, they unconsciously associate this pain with any and all relationships. Through this pain they may try to restore the paradoxical paradise lost, the infant's primal relationship with mother, by filling themselves up with the hurt and anger it evokes in order not to feel alone, empty and incomplete. Without such pain and those who inflict it, sadomasochistic characters will feel not only tense and guilty but also empty and alone. Not only do sadomasochists need their tormentors in order to cling to their parents, they need them to feel whole and alive.

For example, when Dick thought about leaving Ethel, he came to recognize just how unsure he was of himself. He had never been able to be alone, he realized. The teenager had gone from home to college, where he met his future wife during his sophomore year and married her a year later, at twenty. After a mere two years in a dorm room, with a crew of roommates to fill it and him up, Dick was living with Ethel much as he had with his family before her.

He did not exactly go crazy on his business trips apart from her. But he could not sleep well. He found himself masturbating as he had in adolescence to the same sorts of weird fantasies. He worried about his interest in men, again much as he had when he was coming of age. Was he really gay? Sometimes a gal from work or at a hotel bar tempted him. At first, Dick searched his soul about the morality of an infidelity or two. Yet on deeper reflection, he realized he was frightened that he could not perform sexually and uncertain about whether, with his clothes off in the presence of a new and sexual woman, he would really be a man after all. So he never slipped.

Dick needed Ethel. He needed her to be with him always, to help control himself, to remind him who he was: a family man, a hetero-sexual man. He needed her to keep the lid on, to be there to spurn his advances, to protect him from the threat posed to his body and soul in any kind of erotic encounter with a stranger.

Ethel and their life together had become his whole life. To main-tain this, despite his protests, he was more than willing to surrender to what she did to him. Being "done to" was the basic ingredient in his underlying definition of himself, at least his sexual self, and was central to the identity Dick had arrived at after thirty years of mar-ried life. His worse half was his better half, ironically, and what Mac-beth, married to his indomitable Lady, called "the better part of [his] manhood."

Lack of Insight

Most people cannot readily look at and think about themselves. Of-ten they do not like what they see. As I have already suggested, their actions and wishes can make them feel vulnerable, scared, de-pressed, ashamed, guilty and, in the end, angry. So they avert their gazes. Like the patricidal and incestuous King Oedipus, they blind themselves.

In addition, simply from the point of view of intellectual develop-ment, only a small percentage of adults are able to stand back and contemplate themselves. According to the developmental psychol-ogist Jean Piaget, such an achievement requires a capacity to for-mulate hypotheses, deduce their consequences and "decenter" from oneself and one's immediate experience. These abilities, in turn, allow the individual to detach from him or herself, think about the self as an object and imaginatively place him or herself in different circumstances. He is then able to ask questions such as, "If I had done x rather than y, then would B have responded to me (A) by doing z instead of q as he did when I did y?"

In adolescence, certain individuals arrive at this position of per-ceptual and logical detachment. Self-reflection of this order is bound up with the formation of a sense of one's identity during these years, each intellectual or emotional developmental process enhancing the other. Impairments in the bedrock sense of self and/or emotional conflicts, which interfere with the freedom and courage to explore oneself, the kind of impairments that stem, for example, from troubled parental relationships I described earlier, cause the development of insight to falter.

And it does falter in the case of many sadomasochistic characters. Many perpetual victims are either unable or profoundly unwilling to look at themselves. They remain stuck to the concrete, taking each (abusive) moment on its own, isolated from those before and after it, and thus never quite learning from experience. Fragile as so many of them are in their sense of self, they tend to see only the other person and his or her problems. They can look out, but not in. Insight from the outside or even the mere suggestion that they inquire into themselves challenges their defenses and, in many cases, these demands overburden their developmentally limited capacities. Sadomasochists, especially the more narcissistically vulnerable among them, recoil in rage from taking a more philosophical stance because, in the end, it is beyond them.

Of the sadomasochistic characters described so far, Judy seems to have the least insight and capacity for abstract thinking about her own and other people's lives. Amy is the most savvy about herself and, certainly, about other people. But when she is in the grip of her sadomasochistic compulsions, this ability deserts her. Dick demonstrates an ability to think logically and hypothetically in the work arena but not in his personal life. Once he becomes freer to tolerate and contemplate his own wishes, this inherent intellectual capacity will serve him in his personal life.

For sadomasochists such as these, dynamic conflicts and psychological defenses serve to inhibit their capacity for self-reflection and for the more abstract or philosophical frame of mind that goes along with this. Thus, not only does probing these defenses and conflicts help them find ways out of the vicious circles that imprison them; in some cases, it may also serve to release intellectual and imaginative potentials hitherto held in check by conflict. If and when the sadomasochist takes the blinders off and escapes these binds, he or she sees a different world through the eyes of a somewhat different person. In this world, nothing is quite so inevitable as it was before, including herself or himself. Because matters are less predictable, less reassuring and less self-defining, the insight is dizzying and sometimes frightening. The world seems transformed, a buzzing confusion once again, a new frontier without any clear road maps. Morality is less a matter of black and white, and more a function of making personal ethical judgments and responsible choices. When this perceptual shift takes place, other people are not so simple, so two-dimensional or so easily pigeonholed as they appeared, just as the individual is not the person he or she always believed him or herself to be. What may be most unsettling to the sadomasochistic character, particularly to the individual who has long been proud of his or her high-mindedness and propriety, is the discovery of a new dark continent within the self. As defenses and self-deception give way, there emerges from within a rush of wishes and fantasies that, until now, would have seemed alien and depraved as the mad indulgence of the deviate or the practicing pervert.

This brings me to the next chapter, sadomasochism proper.

Chapter

6

```
┌─────────────────────────────────────────┐
│                                           │
│    SADOMASOCHISTIC PERVERSIONS:           │
│  WHAT THEY TELL US ABOUT EVERYBODY ELSE   │
│                                           │
└─────────────────────────────────────────┘
```

DIFFERENT STROKES

HAVING plumbed what clinicians see as garden-variety neuroses, I now turn to a more unusual subject. In this, I hope to discern certain universals that illuminate the wellsprings of the sadomasochism of everyday life.

As I have already noted, sexual practices and society's attitudes toward them change over time. The Puritan ethic of one era, condemning all sexual pleasure, will give way to the libertine ethos of the next that sanctions all erotica, only to be replaced by a renewed conservatism. People have always been ambivalent about sex and what it reveals about themselves. This ambivalence is evident in the changing conventions of the prevailing morality.

One person's pleasure is another person's poison, and the scientists who study sex are not immune to personal subjectivity or changing morality. Scientific attitudes toward deviations from what was once considered the heterosexual norm are biased. Biases are as changeable as any human response to the desires that rule men's hearts—including the sadomasochistic desires that are the subject of this book.

These days, most students of human sexuality tend to conform to what is thought of as a new permissiveness. For example, clinicians and researchers no longer officially classify homosexuality as a sexual deviation. Indeed, it has become anathema to call into question, at times even to examine, an individual's choice of a love object— hetero or homo, straight or gay. "Homosexuality" has been stricken from the American Psychiatric Association's *Diagnostic and Statistical Manual* as a psychiatric disorder. It is now labeled an "alternative lifestyle."

Analyzing sexual object choice—homosexual or, for that matter, heterosexual—in terms of the conflicts that may be associated with it is out of fashion. To attempt to do so, proponents of the new view declare, amounts to a breach of personal freedom. Sexual orientation, many argue, is genetically determined and not the result of regression and deviation. Like it or not, the individual is simply born to one or the other persuasion. Conflicts about homosexuality are not the causes, as earlier clinicians opined, but rather the results of sexual orientation. They are the consequences of homophobia, social condemnation, oppression and the subsequent rage, self-condemnation and inhibition.

It is not easy to grow up stigmatized as a minority. Researchers and clinical practitioners, some say, should not make matters worse by perpetuating the persecution. This holds when it comes not only to gay people but also to any group or individual whose sexual preferences are different from those of the straight majority.

Not only the objects of desire but also the forms of desire must be seen in a new light. While the official mental health institutions have been slower to declassify "perversions," many advocates of sexual freedom and tolerance have called into question the use of such a term to label atypical erotic acts. These acts are ones in which either sexual intercourse is not the route to achieving orgasm or in which some other activity before, after or during intercourse is necessary for the individual to perform and consummate the act. Sexual practices such as fetishism, exhibitionism, voyeurism or sadomasochism proper are, according to these new views, simply forms of a *Different Loving*, as the title of one encyclopedic volume puts it. They are neither worse nor better than the "vanilla sex" practiced by most heterosexuals and homosexuals. They are simply different. More neutral designations such as "paraphilia" convey these differences without implicit value judgments.

In fact, conflicting clinical attitudes toward "deviant," "uncommon" or "special" forms of sexual gratification have a long history. In 1886, Richard von Krafft-Ebing published *Psychopathia Sexualis*. In this encyclopedic volume, the author detailed a gamut of sexual predilections and, as the title suggests, examined these as forms of mental illness.

Shortly thereafter (in 1897), Havelock Ellis began work on the first volume in his more neutrally titled *Studies in the Psychology of Sex*, which he completed in 1928. Ellis's objective was not merely to catalogue the practices he described. He also tried to lift the shame, guilt and repression obfuscating the subject. He sought, he said, to open people's minds. In revealing a vast array of sexual activities, Ellis tried to demystify sex and reclaim his subjects' and his readers' erotic and emotional freedom.

Others have followed Krafft-Ebing and Ellis and fall into different ideological camps. Challenging those conservatives who have steadfastly argued for some sort of heterosexual ideal and cleaved to the concept of deviation have been the self-styled demystifiers of sex. While attempting to open new frontiers of observation, these investigators have espoused an ethic of personal liberty and tolerance above all else. Clinical psychosexual pathologists such as Charles Socarides and Irving Bieber have been opposed by empirical observers such as Kinsey, Money, Masters and Johnson and others. The latter group has tried to strip away the moral strictures masquerading, they say, as objective truth.

Yet they, too, place burdens on the scientific discourse. Attempting to be accepting and inoffensive, clinicians often find it difficult to speak their minds. They can find it even harder to let their patients speak their minds, especially when what these individuals have to say about their sexuality does not conform to their criteria for acceptable discourse. While they have helped liberate minority groups from convention and oppression, the constraints of political correctness can, like the orthodoxies they oppose, prevent the clinical theorists from seeing the phenomena before them.

It is also unfortunate that some of the more liberal sexologists should set up Freud as a straw man and see psychoanalysis today merely as a repository of reactionary and intolerant attitudes toward sexual expression. To be sure, as a man of his times, Freud had significant lapses and rigidities when it came to gender and sexual practices, none of which did him or his followers much credit. These are particularly evident in his starkly chauvinistic views about female sexuality and the place of "penis envy" in the inner life of Victorian women. Freud even referred to the "fact [sic] of her [a woman's] castration" as if she had actually once had a penis—a theory about the little boy's fantasy when he first discovers the anatomical differences between the sexes. However, notwithstanding its initially culturally bound and biased misogyny and other distortions (often personally driven by the conflicts and personalities of its theoretical contributors), psychoanalysis's undying challenge to the limits of social convention and wishful thinking remains true to this day.

It is easy to forget that Freud, more than any scientist before him, lifted the veil of repression to take a good, hard look at what it is that people really want. We must not confuse psychoanalysis's essential approach to psychological experience with the conventionality of its more doctrinaire and less original adherents.

What is most important in the Freudian point of view is the assumption that nothing is obvious, and nothing simply normal. Quite the contrary, what people do, what they think, what they feel and what they believe they want are all motivated and shaped by the conflicting forces of the unconscious mind. In trying to resolve their hidden conflicts and give expression to the competing imperatives of dueling impulses, moral absolutes and realistic constraints, the individual creates compromise formations, as I have suggested in earlier chapters. Even apparently normal heterosexual desires as we know them can be explicated as the consequences of such conflicts and compromises. They are subject, therefore, to psychoanalytic understanding like anything else. They, too, can be decoded.

In such a perspective on subjectivity, norms, if they exist at all, do not matter. The truth does—individual emotional truths.

However, what the lay public often takes to be deviations from accepted convention have an uncanny way of revealing aspects of the unconscious that are raw, direct and riveting. As I have already remarked, Freud himself made such use of phenomena that were dismissed in his day as malingering, the workings of an idle brain and moral degeneracy to plumb what he came to call the "psychopathology of everyday life." Examinations of hysterical symptoms, dreams and the manifestations of both adult and infantile sexuality guided Freud down the royal road to the unconscious. There he found the conflicts and "complexes" governing the thinking and conduct of the most sane-minded men and women.

In this spirit and with this intent I now venture behind closed doors, leading my readers into what is, for most of them, the alien and bizarre worlds of sexual sadomasochism—dominance and submission, bondage and discipline. My aim is to capture the drivenness of these libidinal compulsions and reveal the unconscious fantasies, which serve as essential scripts for the sadomasochism of everyday life. I hope to show how the sadomasochistic pervert gives open and erotic expression to the same scenarios that are enacted in more ordinary relationships in hidden and far less pleasurable ways.

THE EROTIC FORM OF HATRED

"Perversion," wrote the late Robert Stoller, preeminent among modern psychoanalytic sexologists, "is the erotic form of hatred." Perversion is a good word for it, too, Stoller declares unabashedly, since perversion, to the pervert at least, feels like "sinning." Perversion is being "bad," doing something that feels wrong. Pallid neutralities like "paraphilia" are just too clinical to do the trick. Besides, Stoller continues, a perversion is a form of revenge, even when the pervert gets hurt or humiliated in the process. For all the sex involved, a perverse act is an act, he says, of hostility and rage. It is an attack on the sex object—including the self.

Focused on anger and aggression and being a modern man observing modern people, Stoller departed from Freud's original prototype for the perversions and the emotional allegory he saw in it. When Freud first wrote about perversions, he began with fetishism and proceeded from there. Under this rubric Freud included a variety of objects and images such as garter belts, high-heeled shoes, a shiny nose, an obscene recitation, a pictorial scene or a repetitive fantasy—this or that thing or ritual or thought required if the fetishist is to reach orgasm, either alone or in the company of a sexual partner.

Freud's focus derived from his general theory, with its stress on the fear of castration. It led him to think about this particular practice, fetishism, and related aberrations in certain ways. Fetishes, he said, are symbolic penises. In particular, male fetishists (there are very few female ones, for reasons I'll turn to shortly) are uncertain about their masculinity and feel overly identified with their potential female partners. Because of their castration anxiety, they are frightened by women, who do not have penises. In uniting and identifying with them, they risk merging with them and losing their manhood. So they avoid sex with women altogether. Or, more commonly, trying to have their cake and eat it, too, they sometimes add a phallic substitute of their own devising to make intercourse possible. Many later theorists—Phyllis Greenacre, for example—followed suit, stressing penis envy and threats of body damage in the perverse need to repair the self through essentially fetishistic acts.

For those clinicians who have heeded Stoller and who think more about relationships (what psychoanalysts call "object relations"), sadomasochism is the paradigmatic and the most common perversion. The pervert, Stoller argues, not only feels castrated but, more important, is angry because he has been seduced and abandoned, overstimulated and "cockteased." He wants his revenge on the person who was once most important to him or, if not on her then on her surrogates and proxies. So he or she seeks to humiliate and degrade the women (or men), his (or her) partners who take the parent's place later in life. Even in fetishism, this hostility is true to some extent. In an act of secret and subtle betrayal, the fetish becomes more valued than the fetishist's potential lover, whom he implicitly devalues, distances and more or less ignores. However, more clearly than any other perversion, sadomasochism involves violent acts and power plays toward a lover. In sadomasochism, the aggression and hostility do not have to be inferred. The violence and violation are blatant, there for all to see.

Interestingly, both Freud and Stoller talk more about men than women. Empirically, men are more likely to act out perversely than women are, to engage in solitary sexual acts like masturbating and going to massage parlors, peep shows and strip joints. However, women can sometimes seduce and manipulate men in equally perverse ways. In all instances, the penis (or phallus) becomes the focus of excitement. I will return to this gender issue as this chapter proceeds.

SEXUAL SADOMASOCHISM: VARIATIONS ON A THEME

Just as fetishes come in different shapes and sizes, so sadomasochism takes different forms. Its three major categories may overlap and are seen by some of their practitioners as equivalent or synonymous. They include: (1) S&M, or sadomasochism proper, involving inflicting and suffering pain by means of whipping, spanking and related activities; (2) D&S, or dominance and submission, in which one individual orders the other to do his or her bidding; and (3) B&D, or bondage and discipline, in which one individual binds the other with restraints such as ropes and chains and/or punishes him or her for (predictable) transgressions. Further variations on these basic themes include a variety of related practices that have fetishistic, exhibitionistic and voyeuristic components. These include: humiliation; group sex and public exposure; intense and often frustrated genital stimulation; age-play (infantilism, diapering, juvenilism); body mutilations such as scarring or piercing nipples and genitals; so-called body modifications such as corseting and tattooing; cross-dressing; fetishistic dressing (leather, rubber);

water sports (usually involving urination); enemas; and, rarest of all, "scat," a form of fecal play. The combinations and permutations are, in fact, virtually endless.

In these rituals, one individual typically enacts the more active or dominant part (the "top," epitomized by the professional dominatrix) while the other agrees to be passive and receptive (the "bottom"). Individuals may try out different positions, sometimes alternating roles. However, most often the roles remain fixed for a particular coupling, and one individual usually comes to prefer one part to the other. Either role can be assumed by either sex, though, and many men prefer the masochistic position.

Sadomasochistic activities may or may not be accompanied by orgasm. This may occur either during or after the ritual itself, when intercourse may or may not take place. Dominance and submission may be confined to the ritual itself. In this case, an otherwise dominant or submissive individual may assume a diametrically opposing persona. (The powerful CEO or killer litigator who frequents the professional dominatrix is one such example.) Or S&M may characterize a whole lifestyle in which the partners are engaged in a total master and slave relationship.

Generally, the parties involved say that they have won each other's trust. They have agreed in advance how far to go with their otherwise uncomfortable and potentially damaging practices. Acts of debasement, they say, are really expressions of love. They emphasize this love more than hate, claiming that their sexual life has freed them from petty resentments. Most also talk about their S&M relationships in terms of control and their pleasure in exercising or relinquishing it. Sadomasochists further downplay the pain they suffer or inflict and extol the pleasure they find for themselves. Though a sense of the illicit makes these encounters spicy and sinful, participants claim not to feel remorse or shame about what they want from and do to their partner.

S&M practitioners have banded together in recent years. "Coming out," they have complemented their growing numbers of publications and fetishistic supply houses with various support groups, such as the Eulenspiegel Society. Indeed, they idealize what they call "the scene," finding in their predilections, these days at least, a source not of secrecy and shame but of shared purpose and social transcendence. In a newfound communal spirit, they refer to more ordinary hetero- and even homosexual practices as "vanilla sex."

Modern-day S&M practitioners make claims similar to those of early pornographers. Especially before the French Revolution and the downfall of the regimes that ruled most of Europe, the pornographer often saw himself as a social and political commentator whose objective it was to expose the hypocrisy of the ruling class. In this vein, sadomasochists try to refute the feminist protests of writers such as Andrea Dworkin about the degradation and dehumanization of women as "bottoms" in S&M rituals. It is their choice to enact their parts and to be used in these ways. After all, the female bottom controls her pleasures, enacting her fantasies rather than submitting to social pressures and factitious norms, thereby overturning gender stereotypes.

Most people are simply hypocrites, they maintain. The sadomasochist is simply giving heartfelt and ultimately safe expression to hidden universal desires that have been covered up by convention and self-deception. S&M finds its way into everyday sex lives. It has always been there in much of the foreplay of the so-called straight world.

THE BIZARRE BIBLES OF SADOMASOCHISM

As cultists, sadomasochists have dignified certain texts as classics. These texts have even found a certain literary notoriety. Intellectuals see in them a profound challenge to social platitudes and moral illusions.

Among the most influential S&M texts are the eighteenth-century writings of the Marquis de Sade, of which *Justine* is perhaps the most accessible, the nineteenth-century Leopold von Sacher-Masoch's *Venus in Furs* and the modern *The Story of O* by the pseudonymous Pauline Réage, recently revealed as Dominique Aury. These stories will make sadomasochistic perversity come alive for readers unfamiliar with "the scene."

De Sade's Justine

Most celebrated of all sadomasochists is the Marquis Donatien de Sade, the notorious eighteenth-century French aristocrat for whom sadism is named. De Sade's works were initially embraced by many of the leaders of the French Revolution as exposés of the nobility and the clergy. The subsequent overthrow of the monarchy made his politics a cause célèbre while the Marquis continued to rant and rave about the pleasures of pedophilia, sodomy, imprisonment, bondage, flagellation, coprophagia (eating of feces) and other sundry delights. Released from prison and working for the new government, de Sade continued to violate "standards of decency" even after his defiance had a political import. Subsequently viewed in an even harsher light by France's reformers, de Sade spent the last eleven years of his life incarcerated first at the Bastille, where he narrowly escaped amnesty and emancipation, and then at the Charenton Asylum for the Insane. There he wrote and directed the plays that served as the model for Peter Weiss's *Marat Sade* and the Royal Shakespeare Company's famous production of this work in 1964. De Sade died there in 1814.

According to a recent biography by Maurice Lever, de Sade's perverse fiction and lifestyle were based on the author's actual life as a child and an adult. The Marquis eroticized and fictionalized actual events.

Donatien de Sade was the son of a bisexual libertine father. The elder de Sade's aristocratic position saved him more than once from arrest, imprisonment and the guillotine for acts of sodomy and pederasty, but eventually he retired in disgrace from public service. The boy was left to the care of an uncle, a libertine cleric of the kind appearing in many of his nephew's fictional adventures. Whether or not he was seduced by the avuncular priest is unclear. What is clear is that de Sade was exposed to all sorts of licentious works in the cavernous interiors of the family castle presided over by his uncle, including the apocryphal autobiography of Madame de Pompadour. At the age of ten, the boy was enrolled in a Jesuit college for boys. In the classroom, Donatien learned about the classics and the theater as well as theology and religious morality. In the dormitory, however, he learned about sex. Young de Sade was initiated by his schoolmates into the mysteries of whipping, sodomy and the sundry pleasures to be found in inflicting and suffering pain and humiliation. Four years of schooling yielded an abiding love for literature and a lifelong passion for passive penetration and sadomasochistic sex. Experience, literary and real, shaped the boy's imagination.

De Sade's life as an adult followed a predictable course. It was one, moreover, that revealed the inextricability of sadism and masochism, with scenes of his cruelty and his victims' outrage alternating or blending with dramas of his own terrible suffering and severe punishment. For example, only months after his wedding in 1763, the Marquis asked a woman to whip him while he masturbated with a crucifix, which she did, and then submit to anal sex. When she reported him to the authorities, de Sade was jailed for blasphemy and sodomy. In point of fact, the majority of de Sade's victims, like this one, were consenting adults. Most appeared to be prostitutes who agreed to submit to his flagellations for a certain sum of money. However, in 1768, he was arrested again after tying up a female servant, whipping her, cutting her flesh and pouring hot wax into her wounds before she could escape and denounce him.

So on it went, like the monotonously repetitive chapters of his pornographic novels: de Sade seducing his adolescent sister-in-law; de Sade fleeing enraged parents after having violated several male and female teenagers hired as secretaries and servants; de Sade poisoning prostitutes with Spanish fly; de Sade writing an importunate letter in blood to his horrified and estranged mother-in-law who, having saved him from the death sentence more than once, at last becomes his mortal enemy (and, in his words, the prototypical "bitter trollop of a mother"); de Sade attacked by his own peasants; de Sade jailed and seducing guards and nurses; de Sade raving, mad, suicidal; de Sade wretched and dead.

De Sade's life was a tale, like the tales he told, of bestiality—of instinct without love. It was the quintessential tale of sex, hate and self-hatred, of an eroticism careening toward death and destruction. It was indeed a sadomasochistic story.

Most famous of the novels completed and published by de Sade is *Justine,* which appeared in 1791. Described by Napoleon as "the most abominable book ever engendered by the most depraved imagination," it chronicles the fate of the highminded Justine, one of two sisters expelled from a convent for want of funds when the father goes bankrupt. Another novel, *Juliette,* describes the story of the more licentious and callous sibling.

Despite "preferring death to dishonor," Justine is doomed to be repeatedly dishonored. Alone or in the company of other young victims, male and female, she finds herself thrust into one misadventure after another. She is stripped, strapped, chained, sodomized, raped, excreted upon and imprisoned by one or more brigands, nobles and clerics. The cellars and dungeons of the castles and monasteries where the heroine is tortured in these ways bear a remarkable resemblance to the dank halls and tunnels of the family castle where little Donatien de Sade had lived with his uncle—and where his imagination had first been seized by both classic dramas and pornographic indulgences. The pederasty of many of the scenes calls up its author's actual school days. Throughout de Sade reveals an ability to identify with his female protagonist as well as her tormentor and her fellow victims.

Each time she is on the verge of destruction, Justine escapes and recovers from her ordeals and wounds. And each time she remains virtuous and unbeaten in her heart, until a Jovelike bolt of lightning kills her.

Justine's denouement is, I believe, a reference to the Greek mythology, with which de Sade was no doubt familiar—specifically to Euripides' play *The Bacchae.* Semele, daughter of Cadmus, King of Thebes, was killed by lightning—by her impulse to know penetration by the God Zeus in his true form (lightning). The god Dionysus, the sybaritic, bisexual and sadomasochistic spirit of the Greek pantheon, was the fruit of this fatal sexual union between the mortal Semele and immortal Zeus. Virtue's daughter, Justine, is really the bride of Zeus, then. She is thus the mother of a bacchanalian perversity under whose sway men dress as women and are murdered by their mothers (Prince Pentheus was decapitated by

Semele's sister Agave, one of Dionysus' crazed female followers, or maenads). De Sade is telling us that the spirit of Dionysus, like that of Aphrodite, must be recognized and worshiped as much as that of any virtuous god or goddess. To do or pretend otherwise invites disaster. Vice is the child of Virtue.

Some of the scenarios depicted are genuinely erotic. They are disquieting for readers of a more normal persuasion who find themselves aroused by them. Consider the rape of Justine by one of the Benedictine monks who hold her prisoner in their monastery:

> All the women surrounded him, excited him, and added to his bliss. In front of him, the fifteen-year-old girl lifted only my loins with her legs spread apart, offered to his mouth the altar on which he was sacrificing to me, from which he sucked at his leisure that precious sap which Nature had but recently accorded to this young child. One of the old women, kneeling before my conqueror's loins and kindling his desires with her impure tongue, provoked their ecstasy, while to arouse himself still further, the profligate fondled a woman with each hand. There was not one of his senses which was not titillated, not one which did not contribute to the completion of his rapture. He approached at this point, but my undiminished horror for all these infamies prevented me from sharing it, and so he reached it alone. His starts, his cries, everything announced its arrival, and in spite of myself I was inundated with the evidence of a desire I had kindled only as one of six. At last I fell back on the throne on which I had just been immolated, conscious of nothing save my pain and my tears, my despair and *my remorse* [italics mine].

Most men would find the spectacle of the rapist's total pleasuring by so many women sexy in obvious ways. For some women as well, Justine's submission and exposure, sanctioned and sweetened by the threat of harm, the impossibility of resistance and thus the irresponsibility are also erotic. The scene approximates the sexual fantasies of many more normal adolescent girls and young women. As I have suggested earlier, many women, even those who see themselves as most virtuous and purposeful to the extreme or liberated from men's domination, secretly want to be ravaged by men. They wish to be pinioned, overpowered, penetrated, deflowered and potentially immolated. They wish to suffer pleasure while escaping guilt or, in Justine's words, "remorse." But these recognizable desires of theirs soon give rise to others that are more mysterious and, to most so-called normal people, abhorrent.

As the other monks set upon Justine, the sexuality of this first violation quickly degenerates into something sordid and increasingly bizarre. The scenes that follow are disturbing because they follow from the former yet seem so surprising, so unfamiliar, so ugly, so inhuman, so evil, so vicious:

> Clement came toward me armed with switches. One of his arms pressed me to his knee, which exposed more openly the part that was to serve his whims. At first he tested his blows, but soon inflamed with lust, the brute struck with all his might. From the middle of my loins to the calves of my legs the traitor covered every inch. Daring to mingle love with brutality, his mouth sought to inhale the sighs I heaved in my pain. My tears flowed, he swallowed them, and kissing and cursing by turns, he continued to strike. Kneeling in front of him, one of the women played upon him in various ways with both hands. The better she succeeded, the more violent were the blows that reached me. Yet he was impotent. A fresh cruelty decided him: my breasts excited the brute, he set his teeth on them, he bit them, the cannibal. This excess provoked the crisis and the incense was released.
>
> The sated monk yielded me to Jerome. "I shall be no more dangerous for your virtue than Clement," he told me, caressing the bloody (sacrificial) altar. "I want to kiss these stripes. But I want more than that," continued this old satyr, "I want the hen to lay, and I want to eat her egg. Does it exist? Yes, by God! And, how soft it is!"
>
> Jerome's mouth replaced his fingers and I was told what to do, which I reluctantly performed. The odious man was pleased, he swallowed, and making me kneel in front of him, he affixed himself to me in this same position. His ignominious desire was satisfied in a place that silenced all complaint.

In these scenes of violence and coprophagia (devouring feces), the sadomasochist succeeds in transforming the object of his spiteful awe as well as himself into excrement. "Analized," object and subject and their body parts end up diffusing into a fecal mass.

The author's avowed purpose has been to reveal the "monstrous aberrations" of the "human heart." He has sought, he tells the reader, to portray the forces of Vice against which Virtue, often flagging, must stem the tide. But what he has actually done is extol these "natural forces," forces that draw Justine, against her will, toward her destruction. The urges to hurt and be hurt, to overpower and surrender, to abase and be abased are inescapable in a man's nature. They are equally inevitable in the life of the would-be innocent, whatever the latter's protests to the contrary. All men and women are capable of and sometimes desire evil in this view. A Juliette, who exploits her own and others' carnal instincts, fares better than a Justine, who tries to deny them. In fact, de Sade's women are by no means always submissive. *Philosophy in the Bedroom,* for example, features a number of female libertines who are just as aggressive in initiating their pleasures as their male counterparts.

But it is still more complicated than this. Why should de Sade make the female victim his protagonist and narrator? Why should her humiliators themselves "eat shit?" Why is the reader aroused by some scenes and immediately repelled by others?

The bestiality portrayed by de Sade, a sadism that is also masochism, lacks consistency and form. In de Sade's world, mouths and genitals suddenly appear only to dissolve into feces as organs and objects of sexual excitement. The story's episodes are like those of a picaresque novel except that they go nowhere. There is no plot; the narrative is without direction. The roles the characters assume, passive and active, are easily and immediately exchanged. The boundaries between holy man and lecher, decency and immorality, self and other, male and female, one body part and another become blurred. Since the victims recover completely each time from what should be their immolation, reality and imagination also become confounded. For all the focus on pain, there is no real or, at least, lasting harm. Repeatedly, Justine recovers completely from her physical injuries until she finally succumbs to the white light of truth, to her own desires for immolation. In this story, pain is pleasure. Finally, vice becomes virtue. Everything is its opposite. De Sade's *Justine,* for the author and his devotees, is a story of moral insanity. For them this is a divine madness.

For his detractors, Sade's works, like *Justine,* are yet another depiction of the degradation of women. Like others of its kind, they argue, a work such as *Justine* panders to men's inherent sadism and women's conditioned masochism. Sadomasochism is, in this view, merely the politics of gender in extremis.

Sacher-Masoch's Venus in Furs

In fact, the lines are not so clearly drawn. Masochism is not the lot of women alone. Quite to the contrary, masochism is named for Leopold von Sacher-Masoch, whose famous novel *Venus in Furs* is about a man who chooses to surrender to torture at the hands of a woman. He is the masochist, and she is the sadist.

According to reports, the story, which appeared in 1870 and depicted the willing subjugation of its male protagonist to his cruel mistress, was as much fact as fiction. Sacher-Masoch himself had signed a pact of perpetual enslavement and potential death with one Fanny Pistor several years earlier. To Fanny's physical and emotional assaults the author, like his hero Severin, had submitted willingly. A writer of some distinction, a militarist as a child and the son of a police chief, Sacher-Masoch also had a lifelong fascination with what would nowadays be called dominatrices.

Masochistic in his most private life, in public Sacher-Masoch was an early and vociferous feminist. He worshiped women in all their guises, intellectual and otherwise, and devoted much of his work and life to enhancing their active power in society. But what is striking in this particular book is the degree to which he, in the person of his hero, thrusts this power upon them—and in its most violent, virulent and twisted manifestations. In *Venus in Furs,* the male masochist acts to make his mistress into a sadistic mistress. Like its author, the story's protagonist is very much in control—in control of her control of him.

The book's premise is that man and woman are engaged in a war called love. Woman is cruel in the war of love largely because cruelty is what a man wants from her. In the prologue, the figure of the *Venus in Furs* "speaks" to the narrator from a painting upon which he gazes with the "ecstatic eyes of a burning martyr":

> Through man's passion, nature has given man into woman's hands, and the woman who does not know how to make him into her subject, her slave, her toy, and how to betray him with a smile in the end is not wise. . . . The more cruelly she treats him and the more faithless she is . . . the less pity she shows him, by so much she will increase his desire, be loved, worshipped by him. So it has been since the time of Helen and Delilah.

Venus's luxuriant and mysterious furs, covering the figure's alabaster nakedness (and *penislessness* the Freudian would add), enhance the onlookers' excitement. With these, the figure declares, if she comes to life, she can cover up a man completely and make him utterly hers. Where her body and her mien are cool and cruel, the furs enveloping her seem warm and inviting.

A man has only one choice, Severin, the protagonist, tells the narrator as he speaks to his guest while acting the martinet to a girl who serves him. A man must be a woman's tyrant or her slave. There is no passion to be found in stability, tenderness and equality. With this admonition, he begins to recount his story of how Venus in Furs came to be. He relates how he transformed a mild-mannered widow from Lembourg into his cruel Mistress Wanda.

In a surprising act of imagination, Severin brings a statue of Venus to life. Then he transposes, almost mystically, this figure onto the person of the young widow whose rooms happen to be located above his own in a country villa where he is staying. Like the object of all perverse lovers, Venus in Furs is both real person and an illusion—a figment of the pervert's fancy. Soon enough she declares her simple love for him, her wish to be his wife. Severin is unhappy with the young woman's ordinary wish to surrender her heart to him. Instead he encourages her to be cool and rejecting. He wants to surrender to her. He wants to be her "anvil." He wants to submit to her beatings. He wants to worship her.

He tells her that he is a "supersensual martyr." Where women respond to their sensual impulses, as a man he is ruled more by principles than desires. His erotic life resides more in his mental life than in physical sensation. He finds pleasure in deprivation, heartache, suffering and the expectation alone of satisfactions that are never to be his, never to be realized. As in the rhetoric of unrequited love and the Romantic poetry of Keats, reaching after the unattainable object is both more satisfying and sublime than the mere gratification of carnal lust. Severin, Masoch's masochist, finds poetry in the demonic powers and actual abuses of woman. Simultaneously, he keeps his distance from her as a real person.

Slowly, Wanda assents to Severin's entreaties. She promises to beat, humiliate and enslave him. Assenting, she whips him, but then pulls back and covers him with unwanted remorseful kisses. Severin remonstrates: Tenderness is not what he seeks. In a surge of passion, kissing her breast in gratitude, he bites her and draws blood. Becoming more adept at the sadistic part in which Severin has cast her, Mistress Wanda banishes her slave to his cold, bare room. She again relents and this time wraps Severin in her furs, enveloping and smothering him. Drawn into the masochist's web, she weaves hers.

Mistress Wanda drags Severin about Europe as her servant. Along the way, she taunts him with his greatest fear—the specter of rival lovers, one of whom paints her portrait as the Venus in Furs only to succumb himself to her abuses and indifference. At Severin's bidding, he and she enter into a Faustian pact, albeit one without any evident quid pro quo. Severin promises to be Wanda's slave forever. He gives her the right to torture and even kill him. Under no condition will he seek revenge. He cedes everything to her; there is no escape. Severin's only condition is that Mistress Wanda "appear in furs as much as possible," particularly when she intends to administer punishment.

In the penultimate scenes, Wanda seems to relent once more, showering love on her beloved. But she has led Severin on this time, and she treats him to the promised betrayal. Venus takes another lover, a beautiful Greek with black curls. Severin senses that he is a man of "savage masculinity" who can "enchain her, captivate her, subjugate her."

Yet it is not so simple as this. This man, his black velvet coat trimmed with sable, "is a man who is like a woman," particularly in his imperious vanity. He has appeared in woman's dress and been deluged by love letters from scores of male admirers. He is a Greek, a jealous Greek, a curly-haired Greek dressed in furs, a satyr. He is, we learn, Dionysus incarnate. Once more, the ambisexual Dionysus makes his enigmatic appearance on the sadomasochistic scene.

In the climactic pages of the novel, this successful rival whips Severin before the consenting eyes of an adored woman. The "sensation," Severin sighs, "cannot be described." He "almost went mad with shame and despair." Constrained from taking vengeance by his "abominable agreement," Severin returns home from what turns out to be this extended rite of passage. Upon his father's death, he assumes the patriarchal position in real life and so puts on his imperious and phallic "Spanish boots," the trappings of society's dominant male. Venus sends him a letter commending him on his cure. He concludes that "whoever wishes to be whipped deserves to be whipped." His has been, we infer, an initiation rite—a hero's encounter with the Sphinx.

As with de Sade, the confusion of roles and identities is apparent with Sacher-Masoch, whose novel is oddly chaste and mostly devoid of frankly sensual encounters in favor of simply brutal ones. The masochist creates the sadist. He says that he chooses to submit to her violence rather than suffer her betrayal of him and experience the stabs of rejection and jealousy that come with having lost to a rival lover.

Yet his beating at the hands of this rival, a male rival in furs, seems to satisfy him at last while at the same time it destroys his masochistic identity and the peculiar illusion it offers. This real humiliation provokes his misogynistic revenge evident at the tale's beginning and unmasks the man behind the mistress. One interpretation would have it that Severin has been seeking some homoerotic or bisexual gratification all along without knowing it.

Once more the hidden homosexual theme emerges interwoven with the sadomasochistic motif. In this context, ancient Greek myths and rituals again come to mind—the pedophilia of the notorious gymnasium. In these ritualized activities, barely pubescent boys submitted to the nonanal "penetration" of older men. Their mentors stuck erect penises between the initiates' thighs, ejaculating while the boys' penises remained detumescent—as if they had none, indeed, as if they were women. Being womanly and receiving the older and stranger man's phallic power was the first step toward becoming a fully empowered man.

Indeed, the fact that Severin's rival "knows woman" because he is himself womanly only adds to the ambiguities of the masochistic quest. Is this what the protagonist has been seeking for himself all the while: to be enveloped and penetrated by a woman who is really a man and to even *be*, in some sense, a woman? It may very well be the sadomasochist's aim to deny, however sharply, the differences between the sexes and the boundaries between any two people.

Wanda herself is not simply a passive actor in Severin's drama. Wanda does gain some power of her own through the masochistic drama. No doubt, she gets pleasure out of having the upper hand—having female power.

In real life, one female "bottom," Pattie, described her most exquisite torture at the hands of a male "top." He placed clamps over parts of her body, then on the nipples and genital region until at last he "zeroed in on my clitoris." The pain and the orgasmic pleasure were, she said predictably, intense, unbearable, ecstatic. In this man's absolute power, she became a woman without a will of her own. But more than this, Pattie remarked, her clitoris had become so engorged with sexual excitement and the clamps that it looked like a penis. Surrender to a man long enough, she wondered, and one might just become a man oneself. Sadomasochistic caricatures of gender roles and differences have the paradoxical effect of obliterating them.

Réage's The Story of O

Gender roles are once more caricatured with a vengeance in *The Story of O*, arguably the most popular and today the most influential of sadomasochistic parables. The book appeared in 1954 in France.

The novel was written by Pauline Réage, whose identity remained unknown until recently and about whose gender there was great speculation until her identity and her complicated story were revealed in recent years. The book was heralded at the time of its publication as a new cult classic. Winning a literary prize or two, it stirred the imaginations of the French intelligentsia, who proclaimed the work a great advance over the "puerile efforts" of Sacher-Masoch nearly a century earlier. Its heroine's libidinal misadventures eventually found their way into a soft-core pornographic film, which proved to be an inspiration for many hitherto clandestine S&M practitioners. Some of the film's cultists have declared that *The Story of O* moved them to find their true sexual selves and stampede from the closet onto "the scene" with a new sense of vision and mission.

Using a conceit made famous in Dickens's alternative endings to *Great Expectations*, the novel has two beginnings, each with a slightly different twist as far as its heroine's will is concerned. In both versions, however, O, a Parisian fashion photographer, ends up being taken by her lover, René, to a mysterious mansion at Roissy. There she is stripped naked, save for a collar and chains. She is further commanded to keep her legs uncrossed at all times so that the "gentlemen" who inhabit the place—René among them—can have ready access to her. She becomes the "omni-available" woman, in the words of Ethel Person, always open, always lubricated, without needs of her own—a fairly ubiquitous male sexual fantasy and pornographic conceit.

Whipped, sodomized, forced to perform fellatio, O is kept in a cell at night, where her every physiologic function is overseen by a crude peasant who serves as a valet and beats her for good measure. By day, dressed in an old-fashioned gown designed for maximum decolletage and easy penetration, she is forbidden to look at or otherwise challenge her captors. After some weeks, O is released or, rather, remanded to the custody of René. She finds herself transformed.

Back in Paris, René commands O to throw out her underwear and remain sexually accessible at all times. In the first of a series of homoerotic twists, he gives her to his half brother, Sir Stephen. Sir Stephen has a preference, like that of one of Roissy's unseen lovers, for anal penetration. Observing this fascinates René, although, watching, he never indulges in the practice himself. For her part, O, who is long practiced in the ways of lesbianism, in which she takes greater initiative and is generally more dominant, seduces one of her models, Jacqueline. The girl's teenaged sister, Natalie, joining them on a vacation sponsored by this rich Englishman Sir Stephen, comes to worship O. Such lesbian lust is the other standard conceit of male-oriented pornography—one that secretly allows the male viewer to identify himself with the woman as lover.

O is handed over to Mistress Anne Marie for further "modification" and indoctrination. Eventually, she is branded on her buttock while having metal rings inserted into her labia. The Commander, huge and bald like a great phallus, then appears and orchestrates O's final humiliation. Led on a leash by Natalie, her vulva shaved bare, an owl's mask covering her face, her cloak opened to expose her private parts, O becomes a curiosity at a ball. She is ogled and toyed with by the guests until Sir Stephen and the Commander take her rudely on the lawn. From there O will return to Roissy.

The film version of O—soft-core and featuring beautiful actresses—is more erotic than the book, which in its turn was sexier than *Venus in Furs*. As with de Sade, once again the movie's most erotic moments, involving O's exposure and submission to more than one man, are quickly replaced by brutal scenes of whipping and threats of violence. However, the heroine is never so humiliated as she is in the original.

The heterosexual elements are also more salient, for example: O's yielding her model lover, Jacqueline, to René; her being pursued and courted in Paris by the rather handsome and virile valet, her keeper from Roissy; her indulging in a "vanilla sex" interlude with a straight young lover in a hotel room; ultimately, Sir Stephen's falling in love with O and his surrendering himself to her. In the movie, the tinkling clitoris rings are pretty and gold. What is more, O does her share of woman whipping and loves it. In the debacle of the denouement, O is less humiliated than defiant. Her owl's mask is severe, predatory, handsome; her nudity is "insolent;" she is in charge of a gawking crowd. Finally, Sir Stephen yields himself and his power to her. In the movie's last moments, O crushes the glowing tip of a cigarette on the top of his hand, thus complementing his brand on her buttock with a little "o" of her own.

The tides have now turned. The sadism in the masochist, most vivid in the imagery of O's owlish mask, has been unmasked again.

THE SECRET PORNOGRAPHY OF THE MIND'S EYE: "O, JUDY"

Almost everybody responds in some erotic way to a film such as this. For example, the film version of *The Story of O* riveted Judy Gould's attention when she was some two years into her treatment. Her latest, Walter, had suggested that they see it together. Walter himself was into semi-rough stuff, though "not really." He liked tying her up with fake handcuffs now and then—"just for a change"—and half whipping, half tickling Judy with an ostrich feather whip. Oddly enough, he was "more reliable" than any of the "straighter men who had jerked [her] around on a daily basis!"

For her part, Judy had been both tantalized and slightly embarrassed by porno movies in the past. There had been the few that she had actually gone to—most memorably, *Deep Throat* and *Behind the Green Door*. There were the offerings of cable TV, like *The Robin Byrd Show*, which Judy watched when she found herself tormented by some unavailable man and unable to sleep. Was she gay, she wondered? The naked women, more than the men and their pendulous penises, really aroused her.

It was more complicated than this, however. There was something about those women—so exposed on the screen, opened up, splayed open almost, without a shred of remaining privacy, being done to like that, being humiliated. Judy could imagine herself in just such a position, held still, a camera's lens pointed at her dilated vulva, the viewer's eye reaching up into her vagina and beyond. It sent shivers up her spine, the nakedness, the humiliation, the openness of it all.

Shivering, she remembered that once her parents had found her like that—or was it just her father?—at eleven years old. She had been asleep on her bed, without the bottoms of her pajamas, her mother's compact with its mirror lying on the sheets between her legs. She had been exploring herself. Now her father was looking right at her. It made her both nervous and wet just to think about it, like those dreams everyone has of being caught naked outside the privacy of one's own room.

And O was so exposed, so much the object of all eyes, so helpless. Why the letter "O" stood for open, did it not—open to the extreme. O'ed. But it was the last element in *O* that more than anything made Judy squirm when she saw, talked or just thought about it. O's sadism got her. Otherwise, in spite of herself, Judy found herself turned on by the movie and the images, pictures and scenes she kept remembering and reviewing in her mind.

OPPOSITES ATTRACTING

In *Three Essays on Sexuality,* his major contribution to the sexology that was becoming so popular as Victorianism gave way to Naturalism, Freud called neurosis the "negative of perversion." What he meant was that anxious, inhibited, symptomatic people are struggling mightily against aberrant impulses that they fear will lead them down the primrose path. Their symptoms and personality quirks defend against temptation. The phobics, hysterics and compulsives of this world are, in their hearts, fetishists, exhibitionists, and so on. Their secrets, their conflict-laden wishes, may leak from their every pore, at least as far as the psychoanalytic listener is concerned. Yet neurotics themselves bend over backward not to hear them and to deny their deviant desires.

Today the clinician understands that overtly perverse fantasies, rituals and lifestyles are more complicated matters than this simple formula of Freud's would have it. Still his original notion has a core of truth. This is particularly so when it comes to the inverted but inextricable relationship between sadomasochistic sexual practices and what I have characterized as the sadomasochistic relationships and personality types of everyday life. They are opposites, and because of this they are ultimately one and the same.

Consider the following contrasts: Whereas, consciously, the sexual sadomasochist finds endless pleasure in physical pain, the neurotic finds only ceaseless frustration in emotional pain. Whereas the practicing masochist consciously invites and orchestrates his or her subjugation, the "relationship victim" merely feels victimized by the other person. Whereas the self-proclaimed hedonist denies anger, shame and guilt about his or her desires and acts accordingly, the self-styled loser tends to feel no desires at all but only guilt, shame and anger and acts, vainly, to get rid of these unpleasurable feelings. Whereas "perverts" proclaim undying love for those whom they ask to abuse them, neurotics disclaim love for their abusers to whom they nonetheless cling. Whereas sybaritic sadomasochists try, unconvincingly, to disclaim the hatred that is so evident in their erotic imagery and behavior, suffering sadomasochists proclaim their righteous indignation toward those who hurt them.

In the meantime, both are in control of others and out of control of themselves. Both are ruled by urges and wishes in which the love and hate, desire and destruction, have become fused together. Wittingly or not, both make their fantasies come true. Neither really distinguishes their internal life from the realities of the outside world. The people in this outside world are cast as players, again wittingly or not, in both perverse and neurotic sadomasochistic dramas of love and death.

What most clearly distinguishes the neurotic from the pervert are the structures of their very different consciences, their superegos. The former's want of compunction and restraint is matched by the latter's excess of self-punishment and self-denial. Where the disinhibited sadomasochistic practitioner yields to the expression of what looks like raw impulse, the inhibited sadomasochist of everyday life typically nips the possibility of gratification in the bud. Intoxicated by the act itself, the giddy sadomasochistic pervert makes himself or herself unaware of any angst or doubt about the immoral implications of his or her exploitative acts. In his everyday life, the fretful sadomasochistic personality knows only the weight of a malignant conscience, represses his or her immoral impulses and turns his aggression mostly on himself or herself while expressing his or her hostility by covertly seducing aggressors into being punishing and bad without knowing why.

Conscience protects us and others from ourselves. Conscience is the mark of civilization, of a person's personhood—humanity at its most helpful. Its presence is a sign that however confused a person may become, he or she tries to be mindful of others and their separate existence. Though they can backfire, as I have noted, and turn on people's psyches like the body's immune system and thus on others, the forcefulness of such superegos and ego ideals means that people have it in them to strive for something better.

Yielding to a perversion, particularly a sadomasochistic one, means giving up, temporarily at least, on being moral. This is so, it seems, no matter how many claims may be made by the devotees of "the scene" to their sublime status as visionaries of universal truth and social transcendence. The neurotic sadomasochist, who is often subject to some of the same mistreatment as his more impulsive brothers and sisters, knows this. He or she intuits the truth and tries to hold on to his or her decency and dignity, at all costs.

BLOOD BROTHERS: DICK AND ARTHUR

Dick Knight, the repressed and successful CEO first described in chapter 4, had an impulsive and impecunious older brother, Arthur, five years Dick's senior. Dick had suspected that Art was gay for many years. He had joined with his other brother and sisters in shielding their mother from their suspicions and the more obvious facts in support of them. Besides, Dick did not subscribe to homophobia, or so he said. Having glimpsed his own heart, Dick was a tolerant man—tolerant, at least, toward everyone other than himself.

When Art tested HIV positive, the whole truth came out. Not only was Art gay, he admitted to his brother, but he was not "your ordinary homosexual." When he doffed his tweeds and oxford-cloth shirt in the evenings, Art became a leatherist. He had frequented S&M bars such as The Anvil, before the pandemic closed them down. He was into "water sports" and was no stranger to yet another establishment called The Toilet. Art had relished anonymous sex and submitted to unseen anal penetration in dark movie houses and the decaying piers beyond the West Side Highway.

So he told his story to buttoned-down brother one boozy evening after the great confession. These erotic tastes had been Art's undoing. He even had nipple rings, Art added, unbuttoning his pearly white buttons to bare a dark hairy breast. As the pink nipple peeked out at him, Dick felt a shudder not just of horror but of desire. In that flash of flesh, and the revelation of a scary but sensual life, Dick realized that he envied Art his abandon and even the death to which this abandon had sentenced him.

His whole life, his whole sexless and suburban life, Dick had had fantastic pictures drift through his mind that approximated scenes from what he now understood to be his brother's reality. He had fought them off, fought not to give in. He had strained to forget and hold back to the point that he no longer seemed to possess any of the erotic energy that might have led to his undoing. Dick had felt guilty all the same, guilty for his sins of the heart. Guilty, guilty, guilty! The gavel pounded in his head. These sins, like Art's forlorn and somehow invaginated nipple, had winked at him now and then through the veils of disavowal and repression. Dick had recoiled in fear and self-loathing. Better to deprive, incarcerate and unsex himself in joylessness than to surrender to "That!" Better no pleasure at all. Better perpetual punishment. Better a lifeless purgatory than a living hell. Better a dull life than a blistering death.

SADOMASOCHISM is a universal problem. All children, psychoanalysts know, begin their lives in a sensual state of what has been called "polymorphous perversity." Since growing into womanhood and manhood is so very difficult, so fraught, in one way or another, sadomasochists tend to fall back on this familiar sexuality of childhood.

Furthermore, they are angry at the parents and people who have made life's passages difficult and at themselves for foundering. Thus, among all the possibilities, they most often choose erotic forms of hatred. They resort to sadomasochistic modes of relatedness and satisfaction. Then they try to escape their fate. Everybody does this, sometimes, somehow.

In the next chapter, I will explore the allure of an omnipresent erotic destructiveness in the unconscious of all men and women. I will explain the universality and inevitability of sadomasochism in everybody's life.

SADOMASOCHISM IN THE HUMAN CONDITION

A CAVEAT

WE psychoanalysts tend to speak a strange and often alienating language sounding like psychobabble—one that's difficult for the uninitiated to decode and that puts many people off. The important thing is this: Our notions about people are based on what they actually say while free associating in the psychoanalytic session. As their defenses ease, analysands spontaneously utter their hitherto unconscious fantasies and thus some entirely surprising wishes, impulses and ideas. These unconscious wishes are often utterly at odds with what they consciously want yet drive them to feel, respond and behave in ways beyond their understanding and control. Such is the case with the sadomasochism that is an unknown and yet compelling force in all our lives. I thus offer one particular caveat as my readers approach this easily misunderstood subject matter of the pages that follow: Distinguish between the unwanted and unconscious wish and a conscious objective, the two of which may be in considerable conflict with each other.

GODS OF DEATH AND DESIRE

When people think about Freud and psychoanalysis, it is Eros—the god of love, sex and life—that comes to mind before all else. Yet Freud, the dissident Melanie Klein and their various followers struggled just as hard to formulate how Thanatos, god of death, drives people toward their inevitable destruction. They grappled with the uncanny tendency of these opposing powers to come together as strange bedfellows. The fruit of the union of death and desire is, in fact, sadomasochism, in which the forces of life have conjoined with those of destruction.

Ever since de Sade and Masoch lent their names to the perversions first described by Krafft-Ebing, sadomasochism has remained one of the mysteries of the human condition. Clinicians have found it to be a significant factor in virtually all their patients' lives in one form or another. Though they may use different terms to describe it, historians, anthropologists and sociologists have been hard pressed to explain the willingness of people to submit to others in the power politics that govern social relations. Literary critics, film reviewers and other cultural commentators have striven to articulate the hold that so many artists of the grotesque—from Bosch to Bacon and beyond—have had on their spellbound audiences. They, like Freud and then Klein, have inquired into the nature of the death instinct as a driving force in the human psyche.

SADOMASOCHISM AND THE DEATH INSTINCT

Mention Freud or psychoanalysis to many people, and the first words out of their mouths are, "sex . . . Freud said everything was sex." This is a vast oversimplification, of course. For Freud, sex meant much more than sex as it is commonly defined (genital excitement, intercourse and possibly orgasm). It meant sexuality, libido or Eros. It meant the life force within an individual that moves that individual to seek pleasure and, ultimately, to preserve and create life. The oral and anal pleasures of infancy and toddlerhood, centered on nursing and defecating, ensure the survival of the individual by placing a premium on vital bodily functions. The pleasure of eating and excreting helps keep the child alive until he or she becomes autonomous and is old enough to take these functions for granted. The genital pleasures of adulthood and the gratification to be found in sexual intercourse ensure the reproduction and survival of the species. In Freud's teleological view, one that emphasizes the functions and purposes of a phenomenon, sexuality is a powerful force because it guarantees self-preservation and procreation— the creation through sexual union of new life.

In this broad sense, there is a certain truth to the common misapprehension about Freud's understanding of people's fundamental motives. For Freud, initially at least, the libido was the primary, indeed the only, "instinctual drive." Rage and violence were secondary reactions, he said, emotional responses to the frustration of the self-preservative and sexual instincts. For Freud's contemporary, Alfred Adler, an aggressive striving for power lay at the heart of human psychology. But the wish to destroy life had no essential place in Freud's initial view of man's basic nature. Commenting on Adler's notions, Freud remarked that there was no room for love in his theory.

For as long as he could, Freud resisted conceptualizing aggression as a basic human motive or drive in its own right. He struggled his whole working life with the problem of people's penchant for destruction and its eerie manifestation in the form of sadomasochism. Psychoanalysis was already twenty years old when Freud first attempted to fit these phenomena into a theoretical framework.

The Great War confronted Freud with mass destruction. Barraged by news from the front, his sons serving in the Austrian army, he was forced to grant aggression its due as an elemental instinctual drive. Yet even then, he went about his theorizing in convoluted ways.

Human destructiveness, Freud argued in *Beyond the Pleasure Principle* (1919), a book inspired by the phenomenon of shell shock, represents a redirection outward of an inherent self-destructiveness. Human violence toward others derives from the death instinct. People are born to die. Future life requires the death of the old, of the mortal individual whose job it is to harbor and then part with his or her immortal germ plasm, the genes discharged in the sexual act. Whatever we may imagine—and our death is inconceivable to us—the existence of the individual is transitory. Each individual is programmed to die, and this prewiring runs throughout the psyche.

As much as individuals fight for life, they also seek its cessation. They seek to reduce all stimulation and tension within themselves to a minimum. Ordinary people seek what the suicidal Prince Hamlet called that "consummation devoutly to be wished / To die, to sleep." They seek Nirvana. So "beyond the pleasure principle," Freud concluded with a philosophical sigh, lies the "Nirvana principle." Individuals are inherently hell bent on peace of mind through self-annihilation. They are governed by death wishes that primarily target themselves.

This far-reaching and, as it were, perverse purpose underlies a range of mostly undesirable emotional states and behaviors. Of these suicide is the most obvious and ominous example. The *repetition compulsion*—the tendency to relive terrible traumas as in the war neuroses and nightmares Freud was studying at the time—is yet another instance of psychic self-destruction at work. Self-denial and sensual asceticism, manifested in Freud's own relatively sexless existence, are other instances of self-destructiveness at work. People's irrational, tenacious, often unconscious sense of guilt provides yet another case in point. Self-injurious addictions, such as the cigar chain-smoking that caused Freud's jaw cancer, are other examples of the death wish. Masochistic perversions provide further illustration. Even in ordinary sex, orgasm, the acme of ecstasy, has been called the "little death." Everywhere in psychological life, indeed at the very height of life-affirming pleasure, lurks a death wish.

In its primary form, untamed and aimed at the self, such destructiveness can be lethal for both the individual and the species—for the children he or she might otherwise reproduce and the society that relies on human existence and productivity. In order to protect themselves, individuals turn this primary masochism on others as aggression. Hostility, cruelty, intrusion, domination and possessiveness have their roots in the urge to rid oneself of a kind of inner poison. The individual, Freud concluded, wishes to strike out in order to displace and discharge an otherwise noxious self-destructiveness.

THE DEVELOPMENT OF SADOMASOCHISM

To backtrack for a moment: Freud equivocated as to which came first in a child's development—masochism or sadism. Initially, in his highly abstract "metapsychology papers," which began to appear about five years before *Beyond the Pleasure Principle* was published, he had argued that there could be no primary masochism. Until he had articulated his more general theory of the death instinct, it did not make logical sense to him that developing individuals would begin life by wishing to suffer and hurt themselves. Hurting and controlling others, he reasoned, had to come first in a developmental sequence. Primary sadistic impulses could only secondarily be turned back on the self. For instance, when the child bangs its head in frustration, it is taking out on itself its rage toward the powerful caretakers on whom it depends. The urge is primary, and the pain that results secondary.

Freud was then left with a puzzling question. How could somebody aim to inflict pain on somebody else if he or she did not first know what pain was—what it felt like? So he reversed himself. He concluded that masochism, not sadism, must come first after all in the individual's emotional development. Still, the logic was not altogether clear, and Freud continued to contradict himself.

In puzzling over these and other instinctually based desires and their objects, Freud faced one of psychology's great mysteries. He learned that one cannot take the self—the self that does the desiring—for granted. As I suggested earlier, it takes time for someone to know that he or she is an "I" and that others, the infant's mother in particular, are a "they" in a world where the boundaries between objects and persons are drawn only gradually. In the beginning of life, which Freud referred to as a "buzzing confusion," it is unclear where one person ends and the outside world begins. Therefore, it is also unclear which feelings or impulses belong to whom or to what.

This is true when it comes to the ebb and flow of appetite, desire, violence, frustration, pain, power, control and helplessness in this world—the stuff of which sadomasochism is made. After Freud, many of his heirs—Erik Erikson, Margaret Mahler, D. W. Winnicott, Edith Jacobson, Heinz Kohut and others—would focus more and more on the unfolding of identity rather than on the dynamics of desire and would see this phenomenon in light of the primal condition of infancy. They would discern in sadomasochistic aims a variety of paradoxes.

On the one hand, theorists argue, sadomasochists try to plunge back into this boundless beginning. Reviving, if only in part, this amorphous primal state, they attempt to diffuse the lines between the self and other. They create scenarios involving another person in which they are identified with the intentions and feelings of the other in addition to their own. By means of projection (outward) and introjection (inward), the subject is everywhere, even when the sadomasochist casts him or herself in the role of the helpless slave or the overpowering master of the universe. Sadomasochists also suffer the pain and tumult that come with one's psychic skin being torn off. They make themselves permeable, open, utterly vulnerable, unbounded, unprotected, unmodulated—like a helpless and hungry infant melting into its mother's breast. "Masochistic surrender" is how the clinician depicts this peculiar state of mind.

On the other hand, theorists continue, sadomasochists are like babies who pound or push at their mothers in order to define their bodies and themselves. By being angry, aggressive and sadistic, they try to keep other people away, thus reinforcing their own boundaries. Sadomasochists may empower the self, through dominating or assuming an oppositional and negative posture in relation to another person, or they may buttress their boundaries by filling up what they perceive to be their incomplete or insubstantial selves with vibrant sensation—the high pitch of pain. The cliché, "Pinch me, I must be dreaming!" captures the self-defining function of such suffering.

To the extent that sadomasochism revives the diffuseness of self and other characteristics of infancy and early toddlerhood, it also blurs sex differences. As I shall discuss more thoroughly in the next chapter, the development of a sense of self goes hand in hand with a person's sexual or gender identity. It takes time for a child to realize that she or he is not only an individual in a world of others, but also a boy or girl in a world of two sexes. It takes even longer to understand what belongs to whom—to perceive which anatomical parts go with which sex. When gender boundaries are crossed, when the sadomasochistic partners cast a woman in the "top" and stereotypically "phallic" role and a male in the "bottom" or caricatured female role, they are giving expression to the early uncertainty of gender roles, the concrete behavioral attributes growing children come to ascribe to each gender. When they reverse such stereotypes of male and female roles, they are experimenting with, or redefining, both parts—male and female.

In a 1924 paper devoted to masochism, Freud discussed the three evolving forms masochism assumes as the child becomes an adult individual: sexual, feminine and moral. Each has wellsprings in the primal and diffuse sadomasochism of infancy.

Freud saw *sexual masochism,* whose more direct manifestations have been described in the preceding chapter, as the bedrock on which the other forms, which are more psychologically complex and structured, were based. By their very nature, he theorized, pleasure and pain are inextricably linked together. When he first thought about the feeling of pleasure, Freud believed it came from reducing stimulation and tension to a minimum, ideally to nothing at all. However, this early model, which conformed better to the Nirvana principle than the pleasure principle, did not quite work, for it could not account for the seeking out of tense yet subjectively pleasurable experiences such as foreplay, a state of excited, heightened stimulation and exquisite tension. A baby's delicious and expectant inquisitiveness, what researchers have referred to as "stimulus seeking," is another. Being tickled is yet another.

In conditions like these, it is not the absolute quantities but rather the ebb and flow, the *rhythmicity of the stimuli,* that make an experience painful or pleasurable. The balance can tip easily from one subjective experience to the other. The curious, stimulus-hungry baby can quickly become overloaded, frustrated and miserable before completely shutting down, as baby watchers such as T. Berry Brazelton have described. The turned-on teenager, if he cannot discharge his excitement in an ejaculation, develops "blue balls." Too much tickling hurts.

Indeed, like the overloaded infant, many adults try to shun or shut down potential sources of pleasure altogether. For them, experiences of desire and potential satiation are tied to a life history of unbearable excitement and painful frustration. Children are mostly unable to achieve full orgasm, and thus they cannot discharge themselves of mounting stimulation and alleviate painful frustration. Moreover, as they develop, they become subject to the more complex feelings of guilt, shame and anxiety that accompany their sexual and, originally and inevitably, incestuous wishes and feelings. Sexual passion and suffering go hand in hand in an "erotic horror," as I have noted earlier.

Because of the nature of infantile sexuality, then, sexual masochism is an inevitable byproduct of desire and frustration. The poets, blues writers and songwriters have known this on their pulses as have the forlorn lovers whose woes they describe. "Tragic bliss" and "sweet sorrow" are the lover's lot. There can be no pleasure without pain, though later on rational adults try to forget this fact of life.

As Robert Stoller later put it, like it or not, just about everybody harbors conscious perverse, and specifically sadomasochistic, sexual fantasies, which they try to disavow and banish from awareness. We only have to look at ourselves honestly to detect these. Sexual masochism, present from the start but increasingly unconscious in most of us, stays with all of us throughout life.

According to Freud, *feminine masochism* follows from sexual masochism. Growing up, children develop a variety of fantasies about the nature of sexual intercourse between their parents—the so-called primal scene. Freud posited that when a child happens to see or overhear his or her parents engaging in sex, it often seems that the mother, moaning in pleasure, is being beaten or hurt by the father. The watching child links his or her own pleasurable and painful bodily experiences—defecating, getting spanked, having enemas, having his or her temperature taken, being hit by another child—with the mother's feminine position and further conceives of this as masochistic. For the child, to be feminine comes to mean submitting to penetration and domination and suffering pain and humiliation. Clinicians listening to their patients talk about their childhoods have found this to be among several "universal fantasies."

The evidence on which Freud based the above theory (in large part) comes from the "Wolf Man" case, in which his patient recalled observing, as a child—or so Freud inferred—his father and mother in the act of *coitus a tergo*, or rear-entry sex. Children in Freud's era witnessed the copulation of animals frequently enough and developed their sexual theories about human sexual relations not only in response to inference and imaginings about their parents' sex lives, but also on the basis of such natural phenomena. Since animals tend to copulate with the male assuming the dominant position and the female often screeching in apparent pain, children may infer that their parents' sexual practices are not limited to missionary-style sex. In a sense, their experiences with real-life beasts, compounded by highly charged encounters with the sights and sounds of their parents' sex life glimpsed on the sly, led to a view of human sexuality as bestial, with a connection between the feminine position and subjugation. The cognitive understanding of children was further compounded, Freud and other analysts continued, by their own bodily sensations and activities and by the sadomasochistic desires inherent in their instinctual life.

In many of their guilt-ridden, private erotic reveries and early masturbatory activity, children of both sexes—though they are more acceptable and closer to consciousness in heterosexual girls than in heterosexual boys—picture themselves being beaten, immolated, castrated, mortified and even ravaged, loving it all the while. The unabashed ecstasy of Saint Teresa as she receives the stigmata is an example of such suffering. Usually, we repress or reorganize these beating fantasies or rape fantasies along less consequential lines as we grow up. But these secret desires continue to exert powerful influences on our love lives, emerging in wishes to be overpowered, taken, conquered and seduced. This is a central feature in Freud's and later psychoanalysts' theorizing at its most sophisticated. Such theories try to describe not so much material reality, or actuality, as psychic reality, the fantasy life of the child and childhood and the unconscious. When this distinction gets blurred, psychoanalysts can be woefully and dangerously misunderstood.

To some extent, Freud and certainly many of his followers in the 1950s and 1960s, notably Helene Deutsch, came to see feminine masochism as the normal or ideal womanly condition. Women should accept their predestined passivity, castration and suffering, argued Deutsch, rather than accede to their "penis envy" and should not strive to be active and thus, in her formulation, "phallic" and "sadistic," like men. Women, Deutsch wrote, should cede their competitiveness and work ambitions for the sake of a sound adjustment to life's realities. They should prepare for a life as a good and agreeably submissive wife and mother for whom pleasuring a husband represents the highest good. Women should sacrifice their freedom and their very selves to the families they helped create (something, incidentally, the powerful and prolific Deutsch herself did not do). Infant researcher Sylvia Brody went so far as to state that the primary motive for bearing, birthing and rearing babies resided in the prospective mother's wish to be beaten by and submit to her demanding fetus.

However, when he first conceptualized feminine masochism, Freud was talking specifically about boys and men. The male, he stressed, makes a connection between submission and suffering and the female role in the primal scene. He wishes to submit to the violation he imagines a woman experiences in making love, and he imagines himself not only like Saint Teresa, but also like Saint Francis yielding to God's divine stigmatization, or the martyred and beatific Saint Sebastian pierced with arrows. As first conceived, then, feminine masochism was a psychological construct deriving from a universal male fantasy and not a realistic attribute of normal women.

Freud himself only touched on a little boy's awe of his mother and her sex-specific capacities. Only sporadically did he underscore a male's dread and envy of a woman's absolute power—one that was not at all phallic—over his survival and well-being as an infant. Nor did Freud address at length a man's wish to possess a woman's capacity to make and feed babies, or his envy of her breasts and womb. Freud, like other male analysts after him, seemed to have no appreciation of a woman's sexual parts and powers, for instance the multiple orgasmic capacity of the clitoris, which he called an "inferior organ." In the patriarchal family constellations typical of Freud's day, maternal and feminine powers were quickly eclipsed by a paternal authority.

In this defensively misogynistic ethos, a boy's identification with his mother's power over him would be screened by his identification not with this but rather with what he perceived to be his mother's passivity in relation to her husband, his father. Such an identification with a woman reflected a male retreat into inferiority and an identification with the masochism inherent not in her psyche but rather in her sociocultural lot in life. Behind men's attraction to and repulsion from femininity, Freud went on, lies every man's wish to become once again a helpless babe in arms. In other words, in the male view, being like a woman connoted being a dependent baby.

Once established, the male's feminine, masochistic, infantile identification served a variety of purposes, defensive and otherwise. A boy's wish to take a woman's subservient place in the sex act (such as he conceives of it) expresses his homoerotic longing for his father's love and his wish to submit erotically to him and his big, penetrating penis. It derives from a male's wish to be a wife, a woman and a mother, overpowered by a dominant man. Taking in another man's penis, in this fantasy, also represents a passive and therefore safer route to power for the male, especially one who chooses to play the female part with other males rather than engage in a death-defying competition with his stronger superiors. A longing like this may also be exploited and exaggerated to obscure a son's more direct challenge to his father's dominance. Delilah-like, the boy's seduction of his father may serve to avert the father's anger and potential retaliation, get him into a position of weakness, trick and overpower him and steal his adult authority—indeed, to castrate him.

As ethnologists such as Konrad Lorenz point out, submission rituals in primates and other species serve as checks on the full and destructive expressions of male aggression in a given social unit. They help avert battles to the death. Male apes and monkeys allow themselves to be mounted by dominant males in their group when they have lost to them in the fight for sexual access to females in heat. Sometimes they will pay homage by "kissing ass": literally licking the older primate's anus and surrounding parts (which, on baboons, can be quite impressive). A young male wolf will roll over and expose his underbelly and jugular to the pack's Alpha when it becomes clear that he remains the dominant male. Juvenile animals are endowed, Lorenz continues, with foreshortened, beguiling, androgynous and even female faces, a configuration or gestalt that releases the older animals' tenderness and quells their hostility.

The human world is also filled with initiation rites in which male feminine masochism is ritualized in violent and sometimes scary enactments of dominance and submission. In ancient Greece, as I noted earlier, pubescent boys were required to let their mentors use them as if they were female sex partners. They were not sodomized, however. Rather, the initiate had to permit the older male to ejaculate between his legs while he himself remained flaccid, his unerect penis and soft scrotum resembling and symbolizing a woman's softer vulva. This was the only publicly acceptable homoerotic act in the society.

In our own culture, the Judeo-Christian myths of Abraham's near sacrifice of Isaac and Christ's crucifixion as well as rituals like the bris serve as continuing reminders of historically brutal traditions in which the older generation terrorizes the younger. According to Stoller, Spiro and others, in Papua New Guinea, older men wrest their five- to seven-year-old sons from angry mothers with whom they have been living alone since birth. They terrify and beat these boys as they herd them across streams and into their new brotherhood. En route, they jab sharp reedy slivers up the noses of the boys to rid them of any vestiges of their mothers' menstrual blood and feminine soul. Once encamped, they demand that the boys fellate older teenagers and fully grown warriors in order to ingest as much masculinizing semen as possible.

Paradoxically, these rituals are reassuring to the males of both generations. The initiates' submission to a powerful man permits escape from the temptation to submit to and identify with women. By dominating boys, who have been enveloped by women, the older warriors ritualistically reclaim their boys from their mothers' hold, to assert male prerogatives and express their own fantasies of possessing a woman's procreative powers. In some rites, in fact, made famous by Richard Schechner's performing group in the 1960s and 1970s, they pass the initiate through their legs in imitation of a pregnant woman. Being both womanly and maternal, passive and powerful, allows both generations to bond and be male.

The fate of a modern man's feminine masochism is less subject to stereotypic practices and thus more variable, depending on the form it takes. Some men, from de Sade on, have either within their libidinal repertoire or as the dominant feature in their sexuality the yearning to submit to a man's violent penetration as if they were either women or boys. Others, like Sacher-Masoch's Severin, play the slave role in a heterosexual relationship—a circumstance that also allows a man to disguise and gratify his wishes to submit sexually to a man. In these relationships, the traditional male part is given to and enacted by a "cruel mistress" who acts as if she has "balls."

Within their solipsistic framework, clinicians used to call the fantasy figure personified by the dominatrix, the "phallic woman," as if having a penis was the single source of social power. The idea of the so-called phallic woman expresses both men's and women's desires to make her at least part male. Once again, whatever the chauvinism and cultural limits of this construction, whose problems I will turn to in the next chapter when I discuss Karen Horney's challenge to Freud, the phenomenon itself is based on the clinical data. Many little boys, egocentric as all children are, assume their mothers have penises like their own. Later they cling defensively to this notion to protect themselves from the dreaded possibility of losing their own members. But it is striking that whereas the fantasy of the phallic woman is common and perhaps universal in males, this is not the case for females. The sense of castration and consequent "penis envy" of the woman is, in large measure, a male illusion and projection, particularly now in an era of greater numbers of opportunities for women.

Some men, like the various masters of *The Story of O*, conceal and express their feminine masochism by behaving sadistically toward female slaves. In so doing, they identify with women's exposure and vulnerability by projecting themselves into her role and playing out their own masochistic version of femininity. However, in most of the cases presented in the first two chapters of this book, feminine masochism does not retain its original and directly sexual stamp. Rather, it is expressed surreptitiously in heterosexual relationships—as in the vicious circles I have delineated. It may find its way into the workplace, where a man, or a woman for that matter, may submit to the control of higher-ups only to come down hard on subordinates—the daisy chain of authoritarianism of the sort described by Adorno. Pecking orders may be established, in which higher-ups terrorize those lower down in the system while yielding obsequiously to their own bosses.

What is perhaps most interesting, and most problematic, are the ways in which such perceived or imagined external power relations and the hidden gratifications that go along with them become internalized as aspects of one's own personality. When this happens, images of people and relationships are replaced by the "agencies of the mind." Id, ego and superego, roughly the seats of desire, reality and morality, respectively, replace dramas among people (images of the self and the parents, mostly) on the stage of both reality and illusion. The "theater of the mind," as psychoanalyst Joyce MacDougal puts it, gives way to the so-called mind in conflict. In this process of internalization, sexual masochism, pleasure in pain and then feminine masochism, the desire to submit and surrender in the manner of the fantasized mother of the primal scene, become transformed into *moral masochism*, the third major form described by Freud. In moral masochism, the individual's ego or self struggles against and then usually gives in to the sadistic superego.

The superego, or conscience, is heir to both parents in their real and/or imagined roles as the child's omniscient and unrelenting disciplinarians. A lifelong pact, like that between Severin and Wanda, may be established between an individual's self and this vigilant, harsh inner overseer. As a result, that individual will suffer abiding conscious and unconscious guilt in reaction to the merest possibility of happiness in life. Luck in love, work achievement and health itself may risk the wrath of the savage inner god because these gratifications are associated with the forbidden ambitions and desires of childhood. Being whole, human, dignified or joyous become taboo. In success neuroses (Freud's characters "wrecked by success") and a variety of so-called stress-related illnesses and self-inflicted injuries, moral masochists act to punish themselves and thereby to appease a superego that does not permit freedom and fulfillment. They remain slaves of guilt.

Secretly they love it. Despite their complaints, misery makes them happy, or at least content. Masochistic pleasure is present in the disappointments the sufferer brings down on him or herself. But it is so repressed that it can take years to unearth in even the most intensive psychoanalysis. When such pleasure does come to the surface, the feelings that are evoked prove to be profoundly unsettling, for they are tied to the most exotic of forbidden fruits.

The moral masochist's deeply unconscious pleasure in punishment is the very thing he or she has sought to avoid in life. It is associated with fantasies of emasculation, humiliation and even murder at the hands of the parent. In the man's case, these punishments are usually meted out in his unconscious imaginary life by an implacable father, whose real and imagined admonitions provide the basis for the voice of conscience in its final form. In the case of a woman who cannot enjoy her womanhood or work potential, it is usually a critical, intrusive or possessive mother who is felt to torture, invade and imprison her daughter. In both instances, deeply repressed incestuous, homoerotic wishes are also fulfilled.

In fact, the essence of all neurotic conflict resides in the individual's submission to his or her irrational and punishing conscience. Behind this submission lies an erotic and defensive unconscious masochistic surrender to the parent of the same sex. Psychoanalysts refer to this homoincestuous tendency as the reverse or "negative" of the Oedipus complex. By extension, it follows that neurosis in general is shaped by the negative Oedipus complex. In other words, if one looks long and hard enough, one can unearth an unconscious fantasy of sadomasochistic submission to the individual's same-sex parent beneath every inhibition, symptom and state of anxiety.

This is not to say that there are not other conflicts and parental images at work in the neurotic individual's mind. Such people do struggle mightily with their feelings of love, desire and hatred toward parents of the opposite sex, that is, with fears of loss, shame and guilt when it comes to these, the so-called positive Oedipal objects. I merely wish to emphasize the essence of so-called superego-ego conflicts and to understand why "conscience doth make cowards of us all."

Moreover, since neurosis is inevitable and universal, so, too, is moral masochism. As I said in another context, almost all people are moral masochists to one degree or another. This is why—paraphrasing Freud's *The Psychopathology of Everyday Life*—I have referred throughout this book to the "sadomasochism of everyday life." Almost every man and woman must contend with temptations, whose erotic charges are usually unconscious, to cede their autonomy and authority to other and greater powers. Everybody takes pleasure in submission and suffering. This seems true, to one degree or another, in all intimate relations.

Moreover, moral masochism as a ubiquitous phenomenon gives expression to one of the essential paradoxes in the social condition. To paraphrase another of Freud's monographs, being "civilized" carries with it certain "discontents." Being civilized requires that individuals subdue themselves and rein in their impulses, desires and ambitions in ways that are not always rational or useful. Inhibitions ensure our survival as well as the welfare of other people around us. Yet we are also byproducts of a hidden need to harm ourselves and those we love. Being good, being altruistic, feeling pity, sacrificing self-interest to that of the community and working hard all derive in part from this deep-seated general destructiveness and individual self-destructiveness. Some people can be too good for their own good, inviting envy and contempt from others. Some people don't learn when "no good deed goes unpunished."

According to Freud, the superego is a primitive presence close to the id, whose impulses it so energetically opposes. In other words, our most civilized achievements, our adherence to our ideals and our capacity to monitor, criticize and protect ourselves and other people are underlain by primitive sadomasochism. What is most civil and cultivated in people can easily enough degenerate into moral sadism and a scorn for impurity. Moral rectitude can give rise to prejudice, oppression, xenophobia, what Erikson calls "pseudo-speciation," unnecessary violence, demoralization, self-loathing and indiscriminate destruction on a mass scale. Superegos are like smut smashers, secretly drawn to their cause by their own prurience.

We have always known how cruel and uncompromising moral intolerance can be. With greater psychological understanding, we might now begin to see why a Hester Prynn finds herself branded, as if gleefully on her part, with *The Scarlet Letter,* a source of shame but principle. The morality that opposes sadomasochism is fashioned from sadomasochism itself.

BEYOND BEYOND THE PLEASURE PRINCIPLE

Freud's ideas about primary masochism, and the death instinct in particular, were greeted with skepticism by his closest adherents. Melanie Klein and her followers—who dominate psychoanalysis in England, South America and much of Europe—continued to cleave to the notion of a primary and inner badness. In this view, the individual is forever trying to get rid of his or her malignant inner destructiveness by discharging or projecting it upon the outside world. However, most mainstream American clinicians have abandoned this notion in favor of a more straightforward concept of a no-nonsense aggressive drive. Initially, they argue, this aggressive drive is directed outward. But, in the interest of self-preservation and socialization, it gets turned against the self and then sexualized in one or another form of secondary masochism. (Thus, psychoan-

alysts have returned to Freud's earlier and more commonsense notions in which sadomasochism and aggression are understood to
come first in the sequence.)

Over the years, later clinical theoreticians, the so-called classical
Oedipalists, who once dominated American psychoanalysis, further
refined their ideas about the causes and functions of sadomasochism. For example, they suggested that the "defensive" functions of sadomasochism are the result of regression from a position
of so-called Oedipal gratification. All children are fated to give up
the fight and lose heart until adolescence and adulthood provide
them with the power and realism to activate their initiative, and find
and compete for a lover. However, since winning out over rivals in
adult life has mostly unconscious incestuous and patricidal implications, gratification of any kind can prove untenable. It can feel bad
to win anything in life by being powerful, by taking the lead or by
following one's own heart. Rather than put oneself to the test as a
man or a woman, the individual falls back on the "anal" sadism and
masochism of the very young child, which the adult still feels like.
Little boys cannot defeat their powerful fathers and possess their
mothers. Nor can little girls outdo their rival mothers and win their
fathers' favors. Instead of competition, such people resort to a more
passive-aggressive game of the sort seen in a toddler in the throes of
toilet training. Like a terrible two-year-old, blocked and emotionally
infantile people are too frightened to be directly confrontational.
Rather, they try to gain the upper hand by withholding, or alter-
nately by spewing forth abuse. They get locked into power struggles,
and they are constantly jockeying for control. Often enough, they
just give up and give in, like toddlers being retrained.

Most recently, clinicians such as Arnold Cooper and Robert
Stolorow, influenced by Heinz Kohut's "self-psychology," have
stressed the so-called narcissistic functions of sadomasochism. In its
openly sadistic forms, these are obvious. Controlling and even in-
juring another person, though it may be morally distasteful, makes
the sadomasochist feel powerful, at least for a while. However, the
masochistic route to self-aggrandizement is no less significant—if
less obvious and more paradoxical. I have already described the

masochist's identification with and manipulation of the sadist. And I have noted the profound gratification to be found in being good at whatever cost and the masochist's transcendence over his or her own self-destruction. Heady feelings of omnipotence and even revenge go along with surviving injuries, humiliation and near-annihilation and emerging intact, again and again.

These phenomena are explicitly rendered in the more perverse expressions of masochism. Wounded repeatedly, like the characters in a de Sade, Sacher-Masoch or Réage story, but ultimately unharmed, masochists protest, "You're hurting me," but proclaim, "Nobody can hurt me. I cannot be hurt." Ultimately in control, they rob the disciplinarian of power. Sadomasochists take themselves to the edge of the abyss and burn with the fires of hell, but they triumph when they emerge from their ordeals unscathed. What is more, sadomasochists find pleasure and profit in self-abnegation. Particularly in sadomasochistic perversions, forces of guilt are further conquered by exploiting them, eroticizing pain and making punishment itself a source of pleasure.

Thus, sadomasochists are closet thrill seekers who try to soar above life, daring to go where others fear to tread. In this sense, their "different love" conquers all—including those who once subjected them to misery without their consent. Such a sadomasochist is personified by the brutal fighter Jake LaMotta. In a scene made famous in Scorsese's *Raging Bull,* broken and bleeding on the ropes, the defeated ex-champ—noted for his paranoid jealousy and sadism toward women—cried out in defiance at the fighter who was pummeling him and taking his middleweight crown. He told that deft and great Sugar Ray Robinson:

"Ray, ya didn't knock me down. Ya didn't knock me down, Ray. Fuck you."

Finally, since everyone has suffered and been threatened in these ways, most people flirt with sadomasochistic conquests for similar reasons. For all their efforts to avoid discomfort, most people simultaneously hold to the dictum, "No pain, no gain."

THE SOCIOLOGY OF SADOMASOCHISM

Psychoanalysts are poor social theorists, and even more ignorant political scientists. Emphasizing the internal life of the individual, they tend to overlook the concentric social circles in which a person is embedded. In fact, societies and long-lived cultures are structured in such a way as to demand submission and domination on the part of their members—something feminists have made people aware of in their scrutiny of gender politics. As interdisciplinary anthropologists and psychoanalysts such as Ruth Benedict, Margaret Mead and Erik Erikson emphasized in the 1950s, society's demands are filtered through families and childrearing practices that shape character. In this social context, sadomasochistic postures and pleasures make a virtue of necessity.

Social philosophers and sociologists adopt a teleological perspective when it comes to psychological matters. They emphasize how individual behavior patterns and personality characteristics fit into the surrounding social structure. They ask what functions these individual characteristics serve in preserving sociocultural equilibrium. While this emphasis on embeddedness does not tell the whole psychological story, it is an important factor in understanding how a phenomenon as seemingly irrational and destructive as sadomasochism has adaptive value for any given individual.

Seen sociologically, sadomasochism is an expression of the "dialectics of power," an expression of the master and slave relationship governing the human community. This relationship, according to philosophers and social scientists such as Hegel, Weber, and Adorno, lies at the heart of all social relations.

In order to dominate, one social stratum has to count on the willing submission of those strata below it. For the submissive parties, ceding direct power must have certain advantages. At the most primitive level of power brokering, the trade-off has to do with giving up autonomy and freedom for safety's sake—protection, that is, from those "ruling classes" as well as from the surrounding hostile world. At more sophisticated levels, it is the establishment of an external authority—a moral authority whose material as well as spiritual protection can be counted upon. This is gained when the individual yields independence of mind and of action to preexisting and designated superiors.

The parallels between more primitive power relations and the dynamic relations between parents and children are obvious. As I have noted earlier, children are compelled to "roll over" in deference to powerful and threatening parents. By turning a potential antagonist into a powerful ally, they gain further protection from the dangers of the surrounding environment. Similarly, the subordinate individual or group in a social hierarchy bows to the upper echelons in order to survive. In these transactions, the myths, rules of conduct and distributions of labor that govern family relations are maintained as are the genealogical, kinship and other socioeconomic systems that order social systems. If the realistic trade-offs prove inadequate as compensations, then there is still the implicit hope that the disempowered will one day receive their due. Hence, sadomasochism serves to preserve the status quo, guarantee social stability and guard both the individual and the group from outside competitors and predators.

The more sophisticated issues involving sociopolitical authority, rather than mere power, also parallel the personal ethical questions raised by moral masochism. Ultimately, what the moral masochist or social subordinate achieves is the establishment of meaning and moral value beyond what any one individual can hope to construct, expect or achieve for him or herself. However self-abnegating such a stance can be, it provides a certain guarantee against what the French sociologist Durkheim called "anomie"—the sort of mass meaninglessness in a society that leads to despair and even suicide. The attribution of power alone will not suffice to secure existential meaningfulness—one's raison d'être. Individuals must believe in the right of others to rule over them. They must take spiritual and moral pleasure in this conviction.

A higher good—the state, the church—picks up where individual narcissism leaves off, hence the individual's willing submission to such ideals. In this way, sadomasochism helps sanction and secure hierarchies like the class and caste systems. It is woven into the fabric of totalitarian and nationalistic ideologies that are the ironic end products of the revolutions whose aim it was to oppose tyranny. Indeed, it is inherent in all social systems and traditions, including patriarchy and capitalism, as a source of pressure on all individuals. The psychoanalyst or psychologist, who isolates these individuals from their contexts in order to study their inner depths, must also be mindful of these exigencies bearing down from the outside.

To an extent, the masochistic laments and disclaimers of responsibility for fate are true, after all. Forces apart from the individual's personal experience and consequent psychodynamics do conspire to keep sadomasochistic solutions to individual conflicts in place. These abiding forces, which often lie beyond an individual's grasp and influence, make these solutions even harder to detect or to change. Social organizations like biological organisms, are governed by the principle of entropy—the resistance to change.

For example, masochistic stances represent adaptations to the demands and constraints of small, closely knit, yet encompassing and self-protective social groups, such as nuclear families. Parents, siblings, spouses and sometimes even other children require vulnerable young children to give in, suffer at their hands and keep silent. In trying to break free, to reposition themselves in relation to those with whom they are intimate and on whom they have become dependent, to escape vicious circles and other binds and to change themselves, hitherto submissive individuals risk exciting the envy, subsequent hostility and active aggression of family members. Such individuals threaten the dominance, narcissism and self-interest of those with whom they have been interdependent. The people to whom the erstwhile sadomasochist is bound may actually reject or punish and expel him or her because of this new assertiveness. They may fulfill in reality the sadomasochist's worst imaginings while also gratifying his or her masochistic impulses, proving that he or she was right all along. Other people's aggression and their pursuit of power are a reality, and this reality makes it very difficult to escape into sanity and discover a more reasonable pursuit of happiness.

Nor do people want to accept the selfishness, malevolence and, ultimately, the immorality of the caretakers and institutions in which they believe. They will cripple and punish themselves rather than acknowledge the hearts of darkness in those authorities whom they have trusted with their physical and spiritual well-being. Like King Oedipus, they tend to blind themselves—but not only in atonement for their misdeeds or crimes of the heart. They will do so because they do not wish to accept the parents' and parent figures' indiscretions and malevolence—in Oedipus' case, the fact that his father ordered his mother to have him killed. They will do so because they are afraid to be alone, isolated, endangered and hopeless. Thus, sadomasochism allows individuals and the social unit of which they are a part to keep the faith and, when it is threatened, to keep silent.

Summary

In this chapter, I have attempted to conceptualize the persistence and universality of sadomasochism in everyone's mental life. Far from being incomprehensible, sadomasochism makes perfect sense because it is derived from many sources and serves many divergent functions. It typically provides the most efficient form of conflict resolution and maintains equilibrium.

1. To some degree, sadomasochism is an expression of a fundamental death instinct or Nirvana principle in all individuals, all of whom are born to die.
2. It provides one major way of channeling and controlling one's own dangerous aggression toward others and averts their aggression.
3. It portrays the fact that pleasurable stimulation and painful stimulation are always closely associated.
4. Sadomasochism both expresses and defends against the lack of personal boundaries at the beginning of life.
5. It both defends against and expresses a threatening, yet desirable, loss of sexual identity. For a man, it reveals his highly conflicted wish to be a woman.
6. It represents the achievement of moral self-restraint and civilized humanity.

7. It is a regressive alternative to facing the conflicts and difficulties encountered in becoming, as best one can, an independent and responsible man or woman.
8. It empowers the self.
9. It represents a symbolic transcendence over actual death and destruction.
10. It is a cultural requirement of groups and individuals that guarantees social stability and personal protection.
11. It solves many problems. It is a paradox. It is inevitable.

Sadomasochism obeys two basic principles of mental functioning: "overdetermination" and "multiple function." In other words, it has many causes and, once it is in place, serves as many ends.

In the next chapter, I will continue to theorize about sadomasochism, particularly about the ways in which gender organizes its expressions and its significant part in the relations between the sexes.

SADOMASOCHISM AND THE BATTLE OF THE SEXES

To Return to the Femme Fatale

In this chapter, I will discuss at greater length the role of sado-masochism in early sexual identity development and gender relations later in life. Let me begin by returning to one of the new cultural icons described in chapter 3 and asking my readers to conjure up images of the femmes fatales dominating so many of today's movies. These figures and their stories capture not only the struggles of today's gender politics but also their intrapsychic context—primal tensions between the sexes and within all of us from the first years of our lives. These contemporary sirens, who can murder their heroes with their sexuality, play upon the desires, dreads and enduring vulnerabilities of their audience.

The new femmes fatales, the killer women of the media, speak to the potent but forgotten childhood imagery of men's unconscious lives. They incarnate the engulfing symbiotic mother, the phallic woman and the dangerous Oedipal seductress left over from a man's sexually amorphous infancy, ambisexual toddlerhood and erotically driven early childhood. Adult versions of archaic imaginings, they resonate with a little boy's image of woman as an enigmatic and potentially murderous Sphinx. The hero's confusion over both her person and her intent, whether desirous or destructive, is a metaphor for a boy's, and then a man's, efforts to grasp the riddles of gender and the generational cycle. Femmes fatales express a man's repeated rediscovery of his violent hunger and fragility when in the arms of a woman—of mother or lover. The imagery of the hero undone by the siren reminds the male viewer of his tenuous masculine identity.

As far as women are concerned, these stories serve as cautionary tales of crime and punishment. They portray a very little girl's attempts to define herself as a separate being in the white light of her father's admiring gaze. They personify her growing appreciation of the uses of seduction and her unfolding desire to overpower men with her womanliness—men like her father who seem to govern a world from which she has been excluded. They betray a woman's strivings for revenge through the domination of the men who demand her services, sexual and otherwise.

These narratives are exciting without being genuinely revolutionary. They ultimately restrict women's power to the arena of sex and equate sociopolitical power with maleness. Whatever may happen along the way, in the end they reassert the sexual status quo. The spectacles of the temptress's submission and condemnation with which these dangerous stories conclude reiterate that it is bad for a woman to aspire to power, erotic and otherwise. Reminding adult women of their place with regard to men, they call up women's lifelong need for known attachments, to paraphrase feminist theorists Nancy Chodorow and Carol Gilligan. In the end, they imply that a woman, even in a world of sexual consciousness and growing parity, will willingly seek imprisonment, a life sentence, if she is to stay with the man she thinks she needs to protect her from the environment. In other words, dangerous heroines remind a woman that her abiding tendency to take on a posture of helplessness comes not only from without, from a sexist society, but from within, from her need for a man to make her feel whole.

The narratives of the femme fatale tell us all how much the sexes need each other to feel complete and how much each hates the other because of the love that draws them together. In order to understand this particular fact of life, we will have to retrace the steps taken by boys and girls as they develop both their senses of sexual identity and selfhood.

THE CORE OF GENDER IDENTITY

These days, a writer like me is mindful that he or she must use gender neutral language in order to unmask the presence of female subjects behind the pronoun "he." However, this is not easy to do, often requiring stilted, almost inhuman terms such as "it" or "one" for "she" or "he" or the use of plurals when one wishes to talk about an individual. The fact is that virtually every language—with the sole exception of Hungarian—assigns gender to the people and things in the world it describes. Effacing gender from the way we talk is bucking a long-lived and widespread linguistic tradition. Not that we shouldn't do so, but it isn't easy.

Whatever its later meanings, the polarity of gender is there from the start of consciousness. One begins life by being defined and then defining oneself as a female (one of a set or class of women and girls) or a male (men and boys), specifically in relation to the opposite sex. Indeed, at and even before birth, parents define their unknown issue with the declaration that "it's a girl" or "it's a boy." They establish their expectations and set up their childrearing practices accordingly, independent of any biological process unfolding within the child itself.

As a result, the sense of "core gender identity," in Robert Stoller's formulation, means seeing oneself as either a boy or a girl in a human world comprised of males and females. Much will happen later on as children and teenagers find themselves identifying with the femininity or masculinity of "the other" and further finding out what kind of man or woman they will become. Nonetheless, the sense of being and not being male or female is ever-present in people's sense of self and in their subjectivity.

There is an implicit paradox here, one borne out by the observations of experts such as Margaret Mahler, Judith Kestenberg and other investigators of child development. The other as opposite, the other as opposite sex, is omnipresent in the self. Not only is this a matter of logic, but it is inherent in the child's being and becomes a basic, often threatening and repudiated, identification.

FROM THE DUAL UNITY TO THE OEDIPUS COMPLEX

Both boys and girls begin life in their mother's womb; they are flesh of her flesh. As Margaret Mahler discovered, once born into the world, they remain to be born as them*selves*—as individuals in a world of other people, as subjects among objects. Whatever the caretakers do with them in anticipation of their future gender roles, babies reside in a quasi-symbiotic world with which they cling to and feel merged with their mother's body. In this "dual unity," they feel that their mother and, to some extent, all the animate and inanimate objects around them are one. Mother is there, both swaddling the child like a soft sheath (in Latin literally a "vagina") and deep inside the child's viscera, permeating the "body ego" that is the prototype for a later sense of individuality.

In fact, it isn't that simple. As much as baby girls and boys long for bliss in symbiotic self-effacement, they also desire to separate and explore the universe laid out before them. As they grow in capacity and power—turning over, holding their heads higher, thrusting their torsos, pushing at their mother's body and, in her arms or lap, surveying the environment into which they still cannot venture on their own—they mobilize their aggressive energies to separate physically and psychologically from what Carl Jung called the "primordial ooze" from whence they came.

In differentiating themselves from this maternal morass, in striving to define themselves as individuals, they seek out other presences with whom to affiliate and identify. The more different these are the better, and babies of both sexes begin to gravitate toward the deeper vocal tones, larger forms, more abrupt movements and generally higher-keyed style of their fathers and other like presences—toward what Ernst Abelin, a Swiss psychoanalyst and collaborator of Mahler's, called the "male principle." Both boys and girls, secure in the homebase of their mother, are nonetheless drawn to presences like their father, who will come to represent the world other than mother—presences with whom they will identify. This outside world of the father is energized for both sexes by the aggressive drive, first defined not in terms of destruction or harm, but as the urge that is felt in the bones and the muscles to push away and move forward into an unknown and scary, yet intriguing, future.

At some point during the second year of its life, the child begins to walk, explore its environment on its own, utter a few words and communicate needs that in the past were intuited, as if magically, by its primary caretaker. In the past the child knew things as a matter of immediate sensation and illusion, but now the toddler can conjure up images independent of actual perceptions. These images can be projected into a future based on expectations from past experience. The prototypes of symbolization and representation make for greater self-containment and a dawning self-awareness. More of a person, the little boy or girl is able to see others less as extensions of himself or herself and more as distinct individuals in their own right—like the self, in fact, but existing apart from the self.

With these developments, which psychologists refer to as "cognitive milestones" and which constitute the rudiments of subjectivity, two momentous processes begin to unfold simultaneously. The first involves the emergence and basic consolidation of gender identity and, with it, the dawning of primitive and ill-defined genital sensations and awareness as well as the emergence of flirtatiousness and an attraction to the opposite sex.

Believe it or not, a one-and-a-half-year-old girl flirts with her father, plays with her labia and clitoris and is curious about what "others"—boys, men and male animals—possess in the way of anatomy in contrast to her own. It's much the same with boys, who are, however, less advanced than girls—generally slower to acquire control of their anal sphincter, slower to think and speak rather than act— and who are less sexual than aggressive in their basic wants and interests.

Downright destructive aggression is the second such development. Some, such as the Kleinians referred to in the previous chapter, assert that it makes its appearance on the scene earlier. As Erikson put it, with the pain and violence of teething during the first year, "evil" has entered the baby's life. Still other theorists, myself among them, hold that there must be a separate object, defined as such in the mind's eye, before the subject can wish to destroy or simply hurt it. The constitution or mental construction of this object, which in turn gives shape to the unseeable self, requires the maturation of the capacities just enumerated. This can be observed in what infant researchers have called the "rapprochement crisis" of the terrible near-two-year-old. A child of this age typically rushes toward its mother in states of loneliness, newly understood helplessness and desperate need, only to push her away violently because her love and her hold are felt as threats to the child's autonomy.

The thrust away from their mother becomes particularly urgent early on in little boys. Even before he can represent or define it, the boy, according to Stoller, Chodorow and others, is moved to disidentify from his mother and her felt femaleness and consolidate his male identity through disengagement. Long before he has the words for it, the typical baby boy acts—squirming, pushing his mother away, running from her, showing off at a distance—linking up separateness, difference, selfhood and maleness as inseparable qualities. However drawn to her—and, later in life, to other women—the male may be, he is constantly wriggling free if only to be catapulted into her arms once more. The father offers an alternative as another adult power and a more viable object of identification, so the little boy thirsts for and pursues him with a passion described by feminist analyst Jessica Benjamin, following Freud, as "homoerotic identificatory love."

The upheavals of early childhood are far too many and too complex to do justice to in this chapter on sadomasochism and the battle of the sexes. I merely want to stress that a number of psychological fundamentals begin to evolve at the same time, and the quantum leap they create makes for a revolution in consciousness. Thereafter, these imperatives are bound together in a web of inextricable lifelong associations. They include: the articulation of the primal self, the fitful creation of external and internal worlds, the awareness of and interest in one's own gender and that of others, sexual attraction and violent wishes. With such an amalgam, sadomasochism becomes an inevitable force in gender relations and in the uses of the child's and then the adult's sexuality.

In any event, by two and one half years, little boys and girls, mobile and verbal, are becoming ever more curious about the sexes. Their curiosity is fueled not only by inquisitiveness but also by their libidos. Other little boys and girls interest them, to be sure, but their parents, both their mother and father, excite their deepest passions. Though on balance the greatest effort usually will be directed toward the parent of the opposite sex and the most urgent hostility toward the same-sex rival, these children, both boys and girls, want to be both with and like their mothers and their fathers. They are bisexual or, to put it better, ambisexual in their desires and their identifications. In fact, children between three and four years, who are reluctant to give up anything, want to be both sexes.

They are like the mythic Androgynes described by Aristophanes in Plato's *Symposium* on love. Originally, these powerful and hermaphroditic creatures were possessed of both male and female genitals and secondary sexual characteristics, one set on either side of their grotesque bodies. When they attacked the gods, Zeus, enraged and oppressive, punished and crippled the Androgynes by cutting them in half. The creatures became so miserably depressed and frantic about their lost halves that Zeus took pity on them and turned their genitals around so that they might face each other and unite at last in sexual intercourse—just like ordinary women and men.

Freud, as most readers know all too well, stressed a little girl's penis envy and her yearning for the powers associated with fathers and phalluses, discounting what later theorists would call her joy in her "primary femininity." It is no less true that boys, as much as they value their penises and boyishness, covet their mother's visible breasts, mysterious vagina and imagined womb—just as adult men cannot help envying the extraordinary erotic capacity of a woman's clitoris. Neither sex wants to lose anything, and each is resentful of the other for having what it does not. Intrigued and excited by the other's sex and sexuality, they are also angry at the other sex's having just those qualities they wish to have—the femininity and masculinity that they long for and feel they have lost. They feel that they have lost it rather than never having had it, because they began consciousness, if not as two sexes perhaps, then as two persons.

Besides, there is a biological truth to the boy's haunting and later deeply repressed sense of his lost androgyny. The male fetus must be infused with androgens, masculinizing hormones, if its clitoris is to grow into a penis and its labia is to be knit as a scrotum that will house the testicles that descend later. As a result, a boy finds himself in a sort of double jeopardy. It is a bind in which his masculinity feels grafted on, tenuous and fragile so that his bedrock femininity, to which he remains drawn, poses a significant threat to his sense of maleness and selfhood. His pressing and often violent need to separate himself from his mother, described above, takes on more sex-specific meanings. His mother, women and his own femininity become both loved and hated, and the libidinal desire that draws him to them is accompanied by destructive aggression in general and envy in particular. Ambivalent to begin with, much—if not all— of a man's heterosexuality is fated to become sadomasochistic as these poles turn back on themselves and as opposites fuse.

The little girl is also ambivalent toward the mother who has cuddled and enveloped her: ambivalent about her soft contours, about the breasts she nursed from and slept on, about her whole female body and identity. Pushing her mother away, the little girl too will find recourse in her father's presence, which she seeks out and identifies with. His attention helps define her so-called body ego, etching its boundaries more clearly and helping her separate and differentiate herself as distinct. She senses that she needs the maleness of this powerful onlooker because, unlike a boy, she is in fact not anatomically different enough from her symbiotic mother, their bodies being or at least destined to be so much alike. Her mother becomes an embedded object of exhilaration and love and of loathing and contempt while men and their presence at first seem less contaminated, purer, more powerful—altogether more desirable than her own kind.

Yet in turning to the father to fulfill such an imperative, the girl also finds herself in a bind with regard to him. If not immediately, she will eventually resent her need for his affirmation and approbation—the need for male admirers to make her feel whole and complete. Not so privy to a male's self-doubts, it will seem to her that his is the more privileged sex: privileged in seeming more independent and self-contained, and having his superior status socially reinforced. As a result, she will hope for a penis of her own as an illusory means of containing and controlling all possibilities within herself. The problem is that this wish only aggravates her devaluation of her femininity, failing to help her see the gender-specific powers that she, as a future woman, possesses in a more embryonic form. As with boys, so with girls: hatred and self-hatred become powerful currents in their heterosexual relations and sexual identity.

There is another set of characteristics of these parental adults who are the focus of so many of the passions in the child's future adulthood. As Karen Horney validly stressed in her dramatic revisions of Freud's view of male and female development, the child's parents are older, stronger and much bigger than their sons and daughters. This simple generational fact of life implies that the first objects of the heterosexual desires and fantasies that erupt during the Oedipal years—roughly ages three to six—loom large and forbidding in the child's perspective. Their superiority and the fears and fantasies that accompany their status continue into adulthood, affecting a man's and a woman's later dealings with each other. They do not see each other as equals, but rather as awesome and potentially dangerous giants.

Having deconstructed Freud to reveal his misogyny, his fear of women and his own castration anxiety, Karen Horney showed that the enormity of the mother was even more overpowering than the father for both little boys and little girls. In the process, she started a posthumous feminist revolution at the heart of psychoanalysis's theory of development.

As far as the male is concerned, she stated: The little boy is awed by his compelling, alluring and large mother. He imagines that her vagina, like her breasts, which he actually sees, and like the womb that is said to have borne him, is very large. It is, he senses, far too large for his little pink button of a penis—too huge, hairy and wonderful. He wants her but cannot have her. He and his penis are just too small. He could be swallowed up alive. Or he would fail her altogether. He would make a fool of himself.

So, dreading woman and mortified by his paltriness, the little boy denies her vagina's existence. Afraid for his own paltry member, the male child imagines that a woman, his mother first of all, has an illusory penis of her own. In the process, he plugs up her inner recesses and staves off reengulfment. It is the inadequate boy, not the "castrated girl," Horney argues, whose Oedipus complex comes to a close because of a "narcissistic injury."

Once he understands sexual anatomy and sex differences, a boy labels the clitoris an inferior organ, just as Freud did. In acts of defensive contempt, he convinces himself that women, including the woman who bore him, constitute the "second sex." These misogynistic myths thinly disguise an intuitive sense that the male is the "weaker" sex. Crudely, they reverse the facts of life. They allow a man to pretend that Eve, lustrous, sexy and more inviting than God himself, was fashioned from innocent Adam's rib. A lesser soul and more easily tempted, Eve the seductress set Adam on the path toward original sin. Women are more carnal and savage, exploiting their desire to get what they want. Freud suggested that they lack consciences and compunction and that instead of following their own inner light cleave to the values of people who admire them. A woman's feminine sexual powers are also her female weakness, as well as her mate's undoing—or so the wary male believes.

Because of Eve's original sin, man opines, women must thereafter live a life of punishment, bringing forth babies in pain. The most exquisite and exclusive of woman's achievements, the source of her continuing hold on and superiority over males, becomes the most agonizing of her ordeals. Trying to hold his own, a man convinces a woman that it is her lot in life to allow a man to dominate her, impregnate her and make her suffer. Underneath it all, he knows that she can make babies—babies like him at his mother's breast or in her belly.

According to Horney, however, this is a defensive and distorted picture. This sadism inherent in men's misogyny, his "caricature" and "character assassination" of women, guards against a male's feelings of impotence and vulnerability when confronted with the facts of a woman's sexuality and primal procreativity. It prevents a man from hopelessly losing himself to a woman.

Every now and then the truth leaks out, and the mystery is revealed. Every now and then a man revels in his delirious, intoxicating submission to a woman. He throws caution, filialism and moralism to the winds in an eroticism at once sensual and sublime. He bathes in it. He drinks it, like Tristan and Isolde's love potion. But such love cannot be endless love; it is too much to bear. The high pitch of giving in to a woman has to stop sometime and somewhere short of madness.

LIKE those of men, women's sadomasochistic fantasies about the relations between the sexes also find their origins in the Oedipal years. A little girl's wish to excite her father's interest in her body begins in toddlerhood. As development progresses and her Oedipus complex is set in motion at three or four years of age, a girl starts to exploit this inherent flirtatiousness in more directly sexual and aggressive ways. She gets excited at the idea that a father (or any man) will become aroused by her. She wants to wrest a man's attention from her rivals, particularly her mother. Angry at her father because her efforts cannot be successful and because she needs his male presence more than he seems to need hers—because she needs his fickle attention—she also tries to unsettle her would-be admirers. She tries to lay them low with her sex appeal, "knock their socks off" and "make them die for her."

She comes to feel more and more guilty about the competitive, aggressive impulses lurking behind her exhibitionistic play. Through a variety of unconscious maneuvers, a girl's guilt compounds her more violent primal-scene fantasies, making them seem even more dangerous. As Horney remarked in her analysis of a little girl's sexual identity development in general and of her penis envy in particular, a daughter imagines that should she succeed in winning her father after all, she may hurt and displace her mother, thus provoking her mother's retaliation. In addition, should he satisfy his daughter's desires, the daughter imagines, her father will bore into her little vulva with his (to her) huge, hard, erect penis, tearing her apart and destroying her. The fulfillment of the wish and the punishment for it thus become synthesized as one and the same in her unconscious mind. Out of fear and guilt, the girl retreats from her "primary femininity." She exaggerates the fleeting wish for a penis to which she (like the boy who wants a vagina and breasts) inevitably falls prey. By wanting a penis of her own, rather than her father's penis, she is able to keep her distance from him as from her own desires.

The proverbial tomboy stance of what clinicians call the "post-Oedipal" girl, at nine or ten, represents an anxiety-laden and defensive holding position. It is not evidence of a primary quest for masculinity as Freud at his most sexist once believed. In trying to be boyish, in acting male, in striving to have her own penis—in wearing pants and loving horses—a little girl is retreating. Her masculine ambitions derive from this culture's insidious equation of social superiority and power with masculinity and the possession of the phallus. Penis envy of this sort is a silent concession to male chauvinism. It is an indirect expression of the fear of femininity in women and of feminine guilt. Enraged at men for having dominated them for so long, the majority of women later on in their lives simultaneously feel afraid and guilty about their wishes to turn the tables and seize control of men through the exercising not of their masculine strivings but of their feminine capacities. So they play at being male, exaggerating their own wish to be the other sex. I shall return to these themes when I explore their emergence in adolescent and adult heterosexual love.

As their cognitive capacities mature in the manner described by Piaget, reorienting them toward the real world apart from the home—school, friends, hobbies, sports—children retreat from their Oedipus complexes into a period of relative *latency*. This is less true today, in our overstimulated culture, than it was in the Victorian era when Freud first coined the term. Kids are sexier than they used to be. Nonetheless, boys and girls generally become less erotically invested in their actual and imaginary *parents* than in living up to the standards of and demands for their socialization as members of the larger community, in what child psychologist Lois Murphy called "the widening world of childhood."

Among the sociocultural expectations of school-age children are those setting forth their prescribed gender roles as girls and boys, in a process traced by the late Lawrence Kohlberg. These gender attributes have less to do with sexual feelings, which yield to repression, than with certain stereotypical behaviors that the culture teaches us to equate with being a "good girl" or "good boy." Even categories such as these, first formulated by Kohlberg in the late sixties, are subject to historical changes, of course, particularly the changes in childrearing practices brought about by feminism. Nonetheless, as with latency so with the push toward sex stereotyping, the impetus to enact gender roles comes both from the culture and from the developmental process (the latter having a life of its own that makes it less responsive to the ideology of the moment).

Boys are generally more rigid with regard to boyishness than are girls. They energetically remove themselves from their mothers' embraces lest they become "mamas' boys." They exclude girls from their company as well because they are "yukky." Repressing their sexuality, they strive to redefine their masculinity as aggressivity such that being a good boy may, in fact, mean being "Peck's bad boy." The homoerotic aspects of male bonding that drive them to negotiate their world in packs remain far from their consciousness for the most part and for the time being as does their fear of, rather than aversion to, getting close to women. That is, getting too close for comfort, regressing and sinking back into a sexual past in which their mother had power over them. For mostly misogynistic boys between seven and eleven years, sadism toward girls becomes a badge of courage and a means of reasserting that they are not girlish.

Girls this age are generally more relaxed about these matters because they are more secure in their essential or primary femininity than are boys in their fragile and hard-won masculinity. They seem freer to play with male roles, such as that of the tomboy just described, than are their male counterparts, who repudiate anything that smacks of "the sissy boy." While boys retreat from their mothers, many girls still dally and flirt with their fathers. Abetted by a culture that treats women as sex objects and invites them to see themselves as such, girls are more comfortable with other heterosexual yearnings and contacts than are most boys. While they may reject their peers as silly, dirty little boors, they will often cleave to various pop idols or have crushes on older boys or men in their real life. While they may make fun of boys behind their backs and among themselves, their sadistic manipulations are usually confined to their own group, to positioning themselves within cliques and maneuvering female rivals in and out of these groups. They rehearse with other girls some of the ploys they will bring to their later heterosexual life—dancing together, dressing up, experimenting with sex play, teasing boys, dropping them, hurting their feelings. Girls tend to do this sort of thing because, while they may in fact be physically larger than boys at this age, they are less inclined to strike out directly at someone who gets in their way. In the physical realm, they are fated to be designated as the weaker sex, and they must learn to use their intelligence rather than brute force to get their way.

For both sexes, more or less desexualized sadistic displays serve the purposes of defense during middle childhood, keeping the sexes apart and thereby keeping them from knowing their own hearts. With puberty and its rush of sexuality, this stance and the repression that goes along with it become increasingly untenable. In their adolescence, girls and boys rediscover the masochistic half of the sadomasochistic equation as they find themselves living out with each other many of the hitherto repressed phantasmagoria of their Oedipal years—an early childhood hidden behind what psychoanalysts have called "the infantile amnesia."

THE REAL THING: FIRST LOVES AND LATER ENCOUNTERS

It doesn't all go back to childhood, of course. Psychoanalysts who reduce adult sexuality to its prototypes in infantile sexuality have committed "the genetic fallacy" (genetic referring here not to genes or heredity, but to genesis, or origins). As I noted earlier, preadolescent children do not lubricate or ejaculate and rarely engage in intercourse or have full-fledged orgasms. They need to be at least pubescent for their bodies to come to life in these ways. What's more, they don't have the understanding or experience of life needed to engage with other people as new and whole individuals who are more than fantasies. They need to have a history of friendships if they are to have love relationships. They need to be able to step back and think about themselves and others in the world—to have capacities that Piaget called "formal operational logic" or "hypothetico-deductive reasoning"—in order to convert lust into love. They need the metaphoric disposition of the poet, a proclivity and power that emerge only with adolescence and, alas, often end there. They need the anatomy, physiology and minds of adults, and they need some sense of identity if they are to fall in love. They need to "adolesce."

The theorists of adolescence, notably Erikson and Blos, who were cohorts during their teenage years, have described the fitful progression of the teenager toward his or her adulthood: the veiled homoeroticisms, self-conscious intellectualisms and masturbatory narcissisms into which boys and girls retreat before coming together. I will not go into the details of this adolescent passage here, except to say that for all its bravado the male sex, once again, proves to be the more timorous of the two.

For instance, one reason that teenage boys spend much more time masturbating than do girls is that they are afraid of having orgasms with girls, much less within their still mysterious vaginas. They need to reassure themselves repeatedly that they can lose control and remain intact—that they can retain their penises—before they dare to have intercourse with a flesh and blood woman. It is not that males are more libidinally driven than females, although it may take a decade or so for women to shed their inhibitions and immerse themselves in their eroticism. It's that boys have such powerful castration anxiety and, along with their desire, anger at women for making them feel fearful and unmanly.

Nor is their sense of identity, sexual and otherwise, all that solid. Boys sense before the fact that falling in love and uniting with a woman will mean identifying with her. They will find themselves bathed in her womanly aura, osmosing her femininity and assuming her values. They fear they will lose themselves in her and yield their moral absolutes and high-minded principles to a more tolerant ethic, the feminine ethic of care described by Carol Gilligan and associated by young men with womanly ways. (Once again, this picture of women's superior morality, with which some feminists disagree, seems as much a social construction as a fact.) While they may grow up in the process, nonetheless boys and then men angrily try to wrench themselves free from women in order to go about their father's business and pursue their worldly ambitions.

Usually later in adolescence—though the norms are variable—the sexes finally come together. Psychoanalyst Judith Kestenberg has written that many young women are familiar with their clitorises and labia, but penetration by a young man's erect penis allows them to discover certain aspects of their vaginas. Kestenberg suggests that a woman in the making finds, often to her resentment, that she needs a man to help release her sexuality. Thus, while she yearns not only for the male gaze of admiration, but for his sensual touch and penetrating erection as well, the young woman finds herself bridling at the loss of independence and threat to her identity that come with erotic passion. So many essentially heterosexual young women will turn from men for a while, experimenting with masturbation and homosexuality in efforts to reclaim their bodies and their selves as their own.

Both women and men deal with the threats to the self that come with love by way of sadistic and often specifically moralistically sadistic defenses. Hence the threat of rejection on both sides. Hence the battle of the sexes.

However, underneath it all lies the irresistible urge to submit and surrender all to the other. The delirium that comes with union and merger is too sweet to deny. The exhilaration of being bad and defying moral edicts and conventional constraints, painful as the guilt may be, is addictive; even the pangs of jealousy and terror have a masochistic hold on the lovers' sensibilities. The "heaven" is worth the "hell," Shakespeare's sonnet notwithstanding.

All lovers sing the blues. Just look at lyric poetry through the centuries or, for that matter, the lyrics of pop music through the decades. It is as if young people knew ahead of time the sadomasochistic denouements of heterosexual passion.

In fact, passionate love is not the prerogative of beautiful youth. Indeed, many women blossom in their sexual liberation and full orgasmic capacities only in midlife, long after marital and conjugal practices have become routine. Both men and women, including the most monogamous among them, become ripe for love affairs in their forties when such erotic love may pose a real threat to their well-being and that of other people in their lives. Betrayal and deceit, the feelings of being out of control or unable to control others, the limits and degradation of being cast in the role of mistress, paramour or cuckold have their obvious sadomasochistic edge. So, one way or another, most affairs end badly.

In fact, most relationships, including good marriages, are fated to do so. They will culminate, if not in rejection, loss or divorce, then in death. Klein and Freud were right, it seems: Life moves toward death.

But there is a specific twist to all of this these days, which is evident in the icon of the screen sirens with which this book began. Men are hard put to handle women's newfound powers—political powers that they see mostly in sexual terms.

SEXUAL POLITICS

Let's return from the individual development of sexual identity to gender politics and sadomasochism in the culture. Gone are the days when TV ads flagrantly proclaimed the virtues of kitchen cleansers, spotless floors, sinks and dishes, to be scoured by anxious, obsessive and housecoat-wearing housewives whose only aim, it appeared, was to clean and please. Gone are the days when woman actors aspired to the Mildred Dunnock role of long suffering and asexual Linda Loman, helpless helpmate to a pathetic Willy. Now *Working Woman* meets *Mr. Mom* while *Kramer vs. Kramer* in wars of the sexes won mostly by what used to be the second or weaker sex—women. Feminism, which has made inroads in academia, politics, and family law, has found its way more gradually into the marketplace. And yet, old ways die hard and often find themselves dressed in new and deceptive metaphors. In today's commercial world, a woman's seductive person and alluring power has taken over from the homemaker's dust pan.

In the sixties, Masters and Johnson first began to expose men's and women's sexuality for what it was. Their systematic observations of sexual behavior and responsiveness overturned the prevailing psychoanalytic myths about where and to what extent arousal and orgasm take place. To the extent that any collective and consciously accepted truth can penetrate people's personal and individualized defenses, by the 1970s and 1980s, many women found themselves freed from the constraints of the obvious and insidious morality and diminishment imposed on them and their desires by men. No longer could men—Freudian male analysts in particular—induce a female character as in Woody Allen's *Manhattan* to declare: "I have orgasms. But my analyst says they're the wrong kind."

Having bared their subjects' anatomies and parts of their souls in their responsiveness, Masters and Johnson said it was okay for a woman to have clitoral orgasms, after all. In a sense, for all the sexist psychoanalytic willing, they were the only kind. Clitorises were the trigger points for those swelling vaginal paroxysms, which, according to Freud and his followers, were the be-all and end-all of female sexuality. The vagina itself was a fairly unresponsive organ. It had nerve endings only through its first third. The inner two thirds became sensitive only by way of sensations referred from the rectum.

So women were given permission to exercise, experiment with and otherwise exploit and enjoy their clitoral sensuality. When they did, they found out just how remarkable an organ the clitoris could be. Far from being inferior appendages, as Freud had asserted, clitorises opened up erotic vistas like multiple orgasms. The women who possessed them could keep on coming and coming without those refractory periods to which even rutting male teenagers succumb. These clitoral responses spread through a woman's whole elaborate genital and reproductive system and beyond, leaving flushes of arousal all over her body as she convulsed with pleasure. Sexually speaking, a disinhibited woman was capable of leaving the man who loved her in the dust. She, not he, was capable of sustained ecstasy.

Our Bodies, Ourselves became the call to arms of the sexual revolution. Enjoined by the women's movement to look at and lay claim to their genitals, many women began to clear away the fog of prohibition and gaze upon themselves. They studied their sexual anatomy and accepted, indeed celebrated, their erotic appetites. Women's magazines, still pandering to their female readers' willing subjection of themselves to fashionable objectification, came to address women's sexual desires and needs more and more explicitly.

Gradually, men also began to look at women's growing erotic demands differently. Women were no longer innocents to be conquered and deflowered or passive bedmates lying back and taking it. Nor were they whorish handmaidens who participated in sex merely to serve and satisfy men's desires. Women, men acknowledged at last, had powerful erotic drives and obsessions of their own. They were sexual subjects as well as sex objects. They could control and use men as they had been controlled and used in the past.

Rather than merely welcoming this new level of female sensuality and all that it offered them in the way of pleasure and mutuality, men responded with ambivalence. On the one hand, a liberated woman seemed to be there for the asking, and men could find the omni-available woman of their erotic dreams. On the other hand, threatened by women on the work front, men recoiled from the women who awaited them in the bedroom. They felt overwhelmed by women's newly liberated sexuality both in its idealized forms and in its actual manifestations. Men were afraid they could not keep up and felt insecure in their ability to gratify and possess a woman who had been granted the emotional and economic wherewithal to seek satisfaction elsewhere—in the arms of one or more rivals. Feminist Germaine Greer, for instance, had her construction worker—an obvious reference to the sallies of Victorian gentlemen into the ramshackle hovels of the lower classes to find dalliances that sated their lust without taxing their intellect. Greer also came on to men—and to Norman Mailer of all men, and in public!

More significantly, men simply felt inadequate and put upon— not only jealous but envious of and competitive with women as sexual beings and intellectual rivals. Rubbing it in men's faces, formerly demure women's magazines were now serializing books with titles such as *What to Do When* He *Has a "Headache?"* Some periodicals proclaimed that male impotence had become pandemic. In fact, a whole medical industry has recently grown up to aid men in contending with women's sexual demands.

Unsettled, potentially diminished in the sphere of love as in that of work, men tried to regroup. They began to impose on women's sexuality new variants of old misogynist myths, aimed essentially at putting women back in their place. In the media, they reinterpreted her expansive and powerful sexuality according to both the experiences of gender politics and the sadomasochism of everyday life.

Thus in one R-rated cable show combining horror and sex, a young man longs for the sex kitten of his dreams, a chimera played by Mariel Hemingway. He gets her, and with her far more than he bargained for. Welcomed at first, Mariel's sexual demands soon become more than he can handle. He has created a libidinal Frankenstein Monster (originally the brainchild of Mary Shelley, the sister of poet and libertine Percy Shelley). She is too much. Once sexy, she comes to repulse him, and so he repels her. Things get so bad that eventually he throws this sex fiend out the window. Also, since it's a fantasy that is being fulfilled, she doesn't die. Instead, she returns from the pavement below, her face crushed and distorted, but her heart undyingly amorous and monomaniacal. This maimed Mariel will haunt her inventor thus the rest of his days. She is a sex goddess turned avenging angel. The creation of life, even of a sex object, is a woman's and not a man's prerogative—the very message that the original *Frankenstein* tried to convey.

Ambitious at work and rapacious in relationships, women now seemed, to some men, utterly beyond control. They were in control of themselves and so were out of men's control. Like any other men, the men responsible for a woman's public presentation and the creation of her archetypes, the moviemakers and media moguls, tried to represent men's changing and uncertain images of women. But they could not hold on to these pictures for very long in their kaleidoscopic and inchoate forms. Instead, male creators of female images tried to reassert themselves, to take charge again, to interpret, to pathologize, to moralize and manage. They tried to capitalize and intellectualize, literally, on the fact that all women, like the mothers they longed for in their forgotten psychological life, had powerful and insatiable desires of their own.

When women demonstrate their power, boys and men try to deny that the power is that of real women. Such women, males tell themselves, are not real women; they are masculine, or they are trying to be masculine. They are, as Freud argued, men manqués. Either they are like men or they want to be like the men they envy. It's not that they want to be strong women, men aver. They want to have balls. They are ballbreakers. They have penises. They are phallic women. They are wrong, they are sick.

Such women, this logic goes, have to be put in their place, taught what it means to be female and made to give in. Men's surrendering to them has been but a temporary excess, an aberration—a lark, a game, a mistake, an indulgence, a whim whose time passes quickly. Like the Kinski character in *Cat People*, the erstwhile she-cat must roll over in the end and submit to her keepers. She must be killed or caged. She must accept her fate while her lover, the male gorilla (in fact a timid beast), pounds his chest and turns into a caveman with a club.

Like her, he, too, has done it all with love: the force of masculine seductiveness. With men as with women, sex is a weapon, and love conquers all. That's how Heard conquers Kinski, in the end. That was how Odysseus conquered Circe, in the end. Undone by her, he reversed roles and conquered the sorceress with her desire for and surrender to him. If a manly warrior and lover does not get her, then the decent womenfolk of the community will—just like the betrayed and put-upon wife played by Anne Archer who shoots Glenn Close in the conclusion of *Fatal Attraction.*

In fact, focus groups revealed, such a denouement often works best in films. It lets the man off the hook, exonerating any exploitation of his greater physical strength. He isn't the bully after all, the snickering boy pulling his sister's pigtails, the nasty kid destined by his sex to rule the world. He isn't a cad, either. It's the women who want uppity women, home-wreckers, and bad girls put back in their places.

The media's femmes fatales must appeal not only to the men who market them, but also to the women who watch them do their thing. Women buy the most books and see the most movies, take in what the culture has to offer and are willing to pay for it. The scenarios these depict must also excite women's basic and sometimes baser instincts. If men secretly long to take a beating at the siren's hands, women long to mete it out, to beat men, to exact their revenge. And if most men also wish to stand back and become the keeper of the cat, most women find subsequent comfort in giving in, in the long run, and in becoming slaves for love.

REAL SEX AND REAL DANGER

Unclothed, today's antiheroines portray the danger and excitement of sex in an era of renewed sexually transmitted diseases. The brief post-forties respite provided by antibiotics, which silenced syphilis, has come to an end with AIDS. Once more, sex presents the specter of destruction and annihilation. Once more, as in drinking the love potion of Tristan and Isolde, enthralled lovers "drink their death." It seems this will be so for many years to come, without a cure in sight.

The movies play with the interweaving of fear and desire in the offerings of women's sexuality. They exploit the actual dangers that lend reality to the emotional dangers left over from childhood and that make the adult's erotic life so fraught. So thrilling is the result that the viewer fails to notice the political conservatism lurking behind the near pornographic license of mainstream movies.

These movies' femmes fatales—like other manifestations of the sadomasochism of everyday life today—serve the purposes of a collective coverup. Getting people excited and frightened, they are another mass opiate that helps secure the status quo of gender politics in which women are reduced to their sexual tie to, or hold on, the men who desire them. For all their newfound political and professional power, women are to remain sex objects after all. The movies, with their femmes fatales, are our versions of the games of ancient Rome—spectacles that kept the crowd satisfied and politically placid, ensuring the Pax Romana at home and all over the world.

Chapter

9

```
┌─────────────────────────────────────────────────────┐
│ ┌───────────────────────────────────────────────┐   │
│ │                                                 │   │
│ │  SADOMASOCHISM IN THE TREATMENT SETTING:        │   │
│ │               THE CURE                          │   │
│ │                                                 │   │
│ └───────────────────────────────────────────────┘   │
└─────────────────────────────────────────────────────┘
```

SADOMASOCHISM AND THE NEGATIVE THERAPEUTIC REACTION

BECAUSE sadomasochism solves so many problems, is so paradoxical and is therefore inevitable, as I indicated in concluding chapter 7, it is not easy to get over. Its symptoms are not easy to resolve. Once the damage is done, it continues to be done. Wounded and wounding, the sadomasochist keeps on hurting. Thus burdened and undermined, he or she finds the cure can sometimes become as bad as, if not worse than, the disease. Sadomasochism often sabotages the therapy designed to treat it by making the therapeutic relationship yet another vicious circle.

This unpleasant and inconvenient fact led Freud, at sixty-seven, to reformulate his whole theory of the mind's structure when he was twenty-five years into his practice and theorizing. The fact was that some patients who had been provided with all the insight they and their devoted doctor could muster still failed to get better and sometimes even got worse. The reasons for this unfortunate turn of events remained unknown and the motives for it unconscious. Furthermore, the patients' dreams, associations and feelings about and perceptions of the analyst suggested that underneath it all they were feeling very guilty—guilty about getting better. To get better meant to have done something bad or hurtful to others in the first place. They thought they did not deserve the changes in which they had invested so much time and money. So they turned the pursuit of happiness into the pursuit of unhappiness.

What was more, they never seemed to know this was what they were doing. They, Freud reasoned further, must be creatures of their own unconscious guilt. This phenomenon indicated to Freud that rather than existing at the boundary of consciousness as a censor of sorts, the forces of conscience resided deeper in the mind—in the unconscious. Some aspects of what we now call the superego were conscious and others were unconscious, he inferred, as were those functions that belonged to the two other major mental structures, the pleasure-seeking id and the reality-oriented and defensive ego.

His patients' poor outcomes led Freud, first, to an appreciation of unconscious guilt; second, to the conceptualization of the superego; and third, to the construction of the so-called tripartite structural model of mind. Against this backdrop, he was able to identify what I described in chapter 7 as moral masochism, in which the forces of the id, ego and superego find a compromise resolution. Seen in this new light, moral masochism emerged as perhaps the central ingredient and stumbling block in the analysis of everyday neuroses. The individual subject found herself or himself caught in a crossfire between instinctual impulses and moralistic injunctions and, as a result, weighed down by irrational compulsions and self-hatred.

Even then, in the wake of these elegant insights and formulations, consistent success continued to elude Freud and those who followed in his footsteps. Moral masochism still stalled certain therapies and turned others upside down. The unpleasant fact was and still is that the universality of moral masochism makes almost every course of treatment harder and longer than might otherwise be the case.

Let me briefly consider how moral masochism can have a paradoxical effect on the therapeutic process.

Beset by the patient's need to punish himself, the therapeutic process can become counterproductive in what clinicians call "negative therapeutic reactions." Such derailments and deteriorations result from the unconscious sense of guilt, which I have just touched on, and from the resulting tendency to transform the therapist from a helper into a jailer—a cruel mistress or a critical master. Treatments of a particularly inveterate and intractable moral masochist can go on for years. The costs can be considerable, the benefits minimal or nonexistent. The patient will pay large sums of money, lose time and miss opportunities in life while nothing changes or matters get worse—sometimes much worse. Even the best-intentioned therapists, marveling at how their efforts have come to nought, can finally succumb. At a loss, feeling impotent before the tenacity and cruelty of their patients' implacable and irrational consciences, they keep doing what they have been doing all along, but with less and less conviction. Some analysts simply wait for something to happen—for patients to allow themselves to get better. Moral masochism has tended to give psychotherapy and psychoanalysis bad press in recent years, but not for any want of trying on the part of clinical practitioners and theorists, who are forever attempting to refine their technique.

Clinicians are themselves nonplussed by the problem. True moral masochists are more "civilized," almost by definition, than practicing sexual sadomasochists and those with more severe sadomasochistic character disorders, whose consciences are flawed. Because moral masochists have taken the moral high ground and seem more considerate and mature as people and because they are healthier—hypothetically, at least—clinicians used to believe that patients like these had better prognoses. That is, until time and experience proved their predictions wrong. For example, while S&M practitioners are sometimes able to restrict their compulsions to suffer and abuse to delimited and ritualized acts, moral masochists find that their whole lives and the lives of those who depend on them can be infiltrated by such needs, largely without their acknowledging them. High hopes are constantly being dashed in the treatment of people like this, people who seem to have the sensitivity, the insight and the steadfastness to use treatment but mysteriously still lack the wherewithal to heal themselves. Therapy can become a protracted torture for both patient and therapist, a futile bind from which neither can escape, rather like the vicious circles described in chapter 4.

Nor does the understanding of this punishment simply as punishment per se, when imparted to the patient, seem to reverse such trends and release the patient from self-imposed imprisonment and self-torture. As I have suggested in the previous three chapters, punishment like this serves many other internal and external masters, maintaining a psychological equilibrium and the social status quo. There is much more to understand and more to be done, if the patient is to free himself or herself from self-imposed purgatory.

ALTERNATIVES: CULLING FROM THE CULTS OF COMMON SENSE

Faced with past failures and present challenges and seeking the proverbial quick fix in a universe of shorter and shorter sound bites, many practitioners and their patients came to despair of the long-term "talking cure" altogether. Disillusioned by the seeming ineffectuality of self-knowledge, some have advocated not insight but cognitive and behavioral strategies, support systems and self-help programs as rational or commonsense alternatives to inefficient and at times seemingly interminable psychoanalytic therapies. In the process, unbeknownst to the participants, these interventions serve many other needs that had until now been satisfied by perpetual self-punishment. Thus they have gotten results, if only for a while.

In chapter 7, I elaborated on the functions other than the expiation of guilt that are served by perpetual punishment. In so doing, I suggested, masochists surrender to the comfort of a higher authority and hold on to the comfort of known attachments. They heighten their sense of self through the experience of pain while simultaneously diffusing the boundaries between self and other. Theirs is a pleasurable and intimate relationship with suffering. Finally, I noted that in maintaining the hierarchy of master and slave, masochism serves to embed the individual in a protective if tacitly oppressive and exploitative community; the masochistic stance is an adaptive position that secures the social status quo.

Therapeutic strategies that purport to be practical and to change behavior without insight address these needs in other ways—through actions and transactions—without explicitly acknowledging that this is what they are doing. For example, cognitive, behavioral or self-styled "rational emotive" techniques, including certain quickly effective forms of sex therapy, stress the client's capacity simply to take charge of his or her life. But while emphasizing self-possession and self-control, all these strategies in fact amount to forms of suggestion. Such therapists tell clients what to do and not to do, and what to think and not to think. In the process, they set themselves up as counselors, overarching authorities to whom the individual can submit and whose instructions and view of life a client can then assimilate pretty much wholesale. Thus, while ostensibly being encouraged to be more independent and tough-minded, clients actually give over their will to the therapist and yield their capacity for self-determination to the program presented by this therapist. Rather than being driven from within, in accepting the obvious, they are moved from without. Thus, they have externalized once again the sadomasochism within themselves.

Some of the same implicit maneuvers are at work in treatments such as Alcoholics Anonymous, incest surviving, co-dependency groups and a host of other strategies that place self-defeating individuals in an extra-familial support system or a community of fellow lost souls. Some of these modalities have more demonstrable or lasting results than do individual counselors because they also address the sufferer's need, in their suffering, to remain stuck and secure in an oppressive but contained and secure social context. In such settings, individuals believe themselves to be forever recovering. Because of this state of perpetual vulnerability, they remain in need of the ballast and buttressing provided by the reassurance and admonitions of others. They feel safe, and their future seems more certain. With this assurance they can maintain their silent ties to the living past. They come to subsist in a state of abiding patient- or clienthood; they are children in need of supervision and support.

It is much the same with the self-help movement as a whole. The do-it-yourself spiritual/emotional manuals lining the bookstore shelves and sometimes dominating best-seller lists offer the same sort of promise without all the bother and expense posed by a professional contractor. Seeking advice, their readers find not so much ideas as mantras on the printed page. The programs set forth by the unseen authority are often couched in aphorisms, adages and catchwords that are easy to grasp and remember. The author of these formulas and pronouncements, in remaining unseen, can assume almost godlike proportions in the reader's mind. Even while the content of this disembodied counsel goes unheeded, is forgotten or is replaced by newer and trendier cautionaries, the aura of the nonspecific public expert remains. The victims and losers of everyday life tend to flit from one magazine column or bookshelf to another, grazing on self-help guides like groupies or addicts in partially altered states of consciousness and high expectancy. They continually comfort themselves with the hope that through a few choice words—another's words—they can suddenly become somebody else. Thus, practical self-help is a form of mysticism—mass mysticism, in fact, masquerading as pragmatism.

Psychoanalysts have called the more positive results of therapies such as these "transference cures." What they mean is that these changes depend on the relationship to the therapist or expert, who stands in for significant others in the person's life, rather than resulting from self-knowledge and consequent personality reorganization. Since these relationships cannot last, at least not in the form that has encouraged such results in the first place, the results do not last. Indeed, the rate of recidivism, the return to addictive or compulsive patterns once the treatment is concluded, remains high.

Yet the short-term effectiveness of such suggestive treatments, particularly AA and some highly efficient sex therapies, cannot be dismissed easily, especially when compared to insight-oriented therapy. Taking these object lessons at face value, some clinicians have tried to incorporate some of these tactics directly into their own work and modify psychoanalytic and psychotherapeutic technique accordingly. They have varied their therapeutic analytic style, departing now and then from the time-honored stance of neutral or dispassionate listener to give advice or set certain limits for the patient.

There was some precedent for this in the annals of the psychoanalytic discipline. Freud suggested that in the analysis of phobias, once sufficient insight had been gained, the patient should be instructed to put himself or herself in the very phobic situation that he had hitherto avoided (a tactic later referred to by behavior therapists as desensitization or implosion therapy). And with his patient the Wolfman, Freud imposed a deadline, a date when the treatment should terminate in order to rouse his analysand from his lifelong stupor, passivity and dependency. Many years later, Kurt Eissler, former director of the Freud archives and keeper of the most pure Freudian flame, discussed the introduction of various parameters—either limits or support—into the analyses of highly disturbed patients.

These well meaning strategies usually backfired. They failed in typical and predictable ways because they carried with them some of the same transferential implications as those just enumerated—and this within a therapeutic context that was set up to encourage emotional intensity, regression and feelings of dependency and took a long time to establish in the first place. Indeed, if they had openly and honestly examined Freud's or Eissler's actual therapeutic results, analysts might have foretold the future. For example, dismissed from analysis, the Wolfman became an analytic "lifer." He returned to Freud and then to the professor's student analysand and analyst Ruth Mack Brunswick before becoming the virtual ward of the entire psychoanalytic movement. Freud's other patients, Dora and Little Hans, did not fare much better. Nor did Eissler's unlucky analysands fare much better.

Less dramatically, the patients of less extravagant analysts who found themselves treated to doses of common sense and TLC, along with interpretations, tended simply to overstay their welcome. They protracted their courses of treatment, failing to progress and substituting the therapeutic relationship for real-life relationships. Reinforced rather than being worked through and resolved, their so-called transference neuroses, particularly their surrender to their analyst's authority and protection, went on and on with no clear end in sight. Incompletely interpreted and not fully felt, such a transference might run quietly yet desperately wild. The patient in question, mildly seduced and infantilized, refused to face the fact that a therapist is not a parent and that a parent cannot be "had"—conquered, devoured and held on to forever.

The very act of offering advice runs counter to the ingenuity of psychoanalytic method. It is a method devised to draw out and then call into question the omniscience and omnipotence attributed to the practitioner by the patient and to analyze the sources of these illusions in the patient's childish views and expectations of parents. It is a method that leads back to childhood experiences in order to clarify an analysand's responsibility for his or her perpetuation of these in adult life.

If matters were going to change for the better, then it behooved responsible clinicians to learn from their mistakes and treatment failures and those of their colleagues rather than comforting themselves with the illusions provided by seeming innovations and partial successes. Beyond their own field and their own persuasion, they might draw from the remarkable but short-lived results of more manipulative therapies after they analyzed these processes according to their analytic principles. What these fleeting transference cures implied was that underlying the self-punishment of the moral masochist lay the most primitive of dependency needs: the need to empower the self by yielding it to the other, the infantile need to surrender up the self and "to eat and be eaten" as the analyst Bertram Lewin put it. Rather than manage or exploit these demands and longings, with their roots in what clinicians call the "deepest level of early object relations"—those left over from the baby's sinking into the mother's breasts—and their resonances in the checks and balances of the human community, the alert clinician simply had to grant them freedom of expression before interpreting them for what they were. "Ghosts of the past, tasting the blood of the transference," the late Hans Loewald called these primitive personas and relationships formed in the peculiar crucibles of analysis and therapy. Subject to an adult's way of thinking and talking, this form further evolved into something comprehensible to a normal adult mind—something that could be discovered, verbalized, comprehended and, with luck at least, set to rest, not gratified and perpetuated. That is the point: set to rest. This only became possible when the patient could tolerate solitude and mortality as the lonely price to be paid for freedom in adulthood. And that has never been an easy task.

FURTHER ADVANCES: MEANING AND MEDICATION

Responsibility

In this result-oriented contemporary era, the existentialist challenge to determinism of all kinds during the fifties and sixties hardly seems credible anymore and is rarely remembered in therapeutic circles. However, psychoanalysts such as Erik Erikson, Hans Loewald, Roy Schafer and Leonard Shengold have implicitly responded to the wisdom inherent in this perspective on human beings, one in which the individual imposes his or her own meaning on an otherwise meaningless existence through acts of free will. They have emphasized the basic ontological angst in their patients and their search for personal authenticity, responsibility and identity. They have described the active creation in an analysis of one's own life story (or clinical narrative) and stressed "intersubjectivity" in the analyst's and analysand's "construction of truth" about the latter's basic motives. And they have underlined the patient's ownership of his or her own thought processes. The difference has been that they, as psychoanalysts, have tied these existential and implicitly ethical achievements to the unfolding developmental milestones of childhood and adolescence and to the adaptational challenges of adulthood. Genuine insight into one's life history, psychoanalysts now argue, leads to the assumption of individual responsibility. *Insight and Responsibility,* to borrow from the title of one of Erikson's books, are the goals of psychotherapy.

What is most significant for the resolution of masochistic conflicts in this orientation is the psychoanalyst's growing emphasis on the patient's capacity to be alone and to tolerate tension and uncertainty. Patients in treatment seek epiphanies and panaceas. They want simple solutions to felt ambiguities, and they want changes from without that do not place demands on their composure and existing sense of self. They do not want to work at asserting their personal boundaries and taking the initiative. They hope to be "done to." But the existential implications of development and adaptation suggest that in order to be free or independent one must mourn one's past, refrain from taking the paths of least resistance and constantly act to impose one's will on oneself. Well before acts of willpower have become natural and instinctive, the recovering masochist must tolerate frustration and weather the fear and trembling that accompany an appreciation of what is true of the human condition. That is, an adult is not a child to be comforted by illusion; he or she is alone, and alone makes life have meaning.

Psychopharmacology

Another advance in the treatment of more severe sadomasochistic personality disorders has come from an altogether different direction: the discipline of psychopharmacology. In the last few years, literally millions of people have turned to widely publicized drugs like Prozac as cure-alls for what ails them. To some extent, this trend represents yet another form of mass infatuation—another larger scale infantile and oral surrender to higher powers, making for what one author has called a Prozac Nation. Nonetheless, medications, antidepressants in particular, have undeniable uses in the treatment of the less extreme forms of mental illness. What psychiatrists label affective disorders (major depressions and bipolar or manic-depressive illness) and thinking disorders (psychoses, including the schizophrenias) improve with various medications, and the less grave "DSM Axis II" disorders (personality problems) may also respond to chemical intervention when it is judiciously prescribed and just as carefully administered.

More specifically, various antidepressants have been found not only to alleviate profound melancholia and inertia but to have a further impact on a variety of syndromes that have to do, at least in part, with separation anxiety (agoraphobia, panic attacks). One of the infant's basic responses to untoward loss is rage, after the initial rage and evident terror have run their course. Another, often next in the sequence, according to British baby observer John Bowlby, is terror. Another is apathy. Bereft of a mother to "lean on," a baby succumbs to what infant observer Rene Spitz called "anaclitic depression" (from the Greek, "to lean"). It follows that in as much as giving up a masochistic attitude often means abandoning or at least attenuating the individual's attachment to internal images of primary caretakers, easing or attenuating the accompanying depression should facilitate the individual's ability to be alone and, being alone, to get better. The trick is not to fill in for this lost parental figure by fostering an unquestioning dependency on the medicating psychiatrist and his or her pills.

One solution, not without its own risks, is to separate the functions of the psychotherapist and the psychopharmacologist. Even when the former is also a well-trained psychiatrist and thus fully capable of prescribing and monitoring a patient's medication, it may be best to assign to another physician the task of finding the right drug or combination of drugs and the proper dosages for the patient—a sensitive and often protracted process in itself. In this way, the medicating psychiatrist can function like a doctor while the analyst or therapist maintains an interpretative stance. Outside the transference maelstrom, the analyst continues to help a patient understand the meanings of such medical intervention and its resonances with transferences to both practitioners. When the drugs are prescribed by other doctors, therapists can confront and interpret their patients' expectations that something will be done to their body and mind without their own awareness and effort. While patients comply with the psychopharmacological protocol, the analyst can still explore the willingness with which they turn themselves over to another's ministrations. The emotional meanings of being medicated must be made clear if a patient is going to wean himself or herself of substances whose long-term impact and ongoing side effects remain to be fully researched. If this dualistic model is designed and handled correctly—so a primitive polarization of the two practitioners into good/bad or a rivalrous triangulation is anticipated—medication can stimulate depressed and timorous masochists. It can enable them to hear and make use of psychological insight. And the medication can be given up in due course.

But, to repeat, these chemical agents should only be introduced in the context of a therapist's sophisticated understanding of the patient's complex diagnosis and even more subtle psychodynamic conflicts. An untrained physician (like many of the primary-care physicians recently empowered under the new health care system) may miss the exact nature of the depression. For example, when given to an individual who suffers from a bipolar or manic-depressive illness, a drug like Prozac or one of its variants may provoke either a full-blown manic episode or an aggressive and destructive outburst of considerable proportions, posing danger to the patient's and other people's well-being. Less dramatically, and less biochemically perhaps, consider a patient emerging from a melancholic state in which he or she has felt diminished self-esteem and savages him or herself accordingly. He or she may reverse the sequence in a baby's response to maternal absence as described by John Bowlby—a series of emotional reactions proceeding from apathy and despair through renewed anxiety to rage once more. The newly energized sadomasochist may then mobilize more sadistic and narcissistic defenses. Acting suddenly entitled and emboldened, recovering depressives may launch attacks—attacks that are often disavowed—on those around them in efforts both to feel stronger and to exact revenge on others simply for feeling okay. Having punished themselves for so long and to such lengths, they now punish others for having committed a crime of which they themselves are guilty—their self-torture.

People's natural inclination, the course of least resistance, is to act rather than reflect, to do rather than to know, to look at others rather than to look at themselves. So unless the meanings of the changes made by medicine can be accepted and worked through as such, they, too, may have their contradictory effect. Ultimately, patients in the throes of sadomasochistic dilemmas must become, as Shakespeare put it, "masters of their fate" and "of fault[s] not in the stars but in [them]selves." It is tempting *not* to think, and this temptation may be encouraged by the mismanagement of the very drugs that could enable a person to begin to turn his or her life around.

THE COURSE OF TREATMENT

The Beginning Phase

Whatever the common bonds and universal themes that unite them, people are all different. They think, react and act differently in response to common or even universal concerns. They have arranged the hierarchies of the motivations, anxieties and defenses they share with their fellowmen and women in their own unique and complex ways. Given the variation among patients—what exactly brings a person to treatment, how the process unfolds, what benefits it yields and when and how it comes to an end—the course of any one psychotherapy or analysis cannot be predicted with certainty. One may speak of a typical or ideal therapeutic process with the simultaneous recognition that deviations from and variations on this norm are more the rule than the exception. I emphasize this in part to underscore the more extravagant claims to certitude made by many mental health practitioners and to alert my readers about the true nature of any inquiry, however disciplined, into their psyches. Once more, matters are never as clear and simple as we would want them to be.

However, having said this, now let me generalize. I begin with the beginning.

The First Phase

The more masochistic of the sadomasochistic personalities tend to enter therapy reluctantly and fitfully, even though they may later become "addicted" to it. Their friends may have to put some pressure on them to seek professional help as I have noted earlier in this book. Once engaged in the consultation process, they have to be repeatedly persuaded or otherwise helped to stick it out and let the process intensify. In part, this reluctance and fitfulness stem from sadomasochists' stakes in their suffering and ambivalence about giving up these stakes. More to the point here, their hesitancy places a peremptory demand on the therapist from the very outset of their relationship—a demand that the therapist tell the patient what to do, rather than clarify or interpret life patterns and the motives behind them. In threatening to abort or alter their transactions, sadomasochistic patients are unconsciously asking to be restrained and disciplined. In this way, they try to set up the therapist as an authority or parental figure who assumes responsibility for the patients' choices. Once therapists take on such responsibility as sometimes they must temporarily, therapists whose charge it is to expand their patients' consciousness and increase their autonomy find themselves cast in the transference roles of authority, oppressor, jailer and torturer.

GOULD AGAIN   Judy Gould's initiation into therapy and then analysis illustrates this paradox: The patient often attempts to make the cure worse than the disease. Only after Billy finally left her and her cousin and close friend Sally had a baby, did Judy heed the advice of her friends and find a therapist. The loss and hurt and the further sense of "how life was leaving me behind" precipitated Judy's bona fide clinical depression. Her sleepless nights, lack of appetite (for fun as well as food), excruciating self-loathing and suicidal fantasies became unbearable. So Judy relented and went in search of "the pill to cure me," she said bitterly, "of life and love, forever."

Amy had suggested that her friend see a female therapist who, she felt, would more easily empathize with her plight and with whose happiness and success Judy could in turn more readily identify. But Judy, who had come to "hate being a woman," replied that only a man would do. Somehow she felt only men "had it"—an allusion, later analyzed, linking professional and intellectual power with the possession of the phallus. Besides, she added more reflectively, men were her problem, and she would have to work out this problem with one of them.

Thus, Judy found her way to Dr. Cohen, a psychiatrist who had been recommended by Amy's new psychologist, Dr. Kathy Welsh. Judy herself never bothered to check out Fred Cohen's credentials, though fortunately Amy had spent some time selecting Dr. Welsh, who was a graduate of the New York Psychoanalytic Institute and a voluntary clinical assistant professor at Cornell-New York Hospital where Dr. Cohen was a professor of psychiatry on the full-time faculty. A noted researcher on depression and its pharmacological treatment, Fred Cohen was also a training and supervising analyst at The Columbia Center. Through "no fault of my own," Judy got herself "into able hands and not another dill pickle."

After two extended consultations, Dr. Cohen put Judy on twenty and then forty milligrams daily of Prozac. Following her on a weekly basis as the depression began to ease, he continued to admonish her that this phase of treatment was only a beginning and that no drug could cure a relationship or an emotional conflict. She needed to talk—to look at herself long and hard. Judy demurred. She fought. She sputtered. She cried—not the long sobs of earlier months, when she had been so depressed, but those familiar bitter teardrops that crept down her cheeks to the corners of that similarly familiar ironic and self-congratulatory grin.

Finally, Judy relented. Yes, she said, she would come more often and talk. Dr. Cohen reminded her, as he had told her at the start, that he himself did not have this time. He added that it would be better in any case to talk to somebody else. She could continue. . . .

"Oh, no," Judy interrupted him. "So now you're dumping me, too, like everybody else."

No, Dr. Cohen countered, she could continue with him. He would still see her as long as she needed the medication. But someone else, a young and talented analyst, should deal with her mind. Besides, he noted, she had kvetched about his high fee. And she certainly couldn't manage this fee two or maybe four times a week.

"Four times a week?" Judy gasped.

Yes, Cohen said. What Judy really needed was an analysis.

"An analysis, a Freudian psychoanalysis—why, that's *torture!*"

Nonetheless Judy obeyed.

Dr. Cohen referred Judy to Dr. Samuel Richardson, who had just graduated from his institute. Dr. Richardson agreed to take her into analysis, and they met three times in face-to-face sessions before Judy, who liked Dr. Richardson, agreed to get on the couch.

The auspicious Monday morning arrived. Judy entered and gazed in fear at the long black chaise against the far wall. She started forward and stopped.

"Do I have to do it? Can't we talk about it?"

"We have been talking about it."

"I don't know, it seems so foolish, so vulnerable."

"You want me to tell you to do it."

"Okay, okay—I'll do it so long as you don't analyze it!"

And Judy lay down. Within minutes she told him about a dream she'd had the night before about going to the dentist. In the dream, the dentist gave her an extra dose of laughing gas, strapped her to the chair and pulled not the one they agreed on in advance but all of her wisdom teeth. His fee for the torture was $10,000.

"I haven't the faintest idea what it means. Except my father brought me to the dentist once without telling me what he was doing. I was six. The dentist pulled a tooth that wouldn't come out. . . . I was terrified. It hurt horribly afterward. It was mean to trick me, not to tell me that was what they were going to do. . . . But what does it mean now?"

For the time being, Dr. Richardson let it pass. Yet, in these opening moments and in the dream that preceded them, the course of the analysis to come was foretold. Judy wanted to grow up, he conjectured, and lose her wisdom teeth at last. But even in so doing she sought to escape responsibility, to have it done to and for her, without or indeed against her will. She would experience his modest fee as blood money. Her analyst would have to pull teeth, working hard to overcome his patient's recalcitrance, straining, exerting himself, becoming exasperated and potentially angry and vindictive. He would find himself cast in the role of penetrator, torturer, exploiter, deceiver while the analysis would be experienced as a rape, albeit for her own good. In this way—sadomasochistically—Judy would revive her eroticized relationship with her father, a relationship existing both in reality and in fantasy, even though her goal was now to give up her abiding if unconscious tie to him. At some level, Dr. Richardson sensed the existence of not one but two conspirators in the dream, signaling the more shadowy presence of her mother, to whom she had submitted and would continue to submit in other forms—yielding to what another of his female patients had once called her "mother guilt." Resolving this transference neurosis through experiencing and understanding its recreation in the relationship of patient and doctor would be the central task of the analysis.

Alas, it would take some time before such feelings about her doctor would emerge with sufficient clarity to be interpreted and before their force might dissipate under the sway of consciousness and reason. Following the relatively brief introductory phase just described, Judy, like other analysands, would pass through more extended beginning and middle phases of treatment before approaching termination, a final process that is itself fitful and complex. Attempts to let out the stops too quickly and hasten this course usually end up stalling it.

For instance, no patient—at least not one in his or her right mind—is prepared to hear about the deeper levels of his or her conflicts with regard to the analyst and the people whom that analyst comes to represent. Premature attempts to impart such unilateral wisdom, smacking of both arrogance and suggestion, provoke terror and lead to resistances that may compromise the treatment at the outset. If the patient doesn't dismiss them as ridiculous or regress or flee altogether, he or she comes to agree more insidiously with the analyst's suggestions. Intellectualizing defenses then dominate what amounts to a pseudo-analysis in which neither participant acts or experiences the other in a genuine way. Nothing changes in such a parody of the process.

Instead of plunging into the unconscious, the well-trained analyst only listens for a while—simply but carefully. Empathizing with the patient's emotional experience, silently referring it to his or her own life and that of other patients as well as ideas about human development and psychic dynamics, the analyst begins to construct a picture or story that captures the narrative of the patient's life. The analyst brings this story to life in images and scenes that are vivid, evocative and unique. The analyst suspends disbelief and tries not to leap to conclusions about any final and potentially limited half-truths. Instead, thoughtful clinicians, who know enough to know how little they know, willingly accept ambiguity and welcome surprises even when it seems at times that they are hearing the same old story. The Romantic poet John Keats referred to this state of mind in terms of a "negative capability."

In the meantime, in what they actually do say, the analyst or therapist helps the patients define their feelings in the here and now—in the consulting room and in the moment. They underscore their patients' inhibiting anxieties for the most part, their sense of shame and guilt in freely telling their story. They ask patients to pause and wonder why they stop themselves from speaking their mind, to reflect on interruptions in their free associations and in what they choose to tell their analyst. The analyst asks what is scaring patients there and then, at that very instant. By thus alerting patients to the fleeting instants and subtle ways in which they violate the one golden rule of psychoanalysis—to tell all and to be perfectly frank—analysts point out the further existence not only of unwarranted conscious suppression and disavowals of knowledge, but of unconscious defenses such as repression, denial and rationalization. Establishing new ideals and values of personal honesty and self-reflection, the analytic process thus demonstrates the workings of the mind in conflict.

While their relationship deepens, the patient fills the analyst's sympathetic ears with tales of current ordeals and, more and more, of past woes. In the nonjudgmental and friendly atmosphere of this first phase in treatment, a forgotten childhood begins to emerge and, with it, a growing sense of both safety and continuity. In most (if not all) analyses and therapies that get off to a good start, the first year or so is a relative honeymoon period. The therapeutic and working alliance, the good, safe and cooperative relationship of doctor and patient with its roots in the basic trust of a child in its mother, has been established.

DICK KNIGHT IN TREATMENT Only after the Knights' teenage daughter, Alison, got into trouble—she was suspended for smoking pot on the street next to the campus of her girls' day school—did Dick finally seek help. He felt guilty. He also sensed that his and Ethel's problems were somehow a factor in Alison's. He began to see that he was feeling something, doing something wrong, despite his best intentions. Referred by Alison's therapist to Dr. Mildred Smith, a psychoanalyst who was also a professor of psychology at Yale, Dick soon found himself lying on the couch four days a week. "The whole Freudian thing" was hardly what he had anticipated for himself and hardly what the newspapers and cartoons made of the process. Dr. Smith was not some pompous pipe-smoking Viennese with a musty office lined with photos and books of Professor Freud. For one thing, she was a woman, a well-kempt, down-to-earth American lady from a background recognizable to Dick. For another, Dr. Smith was a warm presence during those first months. She was able to attend to Dick's feelings without imposing her own needs on him ("much as Mother did," Dick couldn't help musing). So soon enough he found himself, his hitherto buttoned-down self, "pouring out my heart to her."

Masturbation, homosexual thoughts, his inability to find Ethel's clitoris after twenty-five years of marriage, his excitement at the shadows of his mother's nipples discernible through her translucent negligee, his father's penis in the shower the time "Mother told me to undress 'that foul drunk' and throw some cold water on him"—"every piece of dirty laundry one could think of came out." Or so Dick said to Art on the latter's sickbed during the final weeks of his brother's life, which "Dr. Smith's magic" had made bearable. Somehow, Dick noted, everybody seemed to profit. He handled Alison better than ever before, and before he knew it, this "soft-core delinquent" of his was bound for Princeton.

The Middle Phase

For some clinicians, this first phase represents not a beginning but the be-all and end-all of the treatment process. For example, blending psychoanalysis and the client-centered therapy of Carl Rogers,

Heinz Kohut and his followers, the Self Psychologists, stress empathy in the psychoanalytic process and the feelings of self-esteem and healthy narcissism that come with the patient's conviction in the healer's positive regard. From their perspective, a patient's problems derive from his or her parents' empathic failures and the injuries to the vulnerable child's self-esteem, which result when a so-called self object—the ideal empathetic parent—is out of synch, misses the point and most malignantly, actively exploits, hurts or dismisses that child. To compensate for such developmental insults, the patient fixates on a pathological grandiose self. In treatment, the analyst, cast as a mirror or alter ego of the analysand and/or the analysand's idealized self, undoes the fixation by correcting the inevitable errors in attunement to the patient's needs and feelings. In this welcoming climate, the legitimately boastful and self-absorbed little boy or girl comes out of hiding even as adult patients and their doctors reconstruct a history of subtle abuse and consequent deformation of the so-called self system. As a result, masochism, with its hidden agenda, gives way to healthy narcissism.

It's all very appealing, this exquisite empathy and unconditional support. It is also necessary at the outset of most treatments simply to accept everything a patient has to say. Some patients cannot proceed further into a more uncompromising inquiry into this self. The trouble is, certainly for most of the sadomasochists of everyday life, such gratitude and love—"transference love," Freud called it—does not last. Life, particularly the conflicted life of the mind, is too complicated for that.

Aggression and self-defeat have a way of reasserting themselves. To be sure, therapists can nip their patients' rage and despair in the bud by interpreting or otherwise diffusing their anger and pain before they mount. In so doing, analysts can maintain themselves in the position of the good guy, tacitly enacting the perfect parents the patient never had. As a result, the relationship proceeds smoothly—on the surface at least. However, smothering the patient with such love and killing with kindness deprive the patient of the opportunity to express and explore emotions that well up from within. These emotions come to seem inappropriate, uncalled for and, ultimately, dangerous. Afraid to disrupt the benevolence of the therapeutic relationship and unconsciously guilty and confused by negative feelings that seem unjustified and unjustifiable, such patients suppress their misgivings and misperceptions. In order to keep the peace, they agree with their therapist's agreement with them. This folie à deux reinforces the patients' illusory oneness with the newfound self object. They may find themselves propelled toward getting better but without fully understanding why. And they may get better—for a while. However, once the treatment is over, the old problems will come back; as Freud put it, the "repressed" will "return."

At this point the men are separated from the boys, the women from the girls, the adults from children in general. This juncture is analogous to the developmental moment when a baby begins to teethe, to hurt, and weaning begins. At this point a psychoanalysis proper commences, and well-trained analysts allow their patients the freedom to communicate all their imaginings, good and bad, without censure, correction, solicitousness, constraints of reality or decency or premature closure. Now the journey into the unconscious, the heart of darkness, a voyage that is at once terrifying and sublime, begins.

At this point, the existential courage to be alone is demanded of patient and therapist alike as they separately confront the darkness from within. Patients don't know it yet, but their here-and-now dealings with their doctors have begun to replace the symptoms, character problems and life patterns that brought them to treatment in the first place. Having poured out their guts, their extant past, to their attentive listeners, analysands now begin to relive it. Beset by feelings of rage and terror, the treatment now is as painful and arduous as the life problems and past conflicts that called for it in the first place.

The mid-phase, as a transference neurosis crystallizes, may start innocently enough. Patients begin to be hypersensitive to their doctors. They find themselves balking at perceived slights or hearing and then dwelling on so-called criticisms that in previous months seemed to have been dispelled by a few easy and reassuring clarifications of meaning and interpretations of intent. They become curious about the doctor. They are concerned with the analyst's personal life where previously they had tried to maintain a professional and confessional relationship with the doctor as an expert and unseen authority, sounding board or disembodied voice.

As this curiosity grows, the analyst's person begins to find its way into the patients' daily thoughts and dreams with greater and greater frequency. Sometimes, indeed more often than not, these thoughts and dreams are sexual in nature. Perplexed and decorous patients find themselves recoiling in dismay from the improprieties that come more and more to mind. They find themselves, in spite of themselves, "getting personal." They also find themselves jealous: of other patients first of all, and then, oddly, they think, of anonymous family members, children, spouses, lovers. They find themselves angry for reasons they cannot pin down, which somehow have to do with the fact that there are other people in the analyst's life, people who, the patient laments, are more important and loved than he or she is. Patients feel divided from and envious of this life, which they believe is much better than theirs. Excluded from this imagined life, patients find themselves irrationally preoccupied with the analyst and, if things are going well, simultaneously interested in the nature, sources and resonances of this preoccupation.

DICK KNIGHT YET AGAIN   Eight and a half months into his treatment, Dick Knight had a dream about Dr. Smith that awakened him. For three sessions, he debated whether to tell her about the "silly, dirty little thing." After all, she had been so helpful, was so well-mannered and seemed so entirely proper, that she could not fail to take offense at the workings of Dick's "depraved" mind. But enjoined to be frank and tell all, and scrupulous in this regard as in all contractual matters, he relented and with a sigh confessed:

> In the dream, er, you were walking with your dog, a basset hound, of all things, so squat and ungainly. You were quite impatient with the dog, I remember, particularly when it started to do its *doody*—what an odd word for me to use at my age. And so you started to hit it with

your umbrella. But as if that were not bad enough, this umbrella turned into a . . . penis . . . of all things . . . a big penis . . . your penis. Walking around on a leash—um, shitting? And still you were hitting it—with the penis, no, *your* penis. One penis hitting another and, then, something also bizarre—this boxer came up and mounted the bassett hound. It snarled and barked at you. Then, thank god, I woke up! Am I crazy?

"No," Dr. Smith thought to herself, "most dreams tend to be pretty weird." But she said nothing, simply encouraging her decorous patient to make of her what he would. She asked Mr. Knight to begin to free associate to the images and events in what psychoanalysts call the "manifest dream content," a dream as the dreamer remembers and reports it.

Doing so, Dick Knight again came up with the craziest of ideas. His father's middle name, inherited not by him but by his brother Art, was "Basset—Henry Bassett Knight." This elder Knight had been *a boxer* in his college days, before he married, before everything he did failed and before, falling prey to the booze, he fell from grace. The Knights' first child, Hank, Junior, had also boxed, unlike his less athletic younger brothers, Art and Dick. He'd nearly won a Golden Gloves middleweight title before flunking out of prep school, where he had gone on scholarship and where his maternal grandfather and great grandfather had matriculated before him. Hank had disappeared for two years before returning home, not quite the prodigal son but more a disappointment, like that character Biff in *Death of a Salesman*. During his absence, Dick had filled the failed scion's shoes to some degree, though he'd stayed at home and close to his mother's side.

Deep in this dream lay Dick's rage toward and fear of his mother for what, he now believed, she had done to all the men in her life— Henry Senior, Henry Junior, Art, Dick himself—and done to them in the glorious name of her own dead father. In analysis, Dick displaced this rage and fear onto the otherwise unobjectional person of Dr. Smith, whom he increasingly felt like dumping on and from whom he would seek scoldings and imaginary beatings. Not only did she stand in for his mother, but Dr. Smith at other times represented his lost father and older brother as well, figures whose masculinity survived both Dick's mother's devaluing and castrating assaults on their manhood and their own acts of self-emasculation. To access this lost manhood, however, Dick felt he had to bend over backward and submit to its force embodied by other men. He had to experience with his undeniably female analyst (transferences often fail to discriminate when it comes to the actual gender of the analyst who is, in a sense, gender neutral, and whose presence and voice from behind the couch can be construed in any number of ways) the homoerotic longings and doubts that he had hitherto banished from consciousness, just as Art had been banished from the family.

The honeymoon was over. Or rather, it—the sadomasochistic version of a honeymoon—had just begun. No longer does a patient such as Dick, finding a generally sympathetic listener in the person of Dr. Smith, simply talk about his problems and his past. He now relives them with the person charged with fixing it all, at least up to a point. Without regressing to the sort of state dramatized in the primal scream therapy that was popular a decade and a half ago (a state of mind in which daily functioning, self-inquiry and constructive thinking are impossible) the psychoanalytic patient experiences new feelings. He can do so—feel fully what otherwise might simply terrify him—because in what has been called the "holding environment" of the consulting room he gradually allows himself to cede many of his tried and true defenses. The new emotional experiences that emerge during this middle phase are also old ones. They are "sense memories" that derive from forgotten childhood events and fantasies, both of which carry equal weight in the psychic reality of the patient's unconscious, an inner world that has begun to see the light of day.

Subjected to illumination, examination and adult understanding, this world and the life story it contains can be seen in far greater depth and clarity than anyone—a patient or an analyst, for that matter—could have foreseen at the outset. Perhaps most surprising and disturbing is the dawning realization of what the patient wanted while growing up and continues to pursue as an otherwise mature individual. Not only was the patient a victim, the patient in analysis comes to see. Not only is the patient justified in blaming parents and the other adults charged with his or her care for what they did and didn't do, but now, as the patient feels the same old hurts and disappointments with the analyst who is the innocent object of transferences, the patient comes to see how much he or she wanted and still wants to suffer, to suffer and escape blame.

To say that it all goes back to childhood is to utter a half-truth at best. Indeed, what patients learn is that without knowing it, they still secretly seek to be a hapless child in a childhood they could not control and in which they might have been miserable, but a child nonetheless without responsibility. It is not simply that sado-masochists of everyday life, like typical neurotic patients in analysis, were emotionally abused, imprisoned, hurt and tortured. It is that they loved it and continue to love it. Wherever and however the crack in their psychic worlds began, the fault is now in them.

DICK Knight: "I wanted my mother to beat me. I wanted my father to fuck me up the ass and get me away from her. I wanted to shit all over that lacy nightgown of hers and the tattered family album from her life as a daughter to that blowhard. . . . Ugh, I *want* Ethel to punch me in the balls."

But not just once: Dick must come to such conclusions over and over again, working them through.

JUDY Gould: "I wanted my father to fuck me and *fuck me over.* Over and over I wanted him to slobber all over me with his whiskey breath and throw me by the wayside. . . . I want Bill, all the Bills of the world, to dump me. Even before I met these Bills, I wanted to lose to the other woman. I want to be my mother's daughter forever. I want to be like the Bobbit bitch, get raped and cut the shit's balls off with the whole world watching. I'm a sadistic cunt at heart."

Over and over again.

• • •

A<small>MY</small> Jackson: "I want Ed to yell at me and roll over into oblivion. Just like Dad, dear dead Dad, the Duke of Death like in *Unforgiven.* But I wanted Dad to look at my pussy. . . . Yuck, I can't believe I said it."

E<small>D</small> Jackson: "I want Amy to drop me. I want her to eat me up alive with her tough mouth and her vagina, but it scares me. So I just want her to scream back at me, I guess. That's why I keep acting selfish and stupid and keep provoking her. Hall sex is safe sex. It's sick. No, it's stupid."

Over and over again, alone and together.

Toward Termination

Alas, "Rome was not built in a day," much less unbuilt, demolished and reconstructed. While no individual may be as monumental and diverse from centuries of influences exerted upon him or her or as widespread in his or her influence on others as this Eternal City, still the individual personality is a complex, enduring structure that has evolved over many years. Changing it in any real way and in a manner that safeguards an individual's right to self-determination is thus a protracted and arduous process. It takes longer than any patient or, for that matter, any well-intentioned practitioner might like.

As I noted in chapter 3, when the psychoanalytic method was first devised, most prospective patients, the people most likely to benefit from individual outpatient treatment, suffered from what were called 'symptom neuroses.' In a climate of Victorian and post-Victorian prudery and repression, the majority of individuals expressed their conflicts over unconscious sexual and aggressive wishes in indirect and often symbolic ways. Rather than the depressive moods, generalized anxiety, self-doubt, work inhibitions and repeatedly unhappy relationships that bring contemporary men and women to treatment, these patients suffered from hysterical and obsessional symptoms such as parasthesias and anasthesias (partial or complete loss of sensation in one or more body parts), paralyses, blindnesses, dizzinesses, debilitating neurasthenias (a kind of chronic fatigue syndrome), false pregnancies, sexual dysfunctions, fugue states, sleepwalking, compulsive rituals and intrusive and unwelcome thoughts. Forbidden fantasies and conflicts proved to be embedded in these discrete, if painful, complaints. The sadomasochism of everyday Victorian life was felt in the form of alien visitations, rather like states of demonic possession. As they began to be decoded in the psychoanalytic dialogues, a symptom neurosis was more or less replaced by what came to be called a transference neurosis, in which the analytic relationship was paramount. Once it was more fully felt and interpreted, and repression gradually gave way to conscious awareness and judgment, the analysis and new craziness about the unknown person of the doctor could be understood and fairly well resolved. Essentially, the process granted repressed and inhibited persons a new freedom and self-acceptance so they no longer needed to make themselves unaware of their more troubling feelings and motives.

These days, in the post-Freudian era of expanded consciousness and tolerance, matters have, ironically enough, become more complicated and problematic. Old-fashioned symptom neuroses, apart from certain panic disorders perhaps, are less common and more easily treated in a variety of treatment modalities. However, lifelong bad moods, problems in living, habitual self-defeat—the sadomasochism of contemporary everyday life—do not yield their hold on people so readily. Either as a function of a greater emotional complexity in today's patient population or because clinicians are more sophisticated in their understanding of people's personalities and more ambitious in their goals for them, most analyses have grown in depth, breadth and length. Rather than one clearly defined transference neurosis, a variety of transference paradigms are now seen to emerge in any one treatment, each requiring expression, interpretation and a modicum of resolution. Most practitioners and their patients now concede that symptomatic relief is only a beginning. Indeed, the disappearance of symptoms may be chimeral, an illusion of cure that masks a lack of basic change and permits the return in time of that omnipresent "repressed." A person's character must be dealt with and altered, and character proves most refractory to full analysis and substantial alteration. Changes in a patient's longer-lived and more encompassing patterns of self-deception, self-defeat and self-definition, so-called structural changes in their personalities, require several years to effect. These are years of hard work, of backsliding, of working through and of a sustained effort at maintaining self-awareness.

Nonetheless, life does get better for the well-analyzed patient while the process itself, by which the patient can talk with relative ease about what were once most unsettling psychological secrets, flows more and more smoothly. As resistances let up, ironically it seems the process could go on forever. For patients who once had so little to say, it now seems that there is no end to analysis, to the process of opening up an infinite unconscious for scrutiny. But the demands of time, money and emotional energy weigh heavily. Common sense dictates that analysis, at least within the context of the particular relationship of patient and doctor, must come to a close. Besides, patients begin to realize—often slowly, fitfully, resentfully—this very undertaking, the final separation from their analyst, is itself an important step toward well-being. Having come to get help, they have learned to help themselves. Now they must replace analysis with their own increased capacity for self-analysis. Patients realize that to hang on any longer would be to continue to submit or surrender to the same old false magic, to the same self-imposed fakery that got them into trouble in the first place.

So patient and doctor start talking about finishing up: "termination," in clinical parlance. The patient may have talked about quitting earlier, perhaps even repeatedly, especially when the going got tough. These threats may have been correctly, if irritatingly, ascribed to his or her resistance, to an abiding reluctance to know oneself. But this new talk, unchallenged or even echoed by the therapist, has a different ring to it. It has an aura of finality. It scares, rather than relieves, the patient. He or she is tempted to get "sick" again in order to hold on to the therapist. Once again, the prospect of termination separates the men from the boys and the women from the girls.

Once it is decided, the impending ending exerts new pressures on what transpires in the analysis or therapy. Patients sense, more or less consciously, that there is little time left and much to be done. Old problems and transference issues are reexperienced and worked through more fully. New difficulties also emerge under the constraints of an imminent conclusion, demanding further interpretive efforts and a steadfastness of purpose. Moreover, real life is full of unexpected turns of events. New crises in the outside world— deaths, losses, illnesses, untoward opportunities—have a way of happening during these concluding months. Both parties of this long-standing professional and emotional contract must contend with the temptation to delay the parting of therapist and patient. While it may sometimes be necessary to relent and continue, most often patients must say no: to themselves, to perfection, to the illusion of perpetual parenting, to the subtle sadomasochism of an interminable analysis.

GOULD'S CONCLUSION   For Judy Gould, ending her seven-year analysis was no easy matter. Perhaps the most significant turning point came with her realization of the extent to which she had felt loyal and lovingly bound to her mother in an emotionally fraught relationship that had been obscured by the overt sexiness of her encounters with her father. Her mother, she and her analyst learned, had taken little Judy into bed on those dark and lonely nights when Jim Gould was nowhere to be found. What was more, she discovered, Judy resented these intimacies. They induced guilt that moved her later on to cling to rather than leave her mother and to defer unconsciously to the women rivals for men in her adult life. Understanding these abiding ties began to free her from their grip, and slowly Judy's relationships improved. Always tempted to put men off in the name of truth and commitment, Judy gradually formed an enduring relationship with Walter, a more or less reliable man with whom she could play out the more pleasurable aspects of her erotic fantasies rather than have them silently deform their emotional life together. They got engaged, married and planned to have a child. Judy and her analyst, Dr. Richardson, set a date to finish up. But there was more to be learned.

At this point, as Judy began trying to get pregnant while terminating her treatment, Judy's mother became ill. It didn't help matters, or so it seemed, that it was breast cancer, an assault on Sarah Gould's femininity and motherhood that threatened her life and her daughter's newfound sense of well-being as a grown woman. But Judy had set her termination date months earlier, and with her equally new and uncertain sense of dignity and resolve, she determined to push forward no matter what life might bring.

In this context, as the months passed, with termination but no baby in sight, Judy had a dream, a "real eye-opener." The manifest image was simple and to the point: "Mother wanted me sexually." That was all—one simple declaration of desire. But radiating from this assertion was a whole forgotten history of forbidden and shared passions between the two. Sarah Gould, not Jim, had repeatedly invaded—avowing the best of intentions—her daughter's body. A chronicle of enemas, rectal thermometer insertions, fecal inspection and genital intrusion emerged, climaxing when Judy got her first period at the late age of fifteen. Jim had gone by now, leaving the two women alone. Noting the blood, Mrs. Gould called her sister Becky to proclaim "my little girl is a woman at last." And demonstrating more about womanhood to her daughter, she herself inserted Judy's very first tampon, right there in the living room with the window shades wide open. But what was most disconcerting in all of this, Judy discovered during these last months, was not even the fact that her mother seemed to desire her and to wish to penetrate her innocently evolving body. It was that Judy loved it and loved her mother—she had loved submitting to these invasions and exposures. *Her mother turned her on.* She desired her. Perhaps that was why the fertility procedures to which she now submitted at the hands of her female obstetrician gynecologist had provoked so much anxiety—they excited her. And no doubt this was why she had submitted to what Dr. Richardson, borrowing from his other patient, called her mother guilt.

Sarah Gould had a lumpectomy. Judy got pregnant. Two months after finding this out, she said good-bye to Dr. Richardson. She told him that he had been a father and mother to her, bad as well as good.

BEFORE gender and multicultural factors impinged on liberal, humanistic and surreptitiously bourgeois notions about mental health or even hygiene, therapists and their patients had more definite notions about what was desirable in the way of love and work. Their goals included, predictably, marriage, children and—for men at least—an effective and satisfying career. Today's more tolerant analysts stress states of mind rather than life goals per se, specifically the patients' capacity to bring their latent emotional honesty to life and then to everyday life; something like truth in the process of self-inquiry as in a person's daily dealings and, with some luck, fulfillment in whatever form self-expression takes; an end to the grinding, unacknowledged self-torture and defeat that wear people down and dull their sensibilities and perceptions—these are what patient and doctor can expect. These shifts and thrusts forward need not be dramatic. The point is, they are the patients' own changes and not the inspirations of the doctor or, by extension, of society and its expectations.

DICK'S LIBERATION   Dick left Ethel after their daughter finished her junior year in college. Out on his own, he toyed with the safest of gay sex two or three times before deciding that it, and the loneliness he found therein, wasn't for him. He became engaged to a thirty-three-year-old bond trader, Sam (for Samantha). Sam taught him how to scuba dive and got him skiing again. She was a real pal. At fifty-seven, he planned to have a baby with her. "A boyish woman, and a sweet one, did the trick," he conceded.

ED'S AND AMY'S RAPPROCHEMENT   Ed and Amy continued as usual, adding another child to the hopper while both finished their four-year courses of therapeutic treatment. But they stopped fighting. They added some spa and holistic weekends, in the style of Big Sur's Essalen, to their yearly regimen. The summer before these terminations, the Jacksons vacationed in Greece, on the isle of Paros. Amy went topless and then bottomless much to her husband's (and perhaps a few other onlookers') delight. Less pleasant temptations they resisted mightily. Hall sex became beach sex—sex once again.

What's more, seasoned now, Judy, Dick, Ed, Amy and other analysands are equipped to do the future work on their own.

THE CURRENT IDEOLOGY OF SADOMASOCHISM AND WHAT YOU CAN DO ABOUT IT

OUR FIN DE SIÈCLE

ACCORDING to the pop pundits, ours is an era of disillusionment and cynicism. Many events—Watergate, the Iran-Contra affair, the Vietnam War—have conspired to make American politicians' claims of a higher purpose untenable and often preposterous. Furthermore, the information explosion and, with it, the media's capacity to enter into every recess of public people's private lives have unlocked hitherto closed bedroom doors (Kennedy's, King's, Clinton's) to the public eye. While freeing women to be full-fledged citizens, changing economic realities such as the need for two incomes and the sexual revolution have had more problematic consequences. These include rising divorce rates, the increasing number of single-parent households, and a plethora of alternative lifestyles and parenting choices. In fact and in fantasy, these trends and options have overturned the nuclear family structure, undermined the credibility of fathers and father-figures and belied the family values touted by cynical politicians pandering to their self-deluded constituencies.

In our world, in which technology and science are so vast, intricate and specialized that nobody can grasp all of it, the meaning of life, which depends on a capacity to synthesize past experience, survey present truths and project into an imagined future, becomes fragmented. Overwhelmed by disparate and often contradictory information, most of us can no longer make sense of all the things that bombard us. Things don't add up, leading to a sense of both confusion and disillusion. We seem to exist without a "telos," without conviction or purposefulness. Our era is very different from the latter half of the nineteenth and early twentieth centuries, when it was possible to assimilate and integrate truths from an array of sources and to cull from them ethical implications for conducting oneself within a community and a tradition. With humanism and modernism giving way to mechanistic formulations about human motivation, on the one hand, and a postmodern scepticism about universals, on the other, reasons and ideals are hard to come by.

In the collective state of aimlessness and cynicism that results, morality and the language it entails have become suspect. In this climate, people tend to trust only in its opposite. Hence the "mean men," the antiheroes and the femmes fatales of today's movies first described in chapter 3 become significant. Nihilistic audiences savor the betrayals and atrocities that in the past would have taken them aback. Expecting malevolence, they *want* their leaders and role models to be corrupt.

As the psychoanalyst Leo Rangell recently remarked after surveying the televised spectacles of Watergate and the Iran-Contra scam, the American constituency has become surprisingly uncomfortable with evident integrity and decency. Knowing their own shortcomings and having become inured to the deceit, greed and ruthlessness of their erstwhile leaders, they want to get it—the loss of ideals—over with before it begins. They don't want others to be better than they feel they are. They don't want to be deceived or taken by surprise. They want worlds without superegos. They want "license to kill" and crooks to lead them. In a 1995 episode of *TV Nation,* Michael Moore induced a convicted felon, Louis Bruno, to run for president, having met the two criteria for the job (U.S.-born and over thirty-five). Campaigning in New Hampshire with Robert Dole, he promised the electorate, "I'm Louis Bruno. I'm runnin' for President. I been runnin' all my life. While with other politicians you have to wonder, 'Is he a crook?' with me, ya don't hav ta wonder. I say right out, I'm Louis Bruno, and I'm a crook!"

Bereft of old heroes, ideals and convictions, many people today have made a peculiar virtue of what they hold to be necessity. Not only do they believe that men and women are Hobbesian beasts, loveless and self-serving, they further infer that because this seems so, or is true, it is good. Bad is good. To strive for more is absurd and hypocritical. To exercise constraint is to lie and to betray oneself. Just do it: Act on impulse. Cruelty and selfishness are what human beings are all about, and it is noblest, ironically, to sing their praises—in the hard rock, heavy metal, punk and neo-Brechtian rap that would have been unthinkable back in the fifties, the up-tight and duplicitous fifties before the facades began to crumble. We live the lie of *Twin Peaks* or *Blue Velvet,* the Lynch TV series and film depicting the literal sadomasochism that is the underside of American small-town life. Better to see, even celebrate it actively, Lynch implies, than delude ourselves. Better to have actors such as Richard Beymer and Russ Tamblyn of *West Side Story* reveal themselves for what they have become—not high-minded boys but treacherous old men.

One might have thought that psychoanalysis would flourish in this fin de siècle—more so than in more repressed bygone times, when people generally hid their true desires from themselves. But this is not the case. Quite the contrary, the psychoanalytic process is inherently idealistic and therefore high-minded and out of synch with the times. Emphasizing the expansion of consciousness and the assumption of responsibility as a consequence of insight, the psychoanalytic inquiry values and relies on a person's ability to think, experience and talk rather than to act. Its stress is on personal composure, conscious choice, self-control and individual autonomy. While the psychoanalysis itself is a form of meditation, one in which more obvious goals must not interfere with introspection for its own sake and in which analyst and patient do not play for results, nonetheless it is goal oriented—at least in the long run. Implicit in the undertaking is the notion that people can get better, and that through a relentless search for truths about themselves they can become their best selves. Born of the Enlightenment and Romantic traditions, psychoanalysis is a belief system and a form of treatment wherein truth conquers all. It derives from and upholds the humanism that is now threatened with obsolescence. In this time of tunnel vision, short sound bites, strobe lights and quick fixes, people seem to have lost interest in themselves as sentient and motivated human beings rather than creatures of habit and impulse. So it takes a lot of effort to get them to pause and reflect for a moment or two, much less take the "talking cure"—which, when it comes to the sadomasochism of everyday life, may be the only alternative.

This brings me to the hard part—what should we do about the sadomasochism of everyday life now, or at least what should we think about doing? What can we expect these days? And what can we do? Caught up in what they are doing, vaguely feeling bad, deprived of standards and values, individuals—my readers, in fact—may have a hard time recognizing what their problems are because they don't have yardsticks (however illusory) against which to measure their lives. As a first step, then, let me try to articulate what we can expect from life and from ourselves.

SELF-HELP AND HELP FOR THE SELF IN A SADOMASOCHISTIC SOCIETY

Even if you have been let down, betrayed, or disappointed, there is no logical reason not to want more. Fidelity, love, kindness, passion, ideality, beauty and sensuality can be yours for the asking, in your imagination at least, and perhaps later in reality. With a little bit of luck, and with help from your friends, you might even attain the plateau on which you can find mutual transcendence a good deal of the time with another person; and when you don't, you can still enjoy your solitude and containment.

Your work can and should be meaningful. You may get tired of it at times, when it's not entertaining, but you should be then steadied by the conviction that it matters. You should generally feel authentic in what you do daily, and when you hold back from too much self-expression, it should be for a defined and non-defensive purpose. "All work and no play" doesn't make sense and doesn't work. Yes, effort and realism are requirements for success in life. Ultimately, however, the best work flows effortlessly and gently back into the child's play whence it originated. Hard work should more often than not be exhilarating. It should be play. And for some, it should serve to enhance other people's lot and serve the community. Self-interest is limited because the self is limited. Even in what Christopher Lasch called "the age of narcissism" of the Me generation, narcissism is a dead end.

You cannot simply expect other people or the world in general to be any better than they are, to change in the ways you hope for or to do it for you without your doing something to make it happen. Subject to the conflicts and defenses described in this book, others are mired in miseries of their own and, over the years, become locked in certain personality styles that cannot be shaken. As the Beatles put it—and coming of age in the early sixties, they put many such things very well—the love you take is equal to the love you make. The responsibility for making changes is your own, and in a sense nobody changes anybody else's mind, or heart. Blame is futile. So, while you have the right to feel angry, disappointed, put upon, put down and dissatisfied, don't complain. Or rather, don't just complain. Get mad or sad. But act. Remember, "living well is the best revenge."

I must qualify this: Act once you understand what the action is motivated by and therefore what its consequences are apt to be. Think first. This is the hard part.

In pausing to ponder your motives, you will experience tension and what psychoanalysts call "unpleasure" for a while, often for some time. Defensive maneuvers and the actions that derive from them—what clinicians call "acting out"—aim to avoid conscious anxiety and discomfort. Becoming self-aware necessarily entails becoming aware of the negative feelings and self-punishing tendencies that are always present in hidden places and disguised forms and which most often get expressed in surreptitious and therefore dangerous ways. While it may feel like it at times, as I tell my patients, nobody ever died from feeling bad. Rather, the defenses against experiencing such emotions can be lethal.

The feeling you are most likely to uncover when you try to contain yourself? *Guilt*—guilt in its many aspects. If you find yourself pursuing happiness, finding love and working well, you will feel *irrationally* guilty. When you look into your heart and see there your darkest and deepest desires, your erotic and violent fantasies, what you discover will make you feel guilty, bad. Perhaps worst of all, when you look back on your life, at least your life as an adult, and at all the choices you made for yourself and others, and when you take responsibility for these choices, you will feel guilty—*rationally* guilty.

There is a limit to all of this guilt, of course, since you are not, in fact, omnipotent or omniscient. Other people have a share of the blame, particularly the parents who reared you when you were little, knew little and there was little you could do about your life, when you didn't have choices. Your irrational and primitive conscience notwithstanding, your intentions are not the same as actual deeds, and a sin in the heart remains just that—a sin in the heart and not in real life. At some point, you have to recognize that the free-floating malaise and implicit guilt you experience derive from your inevitable Oedipus complex—from those wishes that are "forced upon us by nature" and yet "repugnant to morality" as Freud first put it. Being human—and this is our essential tragic condition—means living with guilt and suffering, with what the Bible understood to be original sin. A source of misery much of the time, this paradox also makes for basic tensions that are dynamic and potentially creative. Oedipus complexes are there to motivate us, moving some people to achieve great things in love and work and the rest of us to attain our place in the generational cycle. Our most horrific fantasies spur us on, driving us to grow up and become lovers, parents, providers and participants in the life of the community and its future. Knowing these fantasies for what they are frees us to be the best we can be.

The other terrible feelings that must be weathered in the process of self-restraint and self-reflection derive from recognition of our essential solitude. Along with guilt, we must live with, and indeed embrace, a deep sense of loneliness and the anxiety and depression that are evoked by it. Like guilt, these emotions are complex in their sources and nature, and I have elaborated on them at length throughout the book. What I would reiterate here is that there are limits to anyone's love and responsibility for another person. Your parents were as imperfect and selfish as you can be. If you don't take care of yourself in your adult life, nobody else will. If you follow your simpleminded conscience as if it were an external protector and authority, you are cleaving to an illusion. The vast universe in which you find yourself is not a meritocracy meting out rewards for stereotypically good and bad behavior. Whatever values you choose to entertain are your own, and they are values in and of themselves, for their own sake.

Becoming what is commonly called a whole person with a sense of identity, being an "I" who acts, rather than a "me" who is acted upon, means setting yourself apart—apart from others as from your own self. It means detaching yourself not only from others in the flesh but from your own reflexive impulses, inclinations and injunctions. It means standing back in order to survey the field of your life, then making your own choices and living with the consequences. It means an end to all sorts of coddling. It means doing the right thing and relying on nobody else to do it while being glad when they do. To paraphrase Erik Erikson once more, becoming a self-sufficient and therefore lone adult requires that a man or woman replace the morality of childhood with the ethics of the adult.

Help!

But even here there's a limit, another contradiction, another counterpoint. You may *not* be able to do it all on your own. You may not be able to figure it all out. You may need help. Like symptoms, repetitive behaviors and repeatedly disappointing relationships— the sorts of self-defeating patterns and vicious circles described earlier—are unconsciously driven. Because of this, however aware a person may be that she or he has a psychological problem, self-in-

quiry—an attempt to understand the unseen roots of this problem—can only go so far. Unless the individual is already experienced and particularly skilled in the ways of the unconscious and
can catch self-deception or notice a blind spot, an outside observer
and interpreter has to step in. Since he or she is, ideally, not in the
throes of the individual's conflicts and anxieties of the moment,
such an expert is capable of analyzing just enough so the patient
can take over. Once feelings, defenses and basic fears are identified,
patients can discover what they truly want and why they have been
so circumspect about even knowing that this is so.

When seeking psychotherapy or psychoanalysis, you must choose
very carefully. Do not simply rely on a friend's recommendation or
even that of a physician or other health care provider who is not
trained in psychiatry or clinical psychology. You may have the good
fortune to find a counselor who is talented and effective. But you
may very well land in the hands of a relative amateur who can get
you only so far because of his or her personal limitations, blind
spots and inadequate education. Unlike the highly trained seasoned analytic clinician, he or she may not be prepared to understand the complex nature of transference feelings and enactments:
your right to get angry and devalue your therapist, for example;
your need to repeat all the old hurts and outrages until they can be
emotionally understood and interpreted; the ease with which you
can be killed with kindness on the therapist's part not for the sake
of your growth but for his or her own personal comfort and self-esteem. In your hunger for help and advice and for somebody to look
up to, you may even be moved to make decisions that either don't
change anything or may even have disastrous consequences.

Since residencies and psychology graduate programs provide
only the scantiest psychotherapy training these days, you should
seek treatment with a well-credentialed psychoanalyst, a psychiatrist,
psychologist or psychiatric social worker who is certified. This treatment will not necessarily be an exhaustive analysis but treatment of
some kind. Pieces of paper do not guarantee creativity, wisdom or
authenticity, of course, but they are signs of competence, and the
best signs that are available. Even if psychoanalytic training has

taken place elsewhere, it is probably your safest bet to contact the International American Psychoanalytic Association for the institute nearest you. If your financial resources are meager, you will be referred to their treatment clinic at one or another affiliated institutes in your area and referred to a candidate who will see you on a sliding fee scale. This candidate will in all likelihood be an experienced clinician with an advanced degree in clinical psychology, psychiatry or social work (Ph.D., M.D. or M.S.W.) in his or her thirties or forties. If you can afford more, you will be given the names of graduate analysts. Among these, the highest status is that of training and supervising analyst, the analyst who analyzes candidates and supervises their treatment of their cases. You should ask about training, credentials and academic affiliation; check them out and shop around.

How can you decide what and who is right for you, and whether the chemistry is right? You should feel understood by your therapist fairly early in the process. Therapists should maintain what is called the proper "frame." They should confine their contact with you to your sessions and not socialize with you or your friends and family members. They should refrain from burdening you with their own opinions and details about their personal lives. Their fee should fall within reasonable guidelines. They shouldn't promise great things. They should behave in a warm but still basically professional and detached manner, yet they shouldn't be aloof and cold or uninvolved in the name of professionalism. They should not be defensive about your criticisms or observations about their techniques or their persons, but rather invite you to expand on and explore these impressions and reactions. Words, not actions, should be the stuff of your sessions.

But therapists shouldn't be wordy. You should understand what they say even when it's hard to take. Their comments should be pithy enough for you to hear and remember. You should feel safe enough with a therapist to experience a range of uncomfortable emotions in the expectation that they will be understood and the demons set to rest. You should feel challenged rather than gratified by hearing either what you already know or what you want to be told.

While they may seem important at the outset, the fact is that the therapist's gender, race, age and ethnicity don't matter in the long run. His or her humanity and skill are far more important. You shouldn't get impatient, since therapy or analysis usually takes a minimum of five years. You should expect to stall now and then. You should expect to get angry and disappointed. But you should not feel misunderstood or truly mistreated. You should expect to see some results along the way, though more come later. If you stagnate or get worse, you have a right to a consultation with another, preferably senior, clinician. The consultant is in a better position than you are to assess whether your difficulties with your therapy or analysis represent a necessary and temporary regression or impasse—most likely, some transference storm—or a genuine and irreparable treatment failure. If the latter is the case, don't just quit therapy altogether. Change therapists. Understand what went on and what went wrong with your last therapist.

Finally, you should forget it all. Your treatment should come to a close, and there should be an end to all the potentially morbid introspection and endless talk. Some very good analysts err on the side of overintellectualization, excessive ambition and perfectionism and don't let people go until the analysis is complete—completion being an ideal, a fiction. You will do the rest of the job on your own without even knowing that you are doing it sometimes. You will forget much of your analysis. You will have to work at it at times after the treatment, recognizing recurrent and new symptoms for what they are, identifying old relational patterns and picking up on other warning signals. You may need a "touch up" at times of stress—a session here or there, maybe more—which is not a sign of failure. But you should come to accept yourself for who you are.

You should be your best self. You should make the best of it. You should hope for the best.

Epilogue

I n closing, I will offer a personal note. This is one of the toughest books I've ever worked on. It touches on themes in my own life and in the lives of many people whom I've cared about and whose lives have been bound up with mine in troubling ways. I'm glad to be done with it and hope you are too—done with the sadomasochism of everyday life. But in saying so, I'm kidding myself. The sado-masochism of everyday life is unavoidable. I know that because I am, after all, a psychoanalyst.

Bergler, E. (1949). *The Basic Neurosis, Oral Regression and Psychic Masochism.* New York: Grune & Stratton.

Berliner, B. (1958). The role of object relations in moral masochism. *Psychoanalytic Quarterly* 27:38–56.

Blos, P. (1966). *On Adolescence: A Psychoanalytic Interpretation.* New York: Free Press.

———. (1979). *The Adolescent Passage: Developmental Issues.* New York: International University Press.

———. (1985). *Son and Father: Before and Beyond the Oedipus Complex.* New York: Free Press.

Brame, G. G., Brame, W. D., and Jacobs, J. (1993). *Different Loving: An Exploration of the World of Sexual Dominance and Submission.* New York: Villard Books.

Brenner, C. (1990). *An Elementary Textbook of Psychoanalysis.* New York: Anchor Books.

Chancer, L. S. (1992). *Sadomasochism in Everyday Life: The Dynamics of Power and Powerlessness.* New Jersey: Rutgers University Press.

Ellis, H. (1900). *Studies in the Psychology of Sex.* Philadelphia: F. A. Davis.

Erikson, E. (1956). *Childhood and Society.* New York: Norton.

———. (1964). *Insight and Responsibility.* New York: Norton.

———. (1968). *Identity, Youth and Crisis.* New York: Norton.

Freud, S. *The Standard Edition of the Complete Psychological Works of Sigmund Freud*, vols, 1–24, ed. J. Strachey. London: Hogarth Press, 1953–1974. (Abbrev. S.E.)

———. (1900). *The Interpretation of Dreams.* S.E. 4-5.

———. (1915a). Instincts and their vicissitudes. S.E. 12:157–71.

———. (1920). *Beyond the Pleasure Principle.* S.E. 18:3–64.

———. (1924a). The economic problem of masochism. S.E. 19:157–70.

———. (1919e) A child is being beaten. 17:177–204.

Glick, R. A., and Meyers, D. I., eds. (1988). *Masochism: Current Psychoanalytic Perspectives.* New Jersey: The Analytic Press.

Horney, K. (1924). On the genesis of the castration complex in women. *Int. J. Psycho-Anal.* 5:50–65.

———. (1926). The flight from womanhood. *Int. J.Psycho-Anal.* 7:324–39.

———. (1932). The dread of woman. *Int. J. Psycho-Anal.* 13:348–366.

———. (1933). Denial of the vagina. *Int. J.Psycho-Anal.* 14:57–70.

Kakar, S. and Ross, J. M. (1986). *Tales of Love, Sex, and Danger.* New York: Basil Blackwell.

Kernberg, O. (1991). Aggression and love in the relationship of the couple. *J. Amer. Psychoanal. Assn.* 39:45–70.

Kinsey, A. C., Pomeray, W. B., and Martin, C. E. (1948). *Sexual Behavior in the Human Male.* Philadelphia: W.B. Saunders.

Klein, M. (1984). *Envy and Gratitude and Other Works.* New York: Free Press.

Krafft-Ebing, R.V. (1931). *Psychopathia Sexualis: With Especial Reference to the Antipathic Sexual Instinct, a Medico Forensic.* New York: Physicians and Surgeons Book Co.

Lever, M. (1991). *Donatien Alphonse Francois, Marquis de Sade.* Paris: Fayard.

Lowenstein, R. (1957). A contribution to the psychoanalytic theory of masochism. *J. American Psychoanalytic Assn.* 5:197–234.

Mahler, M. (1975). *The Psychological Birth of the Human Infant: Symbiosis and Individuation.* New York: Basic Books.

Masters, W. H. and Johnson, V. E. (1966). *Human Sexual Response.* Boston: Little Brown.

Person, E. (1988). *Dreams of Love and Fateful Encounters.* New York: Norton.

Réage. P. (1965). *The Story of O.* New York: Ballantine Books.

Reik, Theodor. (1957). *Masochism in Modern Man*. Trans. Margaret H. Beigel and Gertrude M. Kurth. New York: Grove Press.

Ross, J. M. (1992). *The Male Paradox*. New York: Simon & Schuster.

————. (1994). *What Men Want*. Massachusetts: Harvard University Press.

Sacher-Masoch, L. V. (1989). *Venus in Furs*. New York: Blast Books.

Sade, M. D. (1988). *Juliette*. New York: Grove Press.

Shengold, L. (1989). *Soul Murder: The Effects of Childhood Abuse and Deprivation*. New Haven: Yale University Press.

Silverman, Kaja. *Male Subjectivity at the Margins*. New York and London: Routledge, 1992.

Stoller, R. (1968). *Sex and Gender*. New York: Science House.

————. (1985). *Observing the Erotic Imagination*. New Haven: Yale University Press.

————. (1991). *Porn: Myths for the Twentieth Century*. New Haven: Yale University Press.

White, E. (1940). *Genet*. New York: Alfred A. Knopf.

Index